MW01040981

aPHR™
Associate Professional in Human Resources Certification Practice Exams

Tresha Moreland, SPHR, SSBBP
Gabriella Parente-Neubert, MLHR, PHR, CLC
Joanne Simon-Walters, MBA, SPHR, SHRM-SCP

Mc
Graw
Hill
Education

New York   Chicago   San Francisco
Athens   London   Madrid   Mexico City
Milan   New Delhi   Singapore   Sydney   Toronto

McGraw-Hill Education is an independent entity from HR Certification Institute™ and is not affiliated with HR Certification Institute in any manner. This publication and CD-ROM are not sponsored by, endorsed by, or affiliated with HR Certification Institute in any manner. This publication and CD-ROM may be used in assisting students to prepare for the Associate Professional in Human Resources (aPHR™) exam. Neither HR Certification Institute nor McGraw-Hill Education warrants that use of this publication and CD-ROM will ensure passing any exam. aPHR is a trademark of HR Certification Institute in the United States and certain other countries. All other trademarks are trademarks of their respective owners.

Library of Congress Cataloging-in-Publication Data

Names: Moreland, Tresha, author. | Parente-Neubert, Gabriella, author. | Simon-Walters, Joanne, author.
Title: aPHR Associate Professional in Human Resources certification practice exams /
  Tresha Moreland, SPHR, SSBBP, Gabriella Parente-Neubert, MLHR, PHR, Joanne Simon-Walters, MBA, SPHR.
Description: New York : McGraw-Hill Education, [2017]
Identifiers: LCCN 2017025655 (print) | LCCN 2017032525 (ebook) | ISBN 9781260026344 |
  ISBN 9781260026337 (set/package : alk. paper)
Subjects: LCSH: Personnel management—Examinations—Study guides. | Personnel management—
  Examinations, questions, etc. | Personnel departments—Employees—Certification.
Classification: LCC HF5549.15 (ebook) | LCC HF5549.15 .M67 2017 (print) | DDC 658.30076—dc23
LC record available at https://lccn.loc.gov/2017025655

McGraw-Hill Education books are available at special quantity discounts to use as premiums and sales promotions, or for use in corporate training programs. To contact a representative, please visit the Contact Us pages at www.mhprofessional.com.

aPHR™ Associate Professional in Human Resources Certification Practice Exams

Copyright © 2017 by McGraw-Hill Education. All rights reserved. Printed in the United States of America. Except as permitted under the Copyright Act of 1976, no part of this publication may be reproduced or distributed in any form or by any means, or stored in a database or retrieval system, without the prior written permission of publisher.

All trademarks or copyrights mentioned herein are the possession of their respective owners and McGraw-Hill Education makes no claim of ownership by the mention of products that contain these marks.

2 3 4 5 6 7 8 9   LCR   21 20 19 18

ISBN: Book p/n 978-1-260-02631-3 and CD p/n 978-1-260-02632-0
of set 978-1-260-02633-7

MHID: Book p/n 1-260-02631-0 and CD p/n 1-260-02632-9
of set 1-260-02633-7

Sponsoring Editor Amy Stonebraker	**Acquisitions Coordinator** Claire Yee	**Production Supervisor** James Kussow
Editorial Supervisor Jody McKenzie	**Technical Editor** Cornelia Gamlem	**Composition** Cenveo Publisher Services
Project Manager Rajinder Singh, Cenveo® Publisher Services	**Copy Editor** Kim Wimpsett	**Illustration** Cenveo Publisher Services
	Proofreader Lisa McCoy	**Art Director, Cover** Jeff Weeks

Information has been obtained by McGraw-Hill Education from sources believed to be reliable. However, because of the possibility of human or mechanical error by our sources, McGraw-Hill Education, or others, McGraw-Hill Education does not guarantee the accuracy, adequacy, or completeness of any information and is not responsible for any errors or omissions or the results obtained from the use of such information.

I dedicate this book to students and first-time human resource professionals who want to propel their careers forward. Success requires courage to take that first step toward greatness. Congratulations on taking that first step.

—Tresha

I dedicate this book to my husband, Steven Walters; my 8-year-old son, Steven Drake Walters II, and my 4-year-old daughter, Farai Chase Walters. There are no words that can adequately express just how much your continual support of everything I do means to me. Thank you for the sacrifices you make for me and for letting me be part of our little family.

—Joanne

I dedicate this book to my loving daughter, Grace. You inspire me to be the best version of myself every day. I hope that in return I inspire you to take on the world wholeheartedly with grace, dignity, and determination. I cannot wait to see all the things you will do!

—Gabriella

ABOUT THE AUTHORS

Tresha Moreland, SPHR, SSBBP, is an executive leader in human resources. She has held senior human resource leadership roles for more than 20 years in multiple industries such as manufacturing, distribution, retail, hospitality, and healthcare.

She has developed a business philosophy of integrating human resources with business strategy, creating a hybrid HR leadership approach. This approach enables organizations to leverage human resources to achieve business results.

Tresha is the founder and principal of HR C-Suite (www.hrcsuite.com). HR C-Suite is an educational and advisory resource that is dedicated to connecting HR to business results.

She received a master's degree in human resource management and a master's degree in business administration. She also earned a Senior Professional in Human Resources (SPHR) certification and a Six Sigma Black Belt Professional (SSBBP) certification.

Gabriella Parente-Neubert, MLHR, PHR, CLC, is a consultant, author, and public speaker. She has 15 years of progressive HR experience. She has unique insights into what makes people successful in their careers and how that impacts the bottom line of an organization.

Gabriella also works to transform lives and careers as a certified life/career coach and as an adjunct professor. Gabriella is also a Certified Gallup Strengths Coach and DDI-certified instructor. Gabriella has a Professional in Human Resources (PHR) certification and is a member of the Society of Human Resource Management (SHRM).

Gabriella received her bachelor's degree in psychology from Heidelberg University and her master's degree in labor and human resources from Ohio State University, graduating *cum laude* from both universities.

Joanne Simon-Walters, **MBA, SPHR, SHRM-SCP,** is a resourceful human resource leader with 20 years of progressive management experience in multiple industries including education, information technology, and financial services. Joanne currently works in an HR leadership role for a healthcare consulting company in the Caribbean. Additionally, Joanne writes and delivers HR content for Lynda.com.

Joanne is pursuing her doctorate degree in creative leadership for innovation and change at the University of the Virgin Islands. Joanne earned a master's degree in business administration with a concentration in technology management and a bachelor's degree in business administration with a concentration in finance. Joanne is Senior Professional in Human Resources (SPHR) certified, a Crucial Conversations Certified Trainer, a certified Prosci Change Management Practitioner, and a trained paralegal specializing in employment law. In the summer of 2017, Joanne will be a speaker at TEDx Saint Thomas, where she will discuss the role of the transformational leader in eliminating workplace bullying.

When Joanne is not working, she is spending time with her husband, 8-year-old son, and 4-year-old daughter on her favorite Caribbean beaches in her birthplace of St. Thomas, U.S. Virgin Islands, and in her parents' native country, Antigua, West Indies.

About the Technical Editor

Cornelia Gamlem, SPHR, is an author, consultant, and speaker. She coauthored *The Big Book of HR* and *The Essential Workplace Conflict Handbook*. Founder and president of the GEMS Group Ltd., she offers her clients human resources and business solutions. Prior to founding the firm, she served in a senior HR leadership role with a Fortune 500 IT services company with a global presence.

Cornelia has served on national task forces that influenced public policy and testified before the Equal Employment Opportunity Commission on three occasions. She served on SHRM's National Board of Directors, chaired its Workplace Diversity Committee, and served on its Global Forum Board of Directors. She has supported HR professionals by serving as an instructor at a number of colleges in the Washington, DC, metro area. She has written many articles and white papers for professional and industry publications.

She is a graduate of Marymount University, where she earned a master's degree in human resource management, and California State University – Sacramento, where she earned her undergraduate degree in business administration. She achieved a Life Certification as a Senior Professional in Human Resources (SPHR) from the Human Resource Certification Institute (HRCI).

CONTENTS

ACKNOWLEDGMENTS

I would like to thank all those who were supportive along my career path journey. Those cheerleaders I've met along my career journey have encouraged persistence and reminded me that believing in yourself is the first step to success.

—Tresha

I would like to thank my parents, David Simon and Ruthella Christian-Simon, and my nine siblings, who collectively taught me to be the author of my own destiny.

—Joanne

I would like to acknowledge my girlfriends, who I am so thankful to call "my sisters." Through the laughter and sometimes tears, we always end up closer. Thank you for the love and support throughout the years.

—Gabriella

PREFACE

Congratulations on your decision to pursue your aPHR certification. The objective of this book is to prepare you for the aPHR exam by familiarizing you with the knowledge areas, style, and difficulty of the questions. The questions in this book explore topics of the human resource Body of Knowledge you may be faced with when you take the aPHR exam.

The best approach to prepare for the exam using this book is outlined here:

1. Take the pre-assessment exam in Chapter 1.

2. Determine your strengths and weaknesses. Decide on first, second, and third priority areas for study so that you can budget your study time effectively. Consider whether you may need an additional self-study resource, such as the *aPHR™ Associate Professional in Human Resources All-in-One Exam Guide*.

3. Review the questions and in-depth answers. Understand not only why an answer is correct but also why the other answers are wrong.

4. Remember that all the questions and in-depth answer explanations in the book are included in the electronic test engine that accompanies the book. We recommend using the test engine to take full-length, timed practice exams as the final step in preparing for the live exam. See Appendix A for more information about the test engine.

Because the primary focus of this book is to help you pass the exam, we cover all knowledge areas of the aPHR exam in this book. It is critical that you use all of these available tools to be successful in achieving your certification.

Because each question in this book features a detailed explanation of why one answer choice was the correct answer and why each of the other answer choices was incorrect, we believe this book will also serve as a valuable professional resource after your exam.

In This Book

We've organized this book so that each chapter consists of a battery of practice exam questions representing each knowledge area, appropriate for human resource concepts. Each chapter covers a knowledge area of the exam, with the answer explanations providing the emphasis on the "why" as well as the "how to" of working with and supporting the human resource concepts.

We've created a set of chapter components that call your attention to the key steps of the testing and review process and provide helpful exam-taking hints. Take a look at what you'll find in every chapter:

- Every chapter includes practice exam questions from one **knowledge area.** Drill down on the types of questions from each area that you will need to know how to answer in order to pass the exam.

- The practice exam **Questions** are similar to those found on the actual certification exam and are meant to present you with some of the most common and confusing problems that you may encounter when taking the live exam. The questions are designed to help you anticipate what the exam will emphasize, and getting familiar with good practice questions will help ensure you know what you need to know to pass the exam.

- Each chapter includes a **Quick Answer Key,** which provides the question number and the corresponding letter for the correct answer. This allows you to score your answers quickly before you begin your review of the explanations.

- Each question is accompanied by an **In-Depth Answers** section, which provides explanations for both the correct and incorrect answers and can be found at the end of each chapter. By reading the answer explanations, you'll reinforce what you've learned from answering the questions in that chapter, while also becoming familiar with the structure of the exam questions.

Exam Objective Map

The following table allows you to reference the official certification exam objective, the chapter in which each objective is covered, and the specific questions pertaining to each objective.

Official Exam Objective	Chapter Number	Question Number
HR Operations (Functional Area 01)	**2**	
01 Organizational strategy and its connection to mission, vision, values, business goals, and objectives	2	1–10
02 Organizational culture (for example, traditions, unwritten procedures)	2	11–20
03 Legal and regulatory environment	2	21–30
04 Confidentiality and privacy rules that apply to employee records, company data, and individual data	2	31–40
05 Business functions (for example, accounting, finance, operations, sales and marketing)	2	41–50
06 HR policies and procedures (for example, ADA, EEO, progressive discipline)	2	51–60
07 HR metrics (for example, cost per hire, number of grievances)	2	61–70
08 Tools to compile data (for example, spreadsheets, statistical software)	2	71–80
09 Methods to collect data (for example, surveys, interviews, observation)	2	81–90

Official Exam Objective	Chapter Number	Question Number
05 Payroll processes (for example, pay schedule leave, time-off allowances)	4	37–45
06 Uses for salary and benefits surveys	4	46–54
07 Claims processing requirements (for example, workers' compensation, disability benefits)	4	55–63
08 Work-life balance practices (for example, flexibility of hours, telecommuting, sabbatical)	4	64–72
Human Resource Development and Retention (Functional Area 04)	**5**	
01 Applicable laws and regulations related to training and development activities (for example, Title VII, ADA, Title 17 [copyright law])	5	1–10
02 Training delivery format (for example, virtual, classroom, on the job, microlearning)	5	11–20
03 Techniques to evaluate training programs (for example, participant surveys, pre- and post-testing, after-action review)	5	21–30
04 Career development practices (for example, succession planning, dual career ladders)	5	31–40
05 Performance appraisal methods (for example, ranking, rating scales)	5	41–50
06 Performance management practices (for example, setting goals, benchmarking feedback)	5	51–60
Employee Relations (Functional Area 05)	**6**	
01 Applicable laws affecting employment in union and nonunion environments, such as laws regarding antidiscrimination policies, sexual harassment, labor relations, and privacy (for example, WARN Act, Title VII, NLRA)	6	1–10
02 Employee and employer rights and responsibilities (for example, employment at will, privacy, defamation, substance abuse)	6	11–20
03 Methods and processes for collecting employee feedback (for example, employee attitude surveys, focus groups, exit interviews)	6	21–30
04 Workplace behavior issues (for example, absenteeism, aggressive behavior, employee conflict, workplace harassment)	6	31–40
05 Methods for investigating complaints or grievances	6	41–50
06 Progressive discipline (for example, warnings, escalating corrective actions, termination)	6	51–60
07 Off-boarding or termination activities	6	61–70
08 Employee relations programs (for example, recognition, special events, diversity programs)	6	71–80
09 Workforce reduction and restructuring terminology (for example, downsizing, mergers, outplacement practices)	6	81–90

Official Exam Objective	Chapter Number	Question Number
Health and Safety (Functional Area 06)	**7**	
01 Applicable laws and regulations related to workplace health, safety, security, and privacy (for example, OSHA, Drug-Free Workplace Act, ADA HIPAA, Sarbanes-Oxley Act)	7	1–9
02 Risk mitigation in the workplace (for example, emergency evacuation procedures, health and safety, risk management, violence, emergencies)	7	10–18
03 Security risks in the workplace (for example, data, materials, or equipment theft; equipment damage or destruction; cyber-crimes; password usage)	7	19–27

INTRODUCTION

Over time the human resource profession has evolved from a back-office administration of paper and processes to one of strategic organizational purpose. Leveraging the workforce to achieve business objectives has become critical for organizations today. The quest to attract and retain top talent is an unquenchable thirst for organizations that want to compete in the marketplace. Understanding how to engage the workforce but within the risk and legal constraints has become a balancing act that human resource professionals must master in today's complex workplace.

Achieving successes in the human resource field can really only begin through proper education and understanding and must continue with the dedicated execution of this knowledge. This book was written to provide a foundation in the many different areas that make up effective human resources.

Take the pre-assessment exam in this book. Don't be fearful. We all have our strengths and weaknesses! Use this information to leverage your study time effectively.

After you've taken the pre-assessment exam, begin to plot out your study strategy. Utilize the practice questions not only to boost your knowledge level, but also to practice how identify what the question is asking in a timely manner. Be sure to read the companion *aPHR Associate Professional in Human Resources Certification All-in-One Exam Guide* before the exam. It will provide you with information about the exam and what to take with you.

We wish you the best of luck on your exam. Write to us and let us know how you did on the exam!

Tresha Moreland (Tresha@hrcsuite.com)
Gabriella Parente-Neubert (gabyneubert11@gmail.com)
Joanne Simon-Walters (HRvistaHR@gmail.com)

CHAPTER 1

Pre-assessment Test

Instructions

This pre-assessment test is designed to help you prepare to study for the HR Certification Institute (HRCI) Associate Professional in Human Resources (aPHR) certification exam. You should take this test to identify your current level of readiness to take the exam, as well as the areas where you should focus your study and preparation.

This pre-assessment test contains 60 questions to be taken in 60 minutes.

The 60 questions are similar in style and format to the questions you will see on the actual exam. As you prepare to take this pre-assessment test, you should try to simulate the actual exam conditions as closely as possible. Go to a quiet place and be sure that you will not be interrupted for the full length of time it will take to complete the test. Do not use any reference materials or other assistance while taking the pre-assessment test. Remember, the idea is to help you determine what areas you need to focus on during your preparation for the actual exam.

The pre-assessment test contains questions divided in proportion to the aPHR exam. Here is a breakdown of the exam content:

Knowledge Area	Exam Weight	Number of Pre-assessment Questions
1.0 HR Operations	38%	20
2.0 Recruitment and Selection	15%	9
3.0 Compensation and Benefits	14%	8
4.0 Human Resource Development and Retention	12%	7
5.0 Employee Relations	16%	10
6.0 Health, Safety, and Security	5%	6

Complete the entire pre-assessment test before checking your results. Once you have finished, use both the Quick Answer Key and the In-Depth Answers section to score your pre-assessment test. You can use the table in the "Analyzing Your Results" section to determine how well you performed on the test.

Are you ready? Go ahead and set your clock for 60 minutes and begin!

1.0 HR Operations

1. The process by which the key stakeholders of an organization envision its future and develop a mission, objectives, and procedures to achieve that future is called:

    A. Goal planning

    B. Future planning

    C. Succession planning

    D. Strategic planning

2. Organizational culture reflects a shared understanding among all who work within the company. What are the common components of organizational culture?

    A. Vision, mission, and values

    B. Structure, systems, and people

    C. Values, beliefs, and norms

    D. Finance, marketing, and operations

3. The Fair Labor Standards Act (FLSA) of 1938 established:

    A. The equitable treatment of all workers

    B. Fair wages for all workers

    C. Overtime and minimum wage requirements

    D. A standard of conduct for supervisors

4. A financial services firm hires a trader who spent the last 4 years in state prison for committing a battery against a coworker. The financial services firm is in Wyoming, but the trader did his jail time in state prison in Arizona. In an effort to reduce costs, HR did a background check, but it was only for the state of Wyoming. How would you safeguard the company from any legal exposure in the future?

    A. This is an example of negligent hiring. The company should conduct complete background and reference checks, including a check of both state and FBI records going forward.

    B. The company should get all candidates' written consent before performing a background check going forward.

    C. The company is guilty of negligent hiring and may be in violation of the Privacy Act of 1974 and should report the situation to the Department of Labor.

    D. Place the employee on leave for not disclosing this information during the interview process, investigate, and determine if the employee should remain employed.

5. Which core business function is responsible for developing and delivering a company's products or services to customers?

   A. Marketing

   B. Finance

   C. Operations

   D. Research and development

6. What qualifies as having a "disability" under the ADA?

   A. A physical or mental impairment that substantially limits three or more major life activities, a record of such an impairment, or you are regarded as having such an impairment.

   B. A physical or mental impairment that substantially limits one or more major life activities, a record of such an impairment, or you are regarded as having such an impairment.

   C. A physical or mental impairment that substantially limits two or more major life activities, a record of such an impairment, or you are regarded as having such an impairment.

   D. A physical or mental impairment that substantially limits four or more major life activities, a record of such an impairment, or you are regarded as having such an impairment.

7. Which of the following is a true statement about measuring days to fill?

   A. Days to fill should be monitored closely because the longer a position remains open, the more likely it is to go unfilled

   B. Days to fill (speed) should be evaluated in relation to cost and quality of hire

   C. It is more cost effective for companies to hire temporary workers once a key position is open for more than 2 months

   D. If it is taking a while to fill a position, a company should adjust the total compensation for the position

8. Computer software that simulates a worksheet used to tabulate data and create graphs based on data is known as what tool?

   A. Presentation

   B. Application

   C. Spreadsheet

   D. Balance sheet

9. Ensuring that a test or a survey effectively measures what it is supposed to measure is known as:

   A. Effectiveness

   B. Quality

   C. Auditing

   D. Validity

10. A graphical representation of data using bars, often in different heights depending on the distribution of numerical data, is called a:

   A. Pie chart

   B. Histogram

   C. Scatter graph

   D. Line graph

11. Which of the following generally describes a security concern where a user deliberately accesses another user's computer without permission?

   A. Hacking

   B. Phishing

   C. E-card

   D. Security alert

12. Which of the following is an important component of an employee record policy?

   A. Retention and destruction timeline expectations

   B. How big the employee record should be

   C. Ensure medical documents are with the general file

   D. HR office hours of which the record can be accessed

13. The Employee Retirement Income Security Act (ERISA) requires employers to file these annual reports on employee benefits offered:

   A. OSHA 300 log

   B. Form 5500

   C. EEO-1 form

   D. LM-1 report

14. Which choice represents an advantage of a "best-of-breed" HRIS solution?

   A. Quicker implementation because of a simpler system

   B. Careful management of vendor relationships

   C. Ease of data integration

   D. Least expensive

15. What is the main reason why an employee who is misclassified as an independent contractor would want to get that corrected as soon as possible?

    A. Miss out on company activities

    B. Miss out on employer-paid taxes and benefits

    C. Miss out on being managed correctly

    D. Miss out on potential training

16. Each essential job function in a job description should consider?

    A. Pay level associated with it

    B. Level of complexity and frequency

    C. Education needed to complete the job function

    D. Work experience of past incumbents in the job

17. Organizational structures were designed to:

    A. Provide a decentralized decision-making process.

    B. Provide a framework for common requirements in the region that are different from other regions.

    C. Provide a framework that keeps the information flowing from functions to employees who need to keep the organization moving.

    D. Provide a formal and rigid process for businesses with a single product line.

18. An HR business process outcome (BPO) is an arrangement:

    A. Where payroll and benefit administration are entirely outsourced

    B. Where employees are leased to an outsourcing company

    C. Where employees are staffed by external recruitment agencies

    D. Where benefits are outsourced only to an external provider

19. Which of the following is the easiest way to recognize passive-aggressive communication in the workplace?

    A. Lack of assertiveness and directness

    B. Employees who have higher seniority

    C. Talking too much in meetings

    D. High absenteeism rates

20. Stating opinions and feelings and firmly advocating for their rights and needs without violating the rights of others is an example of what type of behavior:

    A. Passive-aggressive

    B. Assertive

    C. Aggressive

    D. Passive

2.0 Recruitment and Selection

21. Which of the following statements best describes the Older Worker Benefit Protection Act (OWBPA)?

    A. It is applicable only to public employers.

    B. Older workers can waive ADEA rights if they are given at least 10 business days to consider their options

    C. It prevents hiring discrimination on the basis of age.

    D. It's unlawful to target older workers during a reduction in force (RIF).

22. Which of the following is not specifically mentioned in Title VII of the Civil Rights Act of 1964 but has been interpreted by courts to be inclusive of this protection?

    A. Race

    B. Sex

    C. Gender identity

    D. National origin

23. Which of the following is an example of hiring discrimination?

    A. The applicant tracking system asks a person to disclose his or her race, sex, color, religion, national origin or age.

    B. The applicant tracking system fails to collect genetic and medical history information from all individuals.

    C. The applicant tracking system fails to process applications for those who have self-disclosed their disability status.

    D. The applicant tracking system requires individuals to take a test related to the position they are interested in.

24. Applicant tracking systems can miss out on a large talent pool today if they lack what functionality?

    A. Quality of hire tracking

    B. Ad placement tracking

    C. Cost per hire tracking

    D. Mobile access

25. An internal recruitment method employed by organizations to identify potential candidates from their existing employees is known as:

    A. Independent contractors

    B. Temporary agencies

    C. Job posting

    D. Employee referral

26. What is the main benefit of a job fair?

    A. Employers can quickly meet hundreds of job applicants.

    B. They are cost effective.

    C. Managers do not need to be present.

    D. Employers can pay employees less when recruiting from a job fair.

27. A worker who is self-employed is commonly referred to as a(n):

    A. Independent contractor

    B. Temporary worker

    C. Contingent contractor

    D. Seasonal help

28. Which type of interview uses past performance as a predictor of future behavior?

    A. Structured

    B. Competency based

    C. Behavioral

    D. Stress

29. Pre-offer drug testing could violate which act?

    A. Family Medical Leave Act

    B. Americans with Disabilities Act

    C. Age Discrimination in Employment Act

    D. Title VII of the Civil Rights Act

3.0 Compensation and Benefits

30. Which of the following laws states that the statute of limitations on pay discrimination lawsuits resets as each alleged discriminatory paycheck is issued?

    A. Lily Ledbetter Fair Pay Act

    B. Equal Pay Act

    C. Davis-Bacon Act

    D. Copeland "Anti-Kickback" Act

31. Which of the following identifies a pay adjustment that is given to all employees regardless of employee performance or the organization's financial health?

    A. Differential pay

    B. Market-based increase

    C. Cost of living adjustment

    D. Lump sum increase

32. Which of the following is an example of a tangible reward?

    A. Pat on the back

    B. Public thank-you

    C. Fringe benefits

    D. Development coaching

33. Which of the following is a health and welfare program where an employee may receive incentives to complete a smoking cessation program?

    A. Wellness

    B. Employee Assistance Program (EAP)

    C. Disability

    D. Workers' compensation

34. A bank of hours in which the employer provides time that employees use for sick, vacation, and holidays is known as:

    A. Vacation time off

    B. Personal time off

    C. Sick time off

    D. Paid time off

35. If an organization chooses to focus on the 75th percentile of the market, what type of pay philosophy has it adopted?

    A. Market leader

    B. Lag-lead

    C. Matching the market

    D. Market lag

36. The definition of disability is detailed in which of the following acts?

    A. Title VII of the Civil Rights Act

    B. Americans with Disabilities Act

    C. Age Discrimination in Employment Act

    D. Family Medical Leave Act

37. Which of the following is an example of a compressed workweek?

    A. Working from home

    B. Sharing job responsibilities with another colleague

    C. Working four 10-hour days

    D. Working 20 hours a week

4.0 Human Resource Development and Retention

38. Which type of patent protects new processes, machines, manufacture, or composition of matter?

    A. Design

    B. Plant

    C. Utility

    D. Re-issue

39. Training that is designed to mimic certain processes, events, or scenarios of the participant's job is called:

    A. Lecture

    B. E-learning

    C. Simulation

    D. Classroom

40. A common form of training that utilizes more experienced and skilled employees to train less skilled and experienced employees is called:

    A. E-learning

    B. Simulation

    C. On-the-job training

    D. Scenario

41. Which of the following data gathering methods would help the HR manager determine whether employee behavior has changed after training?

    A. Checklist

    B. 360-degree feedback

    C. Post-measure test

    D. ROI analysis

42. A process for identifying and developing new leaders who can replace leaders when they leave an organization is called:

    A. Strategic planning

    B. Contingency planning

    C. Goal setting

    D. Succession planning

43. _____ is a process that collects information from the employee's supervisor, colleagues and subordinates about an individual's work.

   A. 360-degree feedback

   B. Competency based

   C. Ranking

   D. Forced distribution

44. What is a SMART goal?

   A. Smart, measurable, attainable, realistic, target

   B. Smart, measurable, affirmation, realistic, time bound

   C. Smart, measurable, attainable, realistic, time bound

   D. Smart, meaningful, attainable, realistic, time bound

5.0 Employee Relations

45. A company reaches an agreement with a labor union that states that only union members will be employed with the company. Which of the following laws makes it illegal to establish a closed shop except in the construction industry?

   A. National Labor Relations Act

   B. Wagner Act

   C. Taft-Hartley Act

   D. Labor-Management Reporting and Disclosure Act

46. With respect to sexual harassment, what is quid pro quo?

   A. A favor for a superior in return for a special favor

   B. Hostile work environment

   C. Harassment directed at a female manager by a subordinate

   D. Exchange of sexual favors between peers

47. Which of the following describes an employment-at-will exception?

   A. Employee terminated after filing a workers' compensation claim

   B. A candidate discusses salary range, job title and level with HR

   C. An employee on long-term disability leave is terminated from employment

   D. An employee is fired for no stated reason

48. Surveys that solicit employee ideas and feedback for improving the organization are called:

    A. Competitor surveys

    B. Manager surveys

    C. Opinion surveys

    D. Customer surveys

49. Unwelcome sexual advances, requests for sexual favors, and other verbal or physical conduct of a sexual nature is known as what type of misconduct?

    A. Drug use in the workplace

    B. Sexual harassment

    C. Retaliation

    D. Employee conflict

50. A top mistake in handling complaints or grievances is which of the following?

    A. Conducting a timely investigation

    B. Ensuring objectivity

    C. Ignoring the complaints

    D. Outsourcing the investigation

51. What is the main advantage to an organization using the alternative dispute resolution process?

    A. Decreases HR/management time spent on disputes

    B. Decreases costs related to conducting investigations

    C. Decreases conflict within the organization

    D. Decreases the number of disputes that might end up in court

52. Which of the following is a *not* an HR best practice when terminating an employee or potentially terminating an employee?

    A. Look at all investigation materials and then make a decision

    B. Make a decision on the spot after the accusation has been made

    C. Document witness testimony

    D. Give outplacement information to the employee

53. A procedure that provides clear guidance for supervisors and employees to systematically and fairly resolve complaints is known as which of the following?

    A. An open door policy

    B. An HR resolution policy

    C. A grievance process

    D. A team-building process

54. Which restructuring driver is in place when a company is experiencing a reduction in revenue?

   A. Strategy

   B. Downsizing

   C. Structure

   D. Expansion

6.0 Health, Safety, and Security

55. Drake, the lead groundskeeper, is off the company's premises, cleaning the back access road leading to the company's building. Drake slips, falls, and injures his back. Per the Occupational Safety and Health Act (OSHA), this situation requires:

   A. All employees to be trained on safety protocols

   B. Recording on the OSHA 300 log

   C. The employee to seek medical attention

   D. The employee to be sent home

56. Which of the following requires that a publicly traded company's employment offers consistently meet internal approval requirements, that they are consistent with established salary ranges, and that salary increases are documented and approved in accordance with internal policies?

   A. Occupational Safety and Health Act

   B. Equal Employment Opportunity Commission

   C. Sarbanes-Oxley Act

   D. Fair Labor Standards Act

57. Rumors have been circulating that one of the employees has been receiving threatening calls at work from her former abusive spouse. Which of the following is the best immediate action the employer should take to minimize liability?

   A. Because rumors are circulating at this point, calm employees down and educate them about expectations against spreading gossip in the workplace.

   B. Meet with leadership, develop a "violence in the workplace" policy, and get supervisors involved in training employees on the new policy.

   C. Interview the employee allegedly receiving calls, assess whether there is a danger to her and others in the workplace, and take preventative steps.

   D. Establish an evacuation plan, train all employees on the new plan, conduct regular evacuation drills, and notify local authorities of the drills.

58. Your HR department has been tasked with formulating a disaster recovery plan. What is your first step?

   A. Inventory office equipment.

   B. Make an inventory of all jobs that would need to be relocated to keep the business running.

   C. Send files off-site for backup.

   D. Contact an insurance agent to inquire about necessary coverage.

59. A fake e-mail sent to HR, seemingly from an organization's executive, requesting sensitive information such as Social Security numbers, salary, and dates of birth is known as what type of scam?

   A. Telemarketing scam

   B. Phishing scam

   C. Pyramid scam

   D. Chain letter scam

60. Intellectual property refers to which of the following?

   A. Laptops, computers, tablets, and smart phones

   B. Reports, spreadsheets, presentations, and memos

   C. Internet, intranet, company software, and databases

   D. Patents, trademarks, copyrights, and trade secrets

1.0 HR Operations

1. D	**8.** C	**15.** B
2. C	**9.** D	**16.** B
3. C	**10.** B	**17.** C
4. A	**11.** A	**18.** A
5. C	**12.** A	**19.** A
6. B	**13.** B	**20.** B
7. D	**14.** A	

HR Operations score: _____

2.0 Recruitment and Selection

21. D	**24.** D	**27.** A
22. C	**25.** D	**28.** C
23. C	**26.** A	**29.** B

Recruitment and Selection score: _____

3.0 Compensation and Benefits

30. A	**33.** A	**36.** B
31. C	**34.** D	**37.** C
32. C	**35.** A	

Total Compensation and Benefits score: _____

4.0 Human Resource Development and Retention

38. C	**41.** B	**44.** C
39. C	**42.** D	
40. C	**43.** A	

Human Resource Development
and Retention score: _____

5.0 Employee Relations

45. C	**49.** B	**53.** C
46. A	**50.** C	**54.** B
47. A	**51.** D	
48. C	**52.** B	

Employee Relations score: _____

6.0 Health, Safety, and Security

55. B	**57.** C	**59.** B
56. C	**58.** B	**60.** D

Health, Safety, and Security score: _____

1.0 HR Operations

1. ☑ **D**. The definition of strategic planning is indeed the process by which key
   stakeholders of an organization envision its future and develop a mission, objectives,
   and procedures to achieve that future.
   ☒ **A**, **B**, and **C** are incorrect. **A** is incorrect because establishing goals is a result of
   the larger planning process. **B** is incorrect because although it is true that the larger
   planning process may require looking into the future, that is only a part of the process.
   Although succession planning is an action that may result from the larger planning
   process, **C** is incorrect because succession planning is not the term describing the overall
   planning process.

2. ☑ **C**. Organizational culture is a shared understanding of values, beliefs, and
   norms. These are usually unwritten common understandings for all who work in any
   organization. Organizational culture is not something easily captured in a written
   document. Instead, organizational culture consists of shared values, beliefs, and norms
   that are widely embraced by employees and leadership.
   ☒ **A**, **B**, and **D** are incorrect. **A** is incorrect because vision, mission, and values are
   examples of statements that describe the objectives and priorities of an organization.
   B is incorrect because structure, systems, and people are internal components that make
   up an organization, and **D** is incorrect because finance, marketing, and operations are
   examples of functions within an organization.

3. ☑ **C**. The Fair Labor Standards Act (FLSA) of 1938 is the cornerstone wage and labor
   legislation. The FLSA established the 40-hour workweek, minimum wage, overtime
   guidelines and record-keeping, and child labor standards for both the private sector and
   governments.
   ☒ **A**, **B**, and **D** are incorrect. **A** and **B** are incorrect because the equitable treatment
   of all workers and fair wages for all workers are addressed in other legislation such as
   Title VII of the Civil Rights Act of 1964. **D** is incorrect because standards of conduct
   for supervisors are addressed both by employment legislation and by internal company
   policy; therefore, standards of conduct may vary from organization to organization.

4. ☑ **A**. The company is guilty of negligent hiring and should conduct complete
   background and reference checks, including a check of both state and FBI records going
   forward. Negligent hiring occurs when a company knew, or should have known, that a
   candidate is prone to be a danger to employees, customers, vendors, and anyone else the
   employee comes in contact with. If a thorough background check was done, including
   a search of the FBI database, it could have easily been uncovered that this employee was
   convicted and found guilty of battery.
   ☒ **B**, **C**, and **D** are incorrect. **B** is incorrect because, as it relates to HR, the FCRA
   requires that employers not use information obtained about an applicant's background in
   an adverse manner until certain criteria are met and that employers obtain consent prior

to conducting any background check. **C** and **D** are incorrect because while it is negligent hiring, the Privacy Act of 1974 regulates how information collected is stored, requires that the candidate know what is being collected, and prevents information collected from being used for any purpose other than that which was intended. This does not apply in this case.

5. ☑ **C**. Operations is the function that essentially makes the business go and brings it all together. Operations are responsible for developing, producing, and delivering products and services to the consumer. Marketing and research and development (R&D) defines a product/service, and sales figures out the best way to get consumers to buy the product/service.

   ☒ **A**, **B**, and **D** are incorrect. **A** is incorrect because marketing is responsible for positioning a product or service to the consumer. **B** is incorrect because finance is responsible for processing and documenting the financial resources of the company. **D** is incorrect because research and development is responsible for exploring and developing new products or services that will bring in future revenue for the company.

6. ☑ **B**. Under the ADA, you have a disability if you have at least one of the following: a physical or mental impairment that substantially limits one or more major life activities; a record of such an impairment; or you are regarded as having such an impairment.

   ☒ **A**, **C**, and **D** are incorrect. They are incorrect because the impairment needs only one limit on major life activity.

7. ☑ **B**. Talent acquisition must balance the desire to fill positions quickly with the cost to engage in aggressive recruiting tactics, as well as with the quality of the applicants. Losing focus on all three measures may decrease quality and lengthen the recruiting process.

   ☒ **A**, **C**, and **D** are incorrect. **A** is incorrect because the length that a position is open does not necessarily increase the likelihood that it will go unfilled. **C** and **D** are incorrect because both are recommended strategies to address hiring needs that companies might determine are best given the company's unique situation.

8. ☑ **C**. A spreadsheet is computer software such as Excel or Lotus that simulates a worksheet used to tabulate data and create graphs based on data entered. HR will often use spreadsheets to calculate compensation, employee scheduling, recruitment candidate tracking, checklists, and so on.

   ☒ **A**, **B**, and **D** are incorrect. None of them represents spreadsheet software that calculates data and creates graphs.

9. ☑ **D**. Validity is when a test or a survey effectively measures what it is supposed to measure. The validity of a test describes the degree to which you can make specific conclusions or predictions about people based on how they score.

   ☒ **A**, **B**, and **C** are incorrect. They do not represent the best definition of a valid test. Validity, or content validity, is the best formal answer.

10. ☑ **B**. A histogram is a graphical representation of data using bars, often in different heights depending on the distribution of numerical data. For example, a histogram may be used to display employee distribution by years of service, by age, or by salary.

☒ **A**, **C**, and **D** are incorrect. They are incorrect because a pie chart, a scatter graph, and a line graph display data other than in a bar format.

11. ☑ **A**. Hacking was used to describe exploring technology through trial and error. Today it has grown to mean the act of deliberately accessing another person's computer without their permission.

☒ **B**, **C**, and **D** are incorrect. **B** is incorrect because phishing is specifically the use of e-mails, phone calls, texts, or instant messages masked as originating from a legitimate source with the intent of enticing you to reveal your passwords in order to gain access to your computer and accounts. **C** is incorrect because an e-card usually references an online greeting card delivered via e-mail. Within the context of technological security, an e-card usually appears like a legitimate greeting or job announcement, but when the user opens it, a harmful program is released that could damage your computer. **D** is incorrect because a security alert is an e-mail or pop-up alerting you that your computer has been comprised and purports that clicking the link provided will run a program that will fix the problem. With respect to security risks, this e-mail is fake and will run a program that will infect your computer.

12. ☑ **A**. Retention and destruction timeline expectations are an important part of any employee record policy or procedure. Federal, state, and local laws and regulations require that specific employee records and documents, whether stored electronically or on paper, be kept for a specified period of time, even extending beyond the employee's termination date.

☒ **B**, **C**, and **D** are incorrect. **B** is incorrect because how large an employee file is irrelevant given record retention and destruction legal requirements, **C** is incorrect because medical records should never be kept with the general file documents because of privacy requirements, and **D** is incorrect because HR office hours are irrelevant given record retention and destruction legal requirements.

13. ☑ **B**. The Employee Retirement Income Security Act (ERISA) requires employers to file Form 5500 annual reports on employee benefits offered. Retirement and health benefit plans must file the Form 5500 to report their financial condition, investments, and operations. The due date for the Form 5500 reports is the last day of the seventh month after the plan year ends.

☒ **A**, **C**, and **D** are incorrect. All these options are irrelevant to ERISA reporting requirements.

14. ☑ **A**. A best-of-breed HRIS solution is the use of several smaller systems, each responsible for managing a different HR function. These systems are quicker to implement because they are not as complex as an integrated solution.

☒ **B**, **C**, and **D** are incorrect. **B** is incorrect because vendor management is a disadvantage of a best-of-breed solution. **C** is incorrect because ease of data integration is an advantage of an integrated solution. **D** is incorrect because an integrated solution is less expensive per application than multiple solutions like with the best-of-breed option.

15. ☑ **B.** The employee and the government would miss out on company-paid taxes and insurance

    ☒ **A, C,** and **D** are incorrect. Although they may be factors, none would not be the main reason why you would want to properly classify workers correctly.

16. ☑ **B.** Frequency and complexity should be considered when determining essential job functions.

    ☒ **A, C,** and **D** are incorrect. They are not relevant to the essential job functions.

17. ☑ **C.** Providing a framework keeps the information flowing from functions to employees who need to keep the organization moving.

    ☒ **A, B,** and **D** are incorrect. **A** is incorrect because this is an example of a functional structure. **B** is incorrect as this is an example of geographic structure. **D** is incorrect because this is an example of a divisional structure.

18. ☑ **A.** A business process outcome (BPO) is an arrangement where payroll and benefit administration is entirely outsourced.

    ☒ **B, C,** and **D** are incorrect. **B** is incorrect because this is an example of a professional employer organization (PEO). **C** and **D** are incorrect because they are not examples of a BPO.

19. ☑ **A.** The easiest way to recognize passive-aggressive employees is a lack of assertiveness or directness in forms of communication.

    ☒ **B, C,** and **D** are incorrect. They are not ways to recognize passive-aggressive behavior. They could potentially be factors but not the easiest or most direct way to recognize passive-aggressive employees.

20. ☑ **B.** Stating opinions and feelings and firmly advocating for their rights and needs without violating the rights of others are examples of assertive communication.

    ☒ **A, C,** and **D** are incorrect. **A** is incorrect because passive-aggressive is when individuals appear passive on the surface but are really acting out anger in a subtle, indirect, or behind-the-scenes way. **C** is incorrect because expressing their feelings and opinions and advocating for their needs in a way that violates the rights of others is an example of aggressive communication. **D** is incorrect because passive communication would be when someone exhibits a pattern of not expressing their opinions or feelings, protecting their rights, or identifying and meeting their needs.

2.0 Recruitment and Selection

21. ☑ **D.** The OWBPA amends the Age Discrimination in Employment Act (ADEA) to provide additional protections to older workers. One of those protections is that during a reduction in force, older workers can't be targeted for early retirement.

    ☒ **A, B,** and **C** are incorrect. **A** is incorrect because the OWBPA is applicable to public and private employers. **B** is incorrect because older workers can't waive ADEA rights unless they are given 21 days to consider or 45 days when there is a group termination or a voluntary retirement program is under consideration. **C** is incorrect because the OWBPA does not provide guidelines related to hiring. The overarching legislation, the ADEA, does.

22. ☑ **C.** Gender identity, a person's internal sense of masculinity or femininity, is covered under Title VII due to court decisions but was not specifically included in the act. Title VII refers to sex discrimination, which the EEOC has interpreted to include gender and gender identity.

☒ **A, B,** and **D** are incorrect. They are incorrect because race, sex, and national origin are all specifically named in Title VII.

23. ☑ **C.** When the applicant tracking system fails to process applications for those who have self-disclosed their disability status, this is an example of discrimination. This would be considered disparate impact if it has a disproportionate "adverse impact" against any group based on race, national origin, color, religion, sex, familial status, or disability when there is no legitimate, nondiscriminatory business need for the practice. This is true even when there is an accidental system glitch that causes the disparity.

☒ **A, B,** and **D** are incorrect. None of these is the best answer because none of these answers are an example of discrimination.

24. ☑ **D.** Applicant tracking systems can miss out on a large talent pool today if they lack mobile access functionality. Statistics show a growing majority of talent utilizes smart phones and tablets. Utilizing an applicant tracking database that enables the applicant to apply for jobs from their smart phone gives an organization a competitive advantage in attracting top talent.

☒ **A, B,** and **C** are incorrect. None of these answers is a hiring metric. They are not of interest to potential applicants.

25. ☑ **D.** An internal recruitment method employed by organizations to identify potential candidates from their existing employees is known as an employee referral. The employee referral recruitment method is thought of as one of the most effective methods of recruiting talented people to an organization.

☒ **A, B,** and **C** are incorrect. **A** is incorrect because an independent contractor is someone from outside the organization to do work. **B** is incorrect because temporary agencies are an external agency that fills job openings temporarily for an organization, and **C** is incorrect because a job posting is not an accurate definition of an employee referral program.

26. ☑ **A.** Employers can quickly meet hundreds of job applicants at a job fair.

☒ **B, C,** and **D** are incorrect. These are not factors of a job fair. Managers would still need to be present, employers would still need to pay fair wages, and typically a job fair is not a low-cost strategy.

27. ☑ **A.** A worker who is self-employed is commonly referred to as an independent contractor.

☒ **B, C,** and **D** are incorrect. **B** is incorrect because a temporary worker works for a company only on a temporary basis and could be referred by an agency. **C** is incorrect because it is an incorrect term. **D** is incorrect because a seasonal worker would work only during one time period per year or season when the company is busiest.

28. ☑ **C.** Behavioral interviews include questions such as, "Tell me about a time…" or "Describe a situation…" These questions are designed to get the candidate to describe situations they have encountered in the past and explain how they handled them and the final outcome. The idea is that past behavior will help interviewers predict future behavior.

☒ **A, B,** and **D** are incorrect. **A** is incorrect because a structured interview means that the interviewer asks the same questions of every candidate. **B** is incorrect because a competency-based interview occurs when an interviewer asks questions based on the competencies required for success in the role and candidates are asked to demonstrate an example of the competency. **D** is incorrect because a stress interview is one where a candidate is purposely asked questions to place them on the defensive. The goal of the interview is to analyze how a candidate reacts under pressure. Stress interviews may be used in jobs such as EMT or 911 operators where the candidate will encounter several high-pressure situations on a regular basis.

29. ☑ **B.** Doing pre-offer drugs tests could violate the Americans with Disabilities Act.

☒ **A, C,** and **D** are incorrect. **A** is incorrect because the Family Medical Leave Act requires covered employers to provide employees with job protection and unpaid leave for qualified medical and family reasons. **C** is incorrect because the Age Discrimination in Employment Act protects workers older than 40 against discrimination. **D** is incorrect because the Title VII of the Civil Rights Act prohibits employment discrimination based on race, color, religion, sex, and national origin.

3.0 Compensation and Benefits

30. ☑ **A.** This is the main tenet of the Lily Ledbetter Fair Pay Act.

☒ **B, C,** and **D** are incorrect. **B** is incorrect because the Equal Pay Act prohibits wage discrimination by requiring equal pay for equal work. **C** is incorrect because this refers to establishing prevailing wage and benefit requirements for contractors on federally funded projects. **D** is incorrect because this refers to precluding a federal contractor or subcontractor from inducing an employee to give up any part of the compensation to which is the employee is entitled.

31. ☑ **C.** A cost of living adjustment (COLA) is paid to employees to protect against inflation. A COLA is usually offered in cases where an employee is relocating from a market with a lower cost of living to an area where the cost of living is markedly higher.

☒ **A, B,** and **D** are incorrect. **A** is incorrect because differential pay is dependent on performance and is paid to employees who assume more risk. **B** is incorrect because a market-based increase is a pay strategy where a company increases employees' pay rates to remain competitive with the market. This strategy is often used by companies to attract top talent. **D** is incorrect because a lump sum increase is the same as a performance bonus used to reward employees.

32. ☑ **C**. A fringe benefit is an example of a tangible reward. Health benefits, gift cards, and merchandise are additional examples of a tangible reward.

☒ **A**, **B**, and **D** are incorrect. **A** is incorrect because a pat on the back is not tangible. It is not something that can be converted to cash. **B** is incorrect because a public thank you is also not a tangible reward, and **C** is incorrect because development coaching is also not an intangible reward. While it can be motivating to have the opportunity for career development, it is not considered a tangible reward.

33. ☑ **A**. Wellness programs are established to promote health and wellness. Utilization of wellness programs correlate to a reduction in healthcare premium costs to the employer. Therefore, it is common to incentivize wellness programs.

☒ **B**, **C**, and **D** are incorrect. **B** is incorrect because an EAP is a service employers offer that helps employees work through certain personal matters or work-related matters that may affect performance. **C** is incorrect because disability benefits are paid to employees when they are physically unable to work. **D** is incorrect because workers' compensation pays employees in cases where injuries are sustained on the job.

34. ☑ **D**. Paid time off (PTO) is a bank of hours in which the employer provides time that employees use for illness, vacation, and holidays. It may also be called personal time off. Essentially employers may adopt one of two ways to provide employees paid time off. One way is they may have them in separate banks such as a sick bank and a separate vacation bank. Another way is when the employer combines sick, vacation, holidays, and personal time into one bank called PTO. Typically, the bank of hours is accrued (or earned) every full pay period an employee works for an organization.

☒ **A**, **B**, and **C** are incorrect. While all are time-off provisions, vacation, personal, and sick time stated and accrued separately is not PTO, or an all-in-one bank of hours.

35. ☑ **A**. If an organization chooses to focus on the 75th percentile of the market, it has adopted a market leader compensation or pay philosophy. The 75th percentile indicates that the pay is better than 74 percent of the organizations participating in the survey.

☒ **B**, **C**, and **D** are incorrect. **B** is incorrect because a lag-lead pay philosophy is when an organization chooses to lag in the market the first part of the year and catch up and lead the market the second part of the year. **C** is incorrect because matching the market means the employer intends to align the midpoint of the pay ranges to the 50th percentile of the market, and **D** is incorrect because market lag means the employer intends to align the midpoint of its pay ranges to the 25th or lower percentile.

36. ☑ **B**. The Americans with Disabilities Act broadly defines a disability.

☒ **A**, **C**, and **D** are incorrect. **A** is incorrect because Title VII of the Civil Rights Act prohibits employers from discriminating against employees on the basis of sex, race, color, national origin, and religion. **C** is incorrect because the Age Discrimination in Employment Act protects people who are 40 or older from discrimination because of age. **D** is incorrect because the Family Medical Leave Act requires covered employers to provide employees job-protected and unpaid leave for qualified medical and family reasons.

37. ☑ **C.** Working four 10-hour days is an example of a compressed workweek.

☒ **A, B,** and **D** are incorrect. **A** is incorrect because working from home would be an example of telecommuting. **B** is incorrect because sharing job responsibilities with another colleague would be called job sharing. **D** is incorrect because working 20 hours a week would be considered part-time.

4.0 Human Resource Development and Retention

38. ☑ **C.** A utility patent protects new processes, machines, manufacture, and composition of matter.

☒ **A, B,** and **D** are incorrect. **A** is incorrect because a design patent is granted for the ornamental design of a functional item. **B** is incorrect because a plant patent protects an asexually reproduced variety of plants. **D** is incorrect because a re-issue patent is granted to correct an error in an already issued utility, design, or plant patent.

39. ☑ **C.** Training that is designed to mimic certain processes, events, or scenarios that may occur on the participant's job is called simulation training. Simulation training is used by healthcare professionals, airline pilots, and military professionals to aid in the critical decision-making they need on the job.

☒ **A, B,** and **D** are incorrect. **A** is incorrect because lecture is a one-way information-sharing method typically occurring in a classroom. **B** is incorrect because e-learning is a computer-based or online training that may not involve simulation training. **D** is incorrect because classroom training is in a physical room that may not include training that is based on scenarios that may occur on the job.

40. ☑ **C.** A common form of training that utilizes more experienced and skilled employees to train less skilled and experienced employees is called on-the-job training (OJT).

☒ **A, B,** and **D** are incorrect. E-learning, simulation, and scenario don't necessarily involve using more experienced and skilled workers to train those who are less skilled and experienced. While each of those can be used to train people on the job, one of the most common forms of training seen today is on-the-job training that involves knowledge transfer from a more experienced employee to a less experienced employee.

41. ☑ **B.** A 360-degree feedback process is a data-gathering method that supports Kilpatrick's behavior training effectiveness measure, which is level 3.

☒ **A, C,** and **D** are incorrect. **A** is incorrect because a checklist is a data-gathering method of level 1, reaction. **C** is incorrect because a post-measure test is a data-gathering method for level 2 – learning. **D** is incorrect because an ROI analysis is a data gathering method for level 4, results.

42. ☑ **D.** A process for identifying and developing new leaders who can replace leaders when they leave an organization is called succession planning. Effective succession plans focus on a 1- to 3-year plan that prepares employees for future roles.

☒ **A, B,** and **C** are incorrect answers. **A** is incorrect because strategic planning refers to the overall plan for the organization. **B** is incorrect because a contingency plan refers to a pre-thought-out strategy for addressing scenarios that may disrupt normal business operations. **C** is incorrect because goal setting is individualized or organizational objectives to achieve. Goal setting may be an outcome of succession planning once skill gaps are identified as part of the succession plan process.

43. ☑ **A.** The process that collects information from the employee's supervisor, colleagues, and subordinates about an individual's work is the 360-degree process.

   ☒ **B, C,** and **D** are incorrect. **B** is incorrect because a competency-based system focuses on performance as measured against specified competencies (as opposed to specific tasks or behaviors) that are identified for each position. **C** is incorrect because ranking is a performance appraisal method that lists all employees in a designated group from highest to lowest in order of performance. **D** is incorrect because forced distribution is a performance appraisal method when ratings of employees in a particular group are disbursed along a bell curve, with the supervisor allocating a certain percentage of the ratings within the group to each performance level on the scale.

44. ☑ **C.** SMART stands for smart, measurable, attainable, realistic, and time bound.

   ☒ **A, B,** and **D** are incorrect. **A** is incorrect because target is not correct, as the *T* should be time bound. **B** is incorrect because affirmation is not correct; the *A* should be attainable. **D** is incorrect because meaningful is not correct; the *M* should be measurable.

5.0 Employee Relations

45. ☑ **C.** The Taft-Hartley Act amended the National Labor Relations Act and outlawed closed shops. A closed shop is a company where employees are required to join a union as a condition of employment.

   ☒ **A, B,** and **D** are incorrect. **A** and **B** are incorrect because the National Labor Relations Act, also known as the Wagner Act, established the basic rights of employees to form unions. **D** is incorrect because the Labor Management Reporting and Disclosure Act established reporting requirements for unions, union officers, employees, and employers; set standards for electing union officers; and established safeguards for protecting the assets of labor organizations.

46. ☑ **A.** *Quid pro quo* translates to "this for that" and describes anytime a superior demands a sexual favor of a subordinate in return for special favors such as raises or promotions.

   ☒ **B, C,** and **D** are incorrect. **B** is incorrect because hostile work environment is another type of sexual harassment. **C** is incorrect because it describes a form of bullying or illegal harassment but not sexual harassment. **D** is incorrect because an exchange of sexual favors between peers does not describe quid pro quo; however, if one of the parties is nonconsensual, it could be sexual harassment or sexual assault, which isn't necessarily rape, but would include rape.

47. ☑ **A.** Terminating an employee after filing a workers' compensation claim is a public policy exception to the at-will-employment doctrine.

   ☒ **B, C,** and **D** are incorrect. **B** is incorrect because discussing salary range, job title, and level is not an oral contract that would be considered an implied-contract exception to the at-will employment doctrine. **C** is incorrect because an employee can be terminated while on any leave. This is not an exception to the at-will doctrine.

D is incorrect because firing an employee for no reason is central to the employment-at-will doctrine.

48. ☑ **C.** Surveys that solicit employee ideas and feedback for improving the organization are called opinion surveys. It can also be called an employee engagement or employee satisfaction survey. Often these surveys are conducted periodically, and the results are compared to industry benchmark data to assess the level of employee engagement and determine improvement opportunities.

    ☒ **A, B,** and **D** are incorrect. Competitor, manager, and customer surveys do not solicit feedback directly from employees.

49. ☑ **B.** Unwelcome sexual advances, requests for sexual favors, and other verbal or physical conduct of a sexual nature are known as sexual harassment. The harasser can be any gender and be an organization's supervisor, co-worker, or those who are not an employee of the company such as a vendor or customer.

    ☒ **A, C,** and **D** are incorrect answers. While drug use in the workplace, retaliation, and employee conflict are certainly workplace issues, they may not be sexual infractions as sexual harassment implies. However, retaliation could be a subset of harassment and is considered equally egregious under the law.

50. ☑ **C.** A top mistake in handling employee complaints or grievances is to ignore them. Ignoring employee complaints, no matter the reason, can make a bad situation worse and costly for the employer. This is particularly true if the complaints indicate serious work conditions such as harassment, hostile work environment, or discrimination. As with the case *Walsh v. National Computer Systems, Inc.,* the courts found that HR was neglectful in investigating disparate treatment and hostile work environment complaints from the employee, Shireen Walsh. HR cited the reason for not investigating the complaint was because they "didn't want to take sides" and feared an investigation would lead to more complaints. The cost was a $438,145 judgment against the employer and ultimately a damaged reputation.

    ☒ **A, B,** and **D** are incorrect. Conducting a swift and objective investigation is smart and a "must do" strategy. In addition, some chief human resources officers may choose to outsource highly sensitive investigations, such as a matter relating to a high-ranking executive, to an outside third-party investigator to remove all appearances of bias.

51. ☑ **D.** ADR will reduce the number of disputes that end up in court.

    ☒ **A, B,** and **C** are incorrect. These choices are not the main advantage of using the ADR. Each option is a factor and important but would not be a main advantage.

52. ☑ **B.** Making a decision on the spot after an accusation has been made would not be an HR best practice because it is always prudent to complete a thorough, dispassionate, and objective investigation first before deciding.

    ☒ **A, C,** and **D** are incorrect. **A** is incorrect because looking through all relevant documents and investigation findings before making a decision is the HR best practice. **C** is incorrect because getting all the facts and documenting witness information is prudent before making a decision. **D** is incorrect because giving outplacement information to an employee helps the employee who is being terminated to find another position.

53. ☑ **C.** A grievance process is a systematic and fair procedure for supervisors and employees to resolve complaints that arise. It typically includes timelines, what is eligible, and the decision-making process involved.

☒ **A, B,** and **D** are incorrect. **A** is incorrect because an open-door policy refers to a communication philosophy indicating employees are free to voice their concerns to any level of management at any time. **B** is incorrect because while often supervisors mistake the grievance process as an HR-only procedure, it is a process that should be adopted wholeheartedly by the supervisors for it to be effective. **D** is incorrect because a team building process is an overbroad concept and it does not effectively reflect the grievance process.

54. ☑ **B.** Downsizing is a restructuring driver that is employed when a company is experiencing a decline in revenue.

☒ **A, C,** and **D** are incorrect. **A** is incorrect because a change in strategy is a restructuring driver that organizations employ when they are interested in pursuing new markets. **C** is incorrect because structure refers to when an organization changes its business model to improve efficiencies. **D** is incorrect because expansion refers to when a company expands to accommodate new staff and departments.

6.0 Health, Safety, and Security

55. ☑ **B.** Providing medical assistance and giving time off are good practices; however, they are not considered required practices under the Occupational Safety and Health Act (OSHA). In addition, this scenario describes the employee being off-premises but conducting company business. Because the employee was conducting company business, the location is irrelevant. The employer is required to record this incident on the OSHA 300 log.

☒ **A, C,** and **D** are incorrect. **A** is incorrect because while training employees is a good practice, it is not a requirement upon an injury. **C** is incorrect because seeking medical attention is not a requirement. **D** is incorrect because sending the employee home is not a requirement.

56. ☑ **C.** Section 404 of the Sarbanes-Oxley Act requires that public companies routinely review and test internal financial transaction controls (approval process). Thus, all salary offers, raises, or any other compensation must be documented and follow an established internal signature approval process.

☒ **A, B,** and **D** are incorrect. **A** is incorrect because the focus of the OSH Act is to protect employees from injury or illness. **B** is incorrect because the EEOC is the agency created by Title VII to promote equal opportunities in employment for protected classes. **D** is incorrect because the FLSA is a law that regulates employee status, overtime pay, child labor, minimum wage, record-keeping, and other wage-related administrative issues.

57. ☑ **C.** Under the General Duty Clause of OSHA, the employer is required to provide "place[s] of employment which are free from recognized hazards that are causing or are likely to cause death or serious physical harm to his employees" (General Duty Clause, Section 5(a)(1)). In this case, the employer is hearing rumors of a possible threat that may or may not come into the workplace. The best step is to investigate and determine whether there is a viable threat and take appropriate preventative steps.

☒ **A, B,** and **D** are incorrect. **A** is incorrect because just calming employees down does not effectively address a possible threat to safety in the workplace. **B** is incorrect because while the employer may want to develop a "violence in the workplace" policy and train employees on the new policy as a good long-term practice, it doesn't address a possible eminent threat. **D** is incorrect because developing an evacuation plan is good for the long term but in the short term a threat needs to be assessed and dealt with immediately.

58. ☑ **B.** Taking inventory of all jobs needed for the business to operate is the most important and first thing HR should think about because without the proper staff, the business cannot operate. They should do this by coordinating with all departments.

☒ **A, C,** and **D** are incorrect. While these choices are applicable and needed during the process of disaster recovery planning, they are not the first step.

59. ☑ **B.** A fake e-mail sent to HR or anyone, seemingly from an organization's executive, requesting sensitive information is a phishing scam. Alarmingly, phishing scams are on the rise and unfortunately have been successful in fooling people, including those in HR, to share sensitive employee information. When organizations realize they have an information breach, they are obligated to notify those employees who are affected and will offer identity theft protection monitoring services.

☒ **A, C,** and **D** are incorrect. Telemarketing, pyramid, and chain letter scams are not necessarily in e-mail form.

60. ☑ **D.** Intellectual property refers to patents, trademarks, copyrights, and trade secrets. Intellectual property can be just as valuable to an organization as money in the bank. Organizations that are reliant on intellectual property are best served by having strong policies and limited access protocols in place.

☒ **A, B,** and **C** are incorrect. All other answers may represent property, but in a physical sense of the word and are not necessarily considered intellectual property.

Analyzing Your Results

Congratulations on completing the pre-assessment test. You should now take the time to analyze your results with two objectives in mind:

- Identifying the resources you should use to prepare for the HRCI aPHR exam
- Identifying the specific topics that you should focus on in your preparation

First, use this table to help you gauge your overall readiness for the aPHR examination. Total your score from all the aPHR questions for an overall score out of 60.

Number of Answers Correct	Recommended Course of Study
1–30	If this had been the actual aPHR exam, you probably would not have passed. We recommend you spend a significant amount of time reviewing the material in the aPHR Associate Professional in Human Resources Certification All-in-One Exam Guide before taking the actual exam.
31–44	If this had been the actual aPHR exam, you might have passed, but there is a significant risk that you would not. You should review your scores in the specific functional areas listed next to identify the particular areas that require your focused attention and use the aPHR Associates Professional in Human Resources Certification All-in-One Exam Guide to review that material. Once you have done so, you should proceed to work through the questions in this book.
45–60	Congratulations! If this was the actual aPHR exam, it is likely that you would have passed. You should use the aPHR Associate Professional in Human Resources Certification All-in-One Exam Guide and this book to refresh your knowledge and prepare yourself mentally for the actual exam.

Once you have identified your readiness for the aPHR exam, you can use the following table to identify the specific functional areas that require your focus as you continue your preparation.

Knowledge Area	Weight	Question Numbers in Pretest	High Priority for Additional Study	Medium Priority for Additional Study	Low Priority for Additional Study
1.0 HR Operations	38%	1–20	0–10 correct	11–16 correct	17–20 correct
2.0 Recruitment and Selection	15%	21–29	1–4 correct	5–7 correct	8–9 correct
3.0 Compensation and Benefits	14%	30–37	1–4 correct	5–6 correct	7–8 correct
4.0 Human Resource Development and Retention	12%	38–44	1–3 correct	4–5 correct	6–7 correct
5.0 Employee Relations	16%	45–54	1–5 correct	6–8 correct	9–10 correct
6.0 Health, Safety, and Security	5%	55–60	1–2 correct	3–4 correct	5–6 correct

HR Operations

This functional area includes coverage of the following responsibilities and knowledge objectives:

- **01** Organizational strategy and its connection to mission, vision, values, business goals, and objectives
- **02** Organizational culture (for example, traditions, unwritten procedures)
- **03** Legal and regulatory environment
- **04** Confidentiality and privacy rules that apply to employee records, company data, and individual data
- **05** Business functions (for example, accounting, finance, operations, sales and marketing)
- **06** HR policies and procedures (for example, ADA, EEO, progressive discipline)
- **07** HR metrics (for example, cost per hire, number of grievances)
- **08** Tools to compile data (for example, spreadsheets, statistical software)
- **09** Methods to collect data (for example, surveys, interviews, observation)
- **10** Reporting and presentation techniques (for example, histogram, bar chart)
- **11** Impact of technology on HR (for example, social media, monitoring software, biometrics)
- **12** Employee records management (for example, electronic/paper, retention, disposal)
- **13** Statutory reporting requirements (for example, OSHA, ERISA, ACA)
- **14** Purpose and function of human resource information systems (HRISs)
- **15** Job classifications (for example, exempt, nonexempt, contractor)
- **16** Job analysis methods and job descriptions
- **17** Reporting structure (for example, matrix, flat)
- **18** Types of external providers of HR services (for example, recruitment firms, benefits brokers, staffing agencies)
- **19** Communication techniques (for example, written, oral, e-mail, passive, aggressive)

CHAPTER 2

29

The human resource (HR) operations function consists of the day-to-day tasks essential to meeting the needs of employees and the organization. These tasks involve recruitment, benefits, and compensation; employee records management; and employee and labor relations. Human resource technology has become a large part of how HR manages operations. Successful HR professionals know and embrace HR data, HR metrics, and reporting concepts.

HR operations can entail processing workers' compensation claims, helping employees with their health benefit enrollment questions, analyzing market compensation data, or navigating a multitude of regulatory requirements. At any one time this function may also conduct performance improvement counseling or develop programs that are designed to engage employees.

This section of the book provides a rich collection of practice exam questions relating to HR operations. There are questions that span the 19 sections of the HR Certification Institute (HRCI) Associate Professional in Human Resources (aPHR) exam content outline. Because of the heavy weighting of this functional area on the aPHR exam, nearly 200 questions are dedicated to testing your knowledge on HR operations.

Go ahead and jump in! Use this chapter to gauge your knowledge of HR operations.

Good luck!

Objective 01   Organizational Strategy and Its Connection to Mission, Vision, Values, Business Goals, and Objectives

1. The process by which the key stakeholders of an organization envision its future and develop a mission, objectives, and procedures to achieve that future is called:

    A. Goal planning

    B. Future planning

    C. Succession planning

    D. Strategic planning

2. The process of analyzing and identifying the need and availability of labor resources so that the organization can meet its objectives is called:

    A. Human resource planning

    B. Recruitment requisition

    C. Objective planning

    D. Training needs assessment

3. A unique capability or advantage that differentiates the organization from its competitors is called:

    A. Research and development

    B. Core competency

    C. Providing cheaper products

    D. Hiring talent faster

4. A statement that describes what the future of the organization looks like is known as:

   A. Purpose statement

   B. Vision statement

   C. Financial statement

   D. Benefit statement

5. A description of how an organization will achieve its vision is called:

   A. Job description

   B. Purpose statement

   C. Mission statement

   D. Summary plan description

6. A statement that communicates the organization's top priorities and core beliefs to customers and employees is called:

   A. Code of conduct

   B. Employee handbook

   C. Purpose statement

   D. Values statement

7. The statement "We aspire to be the best widget maker in America" is an example of a:

   A. Vision statement

   B. Financial statement

   C. Mission statement

   D. Values statement

8. A SWOT analysis used for planning identifies an organization's:

   A. Statements, workplace, operations, and technology

   B. Safety, workforce, organization, and terms

   C. Strengths, weaknesses, opportunities, and threats

   D. Salary, wages, objectives, and taxes

9. In Michael Porter's *five forces analysis*, five forces shape the competitive landscape for any industry. What are they?

   A. Budget, workforce, wages, benefits, and leadership

   B. Political/legal, economic, social, technology, and competition

   C. Supply chain, finance, marketing, operations, and human resources

   D. Quality products, best price, fastest service, customer service, and sales

10. Ensuring that each employee within an organization can see the direction for the business and knows how their job fits in the overall picture is known as:

   A. Goal alignment

   B. Mission statement

   C. Performance evaluation

   D. Rewards and recognition

Objective 02   Organizational Culture

11. Organizational culture reflects a shared understanding among all who work within the company. What are the common components of organizational culture?

   A. Vision, mission, and values

   B. Structure, systems, and people

   C. Values, beliefs, and norms

   D. Finance, marketing, and operations

12. While it's not a written policy, while working in a particular organization, it is widely known that there are high expectations of employees to participate in community events such as parades and fundraisers. This is an example of what kind of cultural element?

   A. Values

   B. Objectives

   C. Norms

   D. Beliefs

13. In XYZ organization the leadership team thinks that the expression of humor in the workplace will improve productivity. This is an example of what kind of cultural element?

   A. Norms

   B. Beliefs

   C. Directives

   D. Values

14. What statement can be used to guide an organization's decisions and provides purpose for employees?

   A. Values statement

   B. Financial statement

   C. Goal statement

   D. Norms statement

15. Which of the following techniques is an example of how human resources can effectively shape organizational culture?

    A. Measuring how many applications have been processed within a certain timeframe

    B. Improving on how fast human resource staff members return phone calls and e-mails

    C. Reducing the number of meetings human resources and leadership attend during the week

    D. Establishing a compensation program that rewards employees for certain behaviors

16. Organizational culture can manifest itself in a physical form that often serves as a reminder of something important or a trigger for a special meaning. This element of culture is called:

    A. Rituals

    B. Artifacts

    C. Legends

    D. Beliefs

17. Employees frequently share a story of how the founder rescued the organization from the brink of closure because of an unscrupulous competitor by creating an innovative product and taking it to market quickly. Each time the story is shared, it reminds the employees of the importance of being innovative, quick thinking, and resilient. This is an example of what cultural element?

    A. Rituals

    B. Artifacts

    C. Legends

    D. Beliefs

18. A new-hire orientation and annual awards banquet is an example of what cultural element?

    A. Rituals

    B. Artifacts

    C. Legends

    D. Beliefs

19. A person from inside or outside an organization who assists an organization to transform itself is known as a(n):

    A. Human resource

    B. Executive leader

    C. Contingency worker

    D. Change agent

20. A person's ability to be aware of and control one's own emotions and ultimately successfully handle interpersonal relationships is known as:

   A. Anger management

   B. Emotional intelligence

   C. Human resource development

   D. Training and development

Objective 03   Legal and Regulatory Environment

21. The Fair Labor Standards Act (FLSA) of 1938 established:

   A. The equitable treatment of all workers

   B. Fair wages for all workers

   C. Overtime and minimum wage requirements

   D. A standard of conduct for supervisors

22. The Taft-Hartley Act protects employees from the unfair labor practices of

   A. Unions

   B. Employers

   C. Federal and state governments

   D. Private employers

23. A construction worker union refuses to do business with any company that buys supplies from a particular concrete company. This decision was made to support the workers at the concrete company who have reported multiple violations of the Fair Labor Standards Act (FLSA) with regard to overtime pay. As the HR director at Next Generation Home Builders, what advice would you provide to senior management?

   A. This hot-cargo contract clause is an unfair labor practice as defined by the National Labor Relations Act (NLRA).

   B. This featherbedding contract clause is an unfair labor practice as defined by the Labor Management Relations Act (LMRA).

   C. This yellow-dog contract clause is an unfair labor practice as defined by the Norris-LaGuardia Act.

   D. This iron-clad contract clause is an unfair labor practice as defined by the Labor Management Relations Act (LMRA).

24. Which of the following established that employers can be held vicariously liable for the actions of their employees in sexual harassment cases?

   A. Burlington Industries v. Ellerth

   B. Meritor Savings Bank v. Vinson

    C. Harris v. Forklift Systems

    D. Oncale v. Sundowner Offshore Services, Inc.

25. Jasmine, an African-American woman, resigns her position as account manager citing that she was harassed by the team leader who supervises her on a daily basis. The team leader has no authority to take tangible employment actions in regard to Jasmine. The sales director claims no knowledge of the events leading up to Jasmine's resignation. As the HR director, how would you advise senior management regarding the company's liability in this case?

    A. There is no liability because Jasmine did not report the incidents that led up to her decision to resign.

    B. The company is vicariously liable because the team leader meets the definition of a supervisor as established by the Ellerth and Faragher cases on sexual harassment.

    C. The company is not liable for the team leader's actions because the Supreme Court in *Vance v. Ball State University* narrowly defined supervisor as the person who may take tangible employment actions such as demotion or termination of employment.

    D. The company is liable because the team leader meets the definition of supervisor as established by the Equal Employment Opportunity Commission (EEOC).

26. A reservist was called to active duty for five years. Upon return to the United States mainland, he was informed that the position he left had been upgraded and filled by a permanent employee. Does the employer have any responsibilities to the reservist related to reinstatement of employment?

    A. The reservist has been gone more than 180 days; therefore, the employer has no duty to reinstate him in the same position.

    B. The reservist has 90 days following the completion of service to apply to the employer for reinstatement.

    C. The employer must reinstate the reservist promptly but may terminate his employment for cause within 60 days.

    D. The employer must reinstate the reservist promptly but may terminate his employment for cause after 180 days.

27. Scott, a 57-year-old white male, is interviewing for Director of Urban Affairs at the National Association for the Advancement of Colored People (NAACP). If Scott is not selected for the position, which of the following laws may be applicable?

    A. Norris-LaGuardia Act

    B. Title VII

    C. Landrum Griffith Act

    D. ADEA

28. An employee of a doctor's office often takes a work laptop home. Information about patients is stored on the laptop for the employee's easy reference. While the employee is in a local grocery store, someone breaks into his car and steals the laptop. Which federal law should the employer be concerned about?

    A. Federal Data Protection Act

    B. Sarbanes-Oxley Act of 2002

    C. Health Insurance Portability and Accountability Act

    D. Title 21 Code of Federal Regulations (21 CFR Part 11)

29. What would be the first step for an HR director when an employee requests an accommodation under the Americans with Disabilities Act?

    A. Assess reasonableness of accommodations

    B. Choose job accommodations

    C. Identify job accommodations

    D. Identify the essential job functions and barriers to performance

30. The Consolidated Omnibus Budget Reconciliation Act (COBRA), which provides the continuation of health coverage for a limited time after the loss of a job, is an amendment to which of the following?

    A. Health Insurance Portability and Accountability Act

    B. Uniformed Services Employment and Reemployment Rights Act (USERRA)

    C. Patient Protection and Affordable Care Act (ACA)

    D. Employee Retirement Income Security Act (ERISA)

Objective 04   Confidentiality and Privacy Rules That Apply to Employee Records, Company Data, and Individual Data

31. A financial services firm hires a trader who spent the last four years in state prison for committing a battery against a co-worker. The financial services firm is in Wyoming, but the trader did his jail time in state prison in Arizona. In an effort to reduce costs, HR did a background check, but it was only for the state of Wyoming. How would you safeguard the company from any legal exposure regarding this situation?

    A. The company should adopt a policy of conducting complete background and reference checks, including a check of both state and FBI records, going forward.

    B. The company should get all candidates' written consent before performing a background check going forward.

    C. The company is guilty of negligent hiring and may be in violation of the Privacy Act of 1974 and should report the situation to the Department of Labor.

    D. Place the employee on leave for not disclosing this information during the interview process, investigate, and determine if the employee should remain employed.

32. Jayson, a 20-year-old college student, gets hurt in a car accident in the company's vehicle. He is unconscious. The person in the vehicle with him is the HR manager and accompanies him to the hospital where some members of Jayson's family are already waiting. The HR manager discloses to the doctor and Jayson's cousin that Jayson is HIV positive. Has the HR manager violated the Health Insurance Portability and Accountability Act (HIPAA)?

   A. No, because the HR manager disclosed the information in order to save Jayson's life.

   B. Yes, because the HR manager divulged confidential medical information to Jayson's family member without his written consent.

   C. No, because Jayson's cousin just happened to be near the doctor when the HR manager was updating the doctor. The HR manager is covered by the bystander clause.

   D. Yes, because the HR manager should never disclose confidential medical information to anyone without Jayson's consent.

33. The Electronic Communications and Privacy Act of 1986 establishes:

   A. That an employer can monitor all employee communications

   B. That an employer can monitor employee e-mail without written consent

   C. That an employer can monitor employee electronic communications if the employer can show a legitimate business purpose

   D. That an employer can monitor oral communications only when transmitted via phone

34. There has been a recent uptick in theft at Brisbane Women's Clothing store. The CEO wants to install a surveillance system. As the HR manager, what should you be most concerned with when advising the CEO on the new system implementation?

   A. Is the monitoring system visible to employees?

   B. Are employees aware that there is a new policy?

   C. Are managers trained on how to operate the new system?

   D. Is the monitoring policy narrowly tailored?

35. The Stored Communications Act (SCA) establishes:

   A. That an employer can't intentionally access an employee's e-mails unless they are sent through the employer's server

   B. That an employee has a reasonable expectation of privacy even when accessing personal e-mail from work

   C. That an employer has the right to use any information transmitted via the employer's server if the employer has a legitimate business reason

   D. That an employee may store information on the employer's server as long as they are employed by said employer

36. Latoya resigned from her position as vice president of marketing at Kwesi Engineering. She failed to delete her personal e-mail account from the company iPad prior to returning it on her last day. For the next six months, Latoya's personal e-mail was accessible on the company phone and were read by her former manager. By reading the e-mails, did the manager violate any laws?

   A. Yes, this is a violation of the ECPA.

   B. No, Latoya has no expectation of privacy.

   C. No, Latoya gave implicit consent under the provisions of the SCA.

   D. Yes, under the provisions of the SCA, Latoya's negligence does not constitute authorization.

37. What is the difference between confidentiality and privacy?

   A. Confidentiality is how information is treated. Privacy is an employee's right to freedom from intrusion.

   B. There is no difference between confidentiality and privacy.

   C. Privacy is how information is treated. Confidentiality refers to an employee's right to keep personal matters and public matters separate.

   D. Confidentiality is whether a person has a right to information. Privacy refers to whether an organization has the right to share information.

38. Which of the following is a reason to disclose medical information that was obtained through pre-employment drug testing to a third party?

   A. The manager requests the information in relation to an employee transferring to a school bus driver position.

   B. For a disability claim.

   C. The employee gives verbal approval to release the information.

   D. Evidence of illegal drugs must always be reported to local law enforcement.

39. Jackson, a 47-year-old white male, was extended an offer of employment contingent on a successful drug screen. After 3 weeks on the job, he was released because amphetamines were found in his drug screen. Jackson shared on his application that he had a medical condition for which he was prescribed the amphetamines. Which federal law did the employer most likely violate when Jackson was fired?

   A. Drug-Free Workplace Act

   B. Age Discrimination in Employment Act

   C. Americans with Disabilities Act

   D. Title IV

40. Molly is informed by her new employer that her job offer is contingent on a successful background check. The background check will be conducted by the employer within 30 days. Which of the following statements about the employer's responsibility as it relates to the Fair Credit Reporting Act (FCRA) is correct?

   A. The employer must share with Molly how the information will be used.

   B. The employer is not required to comply with the FCRA.

   C. The employer must get Molly's written permission.

   D. The employer must let the consumer reporting agency (CRA) know that it obtained Molly's permission before conducting the background check.

Objective 05   Business Functions

41. Which of the following performance measures includes metrics in the areas of financial performance, customer satisfaction, efficiency of internal business processes, and company learning and growth?

   A. Balanced scorecard

   B. Benchmarking

   C. HR audit

   D. Lean Six Sigma

42. To provide expert consultation to the organization, an HR professional must understand how other functions in the organization perform their work. Which of the following is a core business function typically found in organizations?

   A. Sales and marketing

   B. Information technology

   C. Operations

   D. All of the above

43. Which core business function is responsible for developing and delivering a company's products or services to customers?

   A. Marketing

   B. Finance

   C. Operations

   D. Research and development

44. Which of the following best describes the difference between the role of finance versus the role of accounting in an organization?

   A. Accounting captures the day-to-day transactions of the business. Finance provides financial modeling and investment advice to the organization.

   B. Accounting and finance are terms used interchangeably to describe the business function led by a chief financial officer (CFO).

C. Finance is responsible for budgeting. Accounting is responsible for tracking expenditures.

D. Finance tracks financial metrics. Accounting ensures the company's books are balanced.

45. Which of the following best describes HR's cross-functional relationship with sales?

   A. Collaborating on ways to manage costs

   B. Managing labor relations in different markets

   C. Aligning incentive programs with local practices

   D. Collaborating with operations to develop staffing plans

46. What is HR's primary strategic value to the organization?

   A. Ability to recruit top talent for strategic initiatives

   B. Intimate knowledge of all core functional business areas

   C. Ensuring that the company is free from litigation

   D. Training and development of staff aligned to key strategic initiatives

47. Which of the following best describes HR's primary contribution to an organization's strategic plan?

   A. HR serves the needs of the entire organization as subject-matter experts (SMEs).

   B. HR provides the executive team with a menu of administrative tasks that it can execute more efficiently.

   C. HR interprets various HR metrics for the executive team to show how HR creates value to the organization.

   D. HR utilizes its "seat at the table" to share how additional HR staff can support the organization by providing better customer service.

48. The executive board of a test preparation company considers franchising. What would be the best organizational structure?

   A. Centralized

   B. Decentralized

   C. Matrix

   D. Functional

49. Why should HR be involved in the strategy formulation, development, implementation, and evaluation of a business?

   A. Staffing projections significantly contribute to a company's strategic direction.

   B. Ensure that HR has a "seat at the table" so that the voice of the people can be heard.

   C. Depending on the strategic orientation of the company, HR's role may differ.

   D. Ensure the strategy is compliant with federal, state, and local regulations.

50. Which functional areas might be a part of the decision-making process regarding the implementation of a new HRIS?

   A. An HRIS is a database to house employee information. Only HR needs to be part of determining how best to do so.

   B. Since this is an information system, it makes the most sense for IT to select the software that will run seamlessly on the company's existing platform.

   C. HR and IT.

   D. HR, IT, finance, accounting, and sales.

Objective 06   HR Policies and Procedures

51. Farough wants to return to work as an administrative assistant 2 days after carpal tunnel surgery on her right hand. She is right handed. The medical certification states that she can use her right hand in 14 days. If her employer agrees, which of the following return to work policies apply in this case?

   A. Reasonable accommodation

   B. Fit-for-duty exam

   C. Modified duty

   D. Interactive dialogue

52. What qualifies as having a "disability" under the ADA?

   A. A physical or mental impairment that substantially limits three or more major life activities, a record of such an impairment, or you are regarded as having such an impairment.

   B. A physical or mental impairment that substantially limits one or more major life activities, a record of such an impairment, or you are regarded as having such an impairment.

   C. A physical or mental impairment that substantially limits two or more major life activities, a record of such an impairment, or you are regarded as having such an impairment.

   D. A physical or mental impairment that substantially limits four or more major life activities, a record of such an impairment, or you are regarded as having such an impairment.

53. How many employees does a company need to have in order to comply with the Americans with Disabilities Act (ADA)?

   A. 25 employees

   B. 15 employees

   C. 20 employees

   D. 10 employees

54. The ADA makes it unlawful to discriminate in employment practices such as:

    A. Benefits

    B. Promotions

    C. Pay

    D. All of the above

55. Deemed a moral and social obligation to amend historical wrongs and eliminate the present effects of past discrimination is a(n):

    A. Code of conduct

    B. Vets 100 report

    C. Affirmative action plan

    D. EEO-1 report

56. Federal contractors above a dollar limit of _____ are required to institute affirmative action plans.

    A. $50,000

    B. $100,000

    C. $25,000

    D. $200,000

57. Who is required to file an annual EEO-1 report?

    A. All private employers that are subject to Title VII and have 50 or more employees

    B. All private employers that are subject to Title VII and have 75 or more employees

    C. All private employers that are subject to Title VII and have 100 or more employees

    D. All private employers that are subject to Title VII and have 150 or more employees

58. A progressive discipline process generally starts with:

    A. Performance improvement plan

    B. Co-worker warning the employee

    C. Verbal warning

    D. Written warning

59. What is the main reason a company would want to have a progressive disciplinary policy?

    A. Investors like seeing proper policies.

    B. It makes the HR department job's much easier.

    C. Marketing and operations require this of the HR department.

    D. Employees are treated fairly and to cultivate a positive corporate culture.

60. A series of increasingly severe penalties for repeated offenses is called:

    A. Performance evaluation

    B. Progressive discipline policy

    C. Performance improvement plan

    D. Formal discipline policy

Objective 07   HR Metrics

61. Ralph is the AVP of infrastructure for a small healthcare consulting company. He is concerned because he has had three employees resign in the last 3 months and his department is right in the middle of a major project deliverable. As his HR business partner, what metrics would be most useful to Ralph as you both determine the next course of action?

    A. Turnover ratio

    B. Number of grievances

    C. Cost per hire

    D. All of the above

62. Which of the following is the best example of a web metric that HR professionals can leverage to support a company's talent acquisition activities?

    A. Tracking referral sources

    B. Tracking number of fans

    C. Tracking number of web site followers

    D. Tracking number of retweets

63. A company operates in a competitive market. To be successful, they need to be able to attract top talent. Part of the objective is to determine whether they are competitive with benefits, compensation, and a reputation as a great place to work. What metric would you use to measure how effective the company is in hiring talent?

    A. Ratios of offers made to acceptances

    B. Involuntary resignation turnover

    C. Hires as a percentage of total employees

    D. Voluntary employee turnover within 90 days

64. A call center depends on the level of sales completed per phone call for its success. An employee's ability to establish credibility and achieve customer satisfaction is critical for optimal performance. The company wants to establish a development program for those who may not be performing to expectations. What metric would you use to measure workforce effectiveness under these circumstances?

    A. Customers per employee

    B. Expenses per employee

C. Revenue per employee

D. Labor cost per employee

65. A public-sector agency is struggling to meet fiscal responsibilities. The concern is that public retirement funds are outpacing revenues being generated. You are being asked to analyze and present your findings to the leadership team. Which metric would be one of the best to measure?

   A. Benefit costs as a percentage of revenue

   B. Benefit costs as a percentage of expense

   C. Retiree benefit cost as a percentage of expense

   D. Compensation as a percentage of expense

66. What is the strategic value of evaluating the relationship of employee salaries to the pay range midpoint?

   A. To determine pay compression

   B. To determine whether pay rates are competitive to the market

   C. To determine the company's overall cost per employee

   D. To establish position pay ranges

67. Which group is experiencing adverse impact?

Group	Applicants	Hired
Native American	22	2
Asian	30	8
Caucasian	120	35
African-American	48	5

   A. Native Americans and Asians

   B. Caucasians and Native Americans

   C. African-Americans and Asians

   D. Native Americans and African-Americans

68. Determine the yield ratio of qualified applicants to job offers extended.

Total Applicants	Qualified	Offers
500	50	10

   A. 20 percent

   B. 2 percent

   C. 10 percent

   D. 1 percent

69. Which of the following is a true statement about measuring days to fill?

A. Days to fill should be monitored closely because the longer a position remains open, the more likely it is to go unfilled.

B. Days to fill (speed) should be evaluated in relation to cost and quality of hire.

C. It is more cost effective for companies to hire temporary workers once a key position is open for more than 2 months.

D. If it is taking a while to fill a position, a company should adjust the total compensation for the position.

70. Which of the following can be used to help management measure employee engagement?

A. Turnover ratio and total revenue

B. Absentee rate and worker's compensation incidence rate

C. Cost per hire and absentee rate

D. Yield ratio and cost per hire

Objective 08   Tools to Compile Data

71. Computer software that simulates a worksheet used to tabulate data and create graphs based on data is known as what tool?

A. Presentation

B. Application

C. Spreadsheet

D. Balance sheet

72. A tool that holds an extensive amount of information such as employee contact information, wages, and benefits is called a:

A. Database

B. Graphs

C. Software

D. Cells

73. Software that allows an organization to use a collection of integrated applications to manage business processes and automate many tactical functions is known as a(n):

A. Applicant tracking system (ATS)

B. Enterprise resource planning (ERP)

C. Time and attendance (TAA) program

D. Learning management system (LMS)

74. A request for information from a database table or a combination of tables is called a:

   A. Memo

   B. Query

   C. Spreadsheet

   D. Graph

75. Which of the following applications would you use if you wanted to see a nonrelational view of data that will be used for frequent calculations and statistical comparisons?

   A. Presentation

   B. Database

   C. Spreadsheet

   D. Report

76. Which of the following applications would you use if multiple people will update the application and run complex queries from it?

   A. Presentation

   B. Database

   C. Spreadsheet

   D. Report

77. Using a spreadsheet you need to combine two lists, one with employee hire dates and salary and the other with department heads and bonus results. What is the name of the function that combines two lists into a single list?

   A. Pivot table

   B. Sorting

   C. Filter

   D. Vlookup

78. A tool found in spreadsheets that can automatically sort, count, total, or average data and display it in a table is called a:

   A. Pivot table

   B. Sorting

   C. Filter

   D. Vlookup

79. A visual display of HR metrics at a high level is called a:

   A. Spreadsheet

   B. Dashboard

C. Presentation

D. Report

80. A statistical analysis tool that gives an overview of variables that tend to go up and down together and in a specific direction, such as data that shows the cost of recruitment rises as the turnover number increases, is called a:

A. Database

B. Filter

C. Spreadsheet

D. Correlation

Objective 09   Methods to Collect Data

81. One of the key benefits of conducting an employee survey is:

A. To stay competitive in driving employee motivation, retention, and productivity

B. To establish an annual routine of asking employees questions about the workplace

C. To keep leaders on their toes about being nice to employees and paying them well

D. To keep employees from complaining about the workplace, leaders, pay, and benefits

82. What is the best way to help employees overcome concerns of confidentiality when using web-based survey tools?

A. There is no security over the Web; have employees use paper-based surveys only.

B. Have leaders or security watch over the computer while employees participate in the survey.

C. Use random protected passwords and third-party administration and establish a good communication plan.

D. Ignore the employee concerns about confidentiality and require employees to participate anyway.

83. When survey results are vague and difficult to determine what employees are saying, which is the best way to validate the data?

A. Re-administer the entire survey; people will understand.

B. Find out how individual employees answered the survey.

C. Conduct focus group sessions to gain further insights.

D. Throw away the survey; anything vague is worthless.

84. A type of interview that depends on job analysis to identify critical job requirements, such as competencies for each position, by focusing on what the person has done in previous situations is called a(n):

A. Phone interview

B. Targeted selection interview

C. Observation interview

D. Panel group interview

85. A structured interview in which the interviewer asks a series of predetermined questions is called a(n):

A. Panel interview

B. Targeted selection

C. Patterned interview

D. Observed interview

86. An interview format in which one participant is interviewed by a group of interviewers at one time is called a(n):

A. Panel interview

B. Targeted selection

C. Patterned interview

D. Observed interview

87. Ensuring that a test or a survey effectively measures what it is supposed to measure is known as:

A. Effectiveness

B. Quality

C. Auditing

D. Validity

88. When a test or survey's measurement consistently measures what it is supposed to, it is known as:

A. Quality

B. Reliability

C. Validity

D. Effectiveness

89. Collecting and analyzing work samplings or reviewing employee logs is an example of what type of data collection method?

A. Observation

B. Panel

C. Structured

D. Semi-structured

90. An interview in which the interviewer determines the major questions beforehand but allows sufficient flexibility to probe into other areas is known as a(n):

    A. Structured interview

    B. Semi-structured interview

    C. Observation

    D. Panel

Objective 10   Reporting and Presentation Techniques

91. A short document, or section of a document, that provides a brief overview of a longer report, proposal, or business plan is known as a(n):

    A. Analysis

    B. Recommendations

    C. Problem statement

    D. Executive summary

92. A graphical representation of data using bars, often in different heights depending on the distribution of numerical data, is called a:

    A. Pie chart

    B. Histogram

    C. Scatter graph

    D. Line graph

93. A type of graph in which a circular shape is divided into sections that each represents a proportion of the whole is called a:

    A. Pie chart

    B. Histogram

    C. Scatter graph

    D. Line graph

94. A type of chart used to visualize the trend of something over time is called a:

    A. Pie chart

    B. Histogram

    C. Frequency distribution

    D. Line graph

95. What is the difference between a histogram and a bar chart?

   A. A histogram plots quantitative data; a bar chart plots categorical data.

   B. A histogram measures quality data; a bar chart measures quantitative data.

   C. A histogram plots quantitative data; a bar chart plots quantitative data.

   D. A histogram measures quality data; a bar chart measures quality data.

96. Comparing an organization's performance against the "best practices" of other leading companies is known as:

   A. Competition

   B. Metrics

   C. Benchmarking

   D. Analytics

97. A performance metric used in strategic management to identify, report, and improve various internal functions of a business and resulting external results is called:

   A. Benchmarking

   B. Balanced scorecard

   C. Performance evaluation

   D. Business intelligence

98. The estimation of the likelihood of an event becoming a reality in the future, based on available data from the past, is known as:

   A. Benchmarking

   B. Forecasting

   C. Metrics

   D. Executive summary

99. Creating statistical models that predict demand for the next year, given relatively objective statistics from the previous year, is known as:

   A. Graph

   B. Metrics

   C. Benchmarking

   D. Trend analysis

100. What provides insight into business trends and patterns and helps improve decisions?

   A. Pie chart

   B. Executive summary

   C. Business intelligence

   D. Histogram

Objective 11   Impact of Technology on HR

101. A hospital has decided to use facial recognition technology to determine which employees are allowed to enter the maternity ward. Advocates state that the added security measures help families feel more secure. Without prior public notice, this collection of biometric data is a threat to what?

    A. Employee privacy and identity theft

    B. Hospital security procedures

    C. Police investigation of unwelcomed hospital visitors

    D. The hospital's customer service ratings

102. Which of the following is a disadvantage of Internet recruiting?

    A. Increase in unqualified candidates

    B. Targets specialized skills

    C. Increases the candidate pool

    D. Improves candidate mapping

103. An employee of a national coffee reseller was recently denied a promotion. Since then, he has made several negative statements about the company culture, pay, and promotional opportunities via multiple social media web sites. The facilities manager wants HR's support in discouraging this type of communication by other employees. As the HR director, how would you address this concern?

    A. Train supervisors on the provisions of the Electronic Communications and Privacy Act

    B. Develop a company privacy policy that clarifies what is expected of the employee in regard to social media

    C. Train staff on the provisions of the Privacy Act of 1974

    D. Develop a company privacy policy that details Internet use

104. What is one benefit of big data to HR?

    A. Help identify more consumers.

    B. Improve sales forecasting accuracy.

    C. Provide easier access to employee data.

    D. Predictive analytics result in better employment risk management.

105. Which of the following will help a company minimize any negative impact to data integrity?

    A. A policy that prohibits the sharing of passwords and the utilization of monitoring software that tracks and blocks the attempted download of phishing programs or malware

    B. A policy that prohibits the use of social networking sites

C. A policy that prohibits the sharing of confidential information with competitors

D. A policy that prohibits sending unsolicited e-mails to outside vendors

106. Which of the following generally describes a security concern where a user deliberately accesses another user's computer without permission?

    A. Hacking

    B. Phishing

    C. E-card

    D. Security alert

107. Which of the following is the best description of software that is managed remotely where the organization is charged only for the number of users and the bandwidth they use?

    A. Cloud computing

    B. SaaS

    C. ASP

    D. SLA

108. Which of the following is true with regard to effective technology communication policies?

    A. ISO 9000 compliant.

    B. Employees are aware that they are free to make online postings so long as they are anonymous.

    C. The organization reserves the right to monitor all technology use from or to company equipment.

    D. Lists all the technologies available to employees.

109. A personal concierge service recently started a blog. What might they want to consider when determining their social media approach and policy development?

    A. How often the design of the blog can change

    B. Which employees may post

    C. Will the blog be used for customer contact?

    D. Will the blog be used to connect employees in different geographic regions?

110. Which of the following collaborative software platforms provides users with a near in-person integrated experience?

    A. Webconference

    B. Multifaceted groupware

    C. Telepresence

    D. Videoconference

Objective 12 Employee Records Management

111. Which of the following is an important component of an employee record policy?

   A. Retention and destruction timeline expectations

   B. How big the employee record should be

   C. Ensure medical documents are with the general file

   D. HR office hours of which the record can be accessed

112. The best reason for restricting access to employee records to only those who have a "need to know" is:

   A. Because only human resources should have access to employee records

   B. So that filing doesn't have to be updated immediately, saving time

   C. To prevent employee records from getting lost or accidently deleted

   D. To prevent discrimination, identity theft, and privacy breaches

113. Which records should the hiring manager have access to?

   A. Drug tests

   B. Applications

   C. Background checks

   D. I-9 forms

114. How long should an organization keep an I-9 form for a terminated employee?

   A. There is no need to keep an I-9 form for an employee who is no longer with the organization.

   B. Three years from date of hire or 1 year following termination of employment, whichever is later.

   C. The I-9 form can be destroyed after 1 to 5 years from the date of hire.

   D. The I-9 form can never be destroyed and must be kept as long as the organization is operating.

115. If an employer is a federal contractor of more than 150 employees and greater than $150,000 in federal contracts, how long should pre-employment documents such as résumés, applications, interview notes, and other related hiring materials be kept for applicants not hired?

   A. Ten years

   B. Forever

   C. Not at all

   D. Two years

116. If an employer receives an Equal Employment Opportunity Commission (EEOC) charge regarding an employee who has just resigned, what should be done with the employee record and EEOC documents?

    A. Shred or delete all records per the normal retention or destruction timeline.

    B. Shred or delete all records immediately as the employee has left employment.

    C. All records must be kept until the final disposition of the charge.

    D. Immediately send all employee medical records to the EEOC.

117. How long does the Equal Employment Opportunity Commission (EEOC) regulations require employers to retain records for an employee who has been involuntarily terminated?

    A. Retain the record for an indefinite period of time.

    B. There is no need to retain the record.

    C. One year from the date of termination.

    D. Five years from the date of termination.

118. The Federal Labor Standards Act (FLSA) requires employers to retain payroll records for how long?

    A. Three years

    B. After the pay period ended

    C. Ten years

    D. When the year ends

119. The Occupational Safety and Health Administration (OSHA) requires the OSHA 300 log to be retained by the employer for how long?

    A. Two weeks following the end of the calendar year in which the record occurs.

    B. There is no required timeline as most likely the health concern is resolved.

    C. Five years following the end of the calendar year in which the record occurs.

    D. Thirty days following the end of the calendar year in which the record occurs.

120. When converting hard-copy employee records to electronic format, what is an important consideration?

    A. Records should be able to be accessed through a smart phone.

    B. Destroy paper copies after conversion to an electronic format.

    C. Keep all paper records after conversion to an electronic format.

    D. The computer storing the records must be a particular brand.

Objective 13 Statutory Reporting Requirements

121. The Employee Retirement Income Security Act (ERISA) requires employers to file these annual reports on employee benefits offered:

    A. OSHA 300 log

    B. Form 5500

    C. EEO-1 form

    D. LM-1 report

122. Under Title VII, the form that employers must file indicating the number of employees by specific covered protected categories is called:

    A. OSHA 300 log

    B. Form 5500

    C. EEO-1 form

    D. LM-1 report

123. Which regulation requires employers with a self-insured health plan to complete and file Forms 1095-B and 1094-B with the IRS, as well as provide employees with a copy of Form 1095-B?

    A. Patient Protection and Affordable Care Act (PPACA)

    B. Americans with Disabilities Act (ADA) of 1990

    C. Employee Retirement Income Security Act (ERISA)

    D. Occupational Safety and Health Act (OSHA)

124. The Patient Protection and Affordable Care Act (PPACA) reporting requirements apply to which type of organizations?

    A. Those that employ fewer than 50 full-time employees on average

    B. Those employers that do not offer any health benefit plans

    C. Those that employ 50 or more full-time employees on average

    D. Those employers that have 50 or more physical locations

125. Which type of organization must submit an EEO-1 report?

    A. This report applies to employers with 100 or more employees.

    B. This report applies to employees with 50 or more locations.

    C. Employers who have employees in more than one country.

    D. Employers with 100 employees and federal contractors with 50 or more employees.

126. The EEO-1 report includes specifically what type of information?

    A. Employees' race, ethnicity, and sex

    B. Employees' workplace injuries or illnesses

    C. Medical, dental, and vision benefit plans

    D. Number of full-time employees hired

127. Which of the following requires employers to report to the Occupational Safety and Health Administration (OSHA)?

    A. Employees who cannot produce proper identification

    B. All workplace fatalities

    C. Medical, dental, and vision benefit information

    D. How many employees are hired

128. When an employee becomes hospitalized because of a workplace injury, when must the employer report the event?

    A. Within 30 days of learning of it.

    B. Before the calendar year ends.

    C. There is no need to report it.

    D. Within 24 hours of learning of it.

129. Employers may have to file Form 1099-MISC to the Internal Revenue Service (IRS) when:

    A. An employee is offered a medical, dental, and vision benefit plan

    B. A full-time employee is paid for regular duties and responsibilities

    C. Someone who was not an employee was paid at least $600 for services

    D. An employee works overtime every week for a year

130. Employers must file copies of employees' W-2s with which agency by the end of February every year?

    A. Social Security Administration (SSA)

    B. Occupational Safety and Health Administration (OSHA)

    C. Department of Labor (DOL)

    D. National Labor Relations Board (NLRB)

Objective 14 Purpose and Function of Human Resource Information Systems (HRISs)

131. A healthcare consulting company has almost quadrupled in size in the last 5 years, from 68 employees to 220 employees. The chief HR officer decides to implement an HRIS system to provide key leaders with better data for use in making strategic decisions. What HR functions can an HRIS effectively handle?

A. Benefits administration.

B. An HRIS can support most HR functions with data.

C. Payroll processing and employee self-service.

D. An HRIS handles administrative HR functions only.

132. One of the competitive advantages of a small marketing company is its highly capable IT department. The company has been able to leverage the IT competencies to secure additional client business and has a dozen projects on the horizon. HR in collaboration with IT has determined that it is time to implement an HRIS. At this stage of development, the organization's needs are relatively standard. Which of the following would be the best choice in this scenario?

A. Outsource the project

B. Build an HRIS in-house

C. Customize an off-the-shelf solution

D. Build portions of the system and outsource the rest of the work

133. A financial services company expects 30 percent growth each year for the next 5 years, which means an increase in staff by 200 percent. Which of the following is the key consideration in selecting a human resource information system (HRIS) in this case?

A. Scalability

B. Cost

C. Usability

D. Extensibility

134. What is the primary benefit of the continuous integration approach when implementing an HRIS?

A. Integration takes place after all components are complete.

B. Most problems can be identified and fixed as they manifest themselves.

C. All components are implemented at once.

D. All bugs are fixed during testing, so integration is always flawless.

135. Which choice represents an advantage of a "best-of-breed" HRIS solution?

A. Quicker implementation because of simpler system

B. Careful management of vendor relationships

C. Ease of data integration

D. Least expensive

136. Which statement best describes decision-maker access through an HR portal?

A. Ability to change tax withholdings

B. Ability to approve paid time off

C. Ability to generate reports for strategy session

D. Ability to apply for internal job posting

137. Converting data into a format that masks the intended meaning is known as _____.

   A. Data mining

   B. Encryption

   C. Hypertext Transfer Protocol

   D. DBMS

138. When is it best for HR to collaborate with other departments to build an HRIS in-house?

   A. A robust customized solution is needed.

   B. There are off-the-shelf systems that could meet the need.

   C. The organization has unique business needs and the functional and technical skills in-house.

   D. The organization has standard business needs.

139. In terms of HR technology delivery, which of the following describes a hosted approach?

   A. Purchased software

   B. Managed from the vendor's site

   C. Subscription service

   D. Supported by company's IT department

140. What is the major disadvantage of the "big bang" approach to HR system integration?

   A. All systems are integrated simultaneously.

   B. Developers can verify performance in a working environment.

   C. Several builds are implemented incrementally.

   D. It is difficult to find the root cause of system failures.

Objective 15   Job Classification

141. Which of the following factors are *not* generally considered when determining whether a worker is an employee as opposed to an independent contractor?

   A. Reasonableness of the work accommodations

   B. The permanency of the worker's relationship with the employer

   C. The extent to which the work performed is an integral part of the employer's business

   D. The relative investments in facilities and equipment by the worker and the employer

142. What is the main reason why an employee who is misclassified as an independent contractor would want to get that corrected as soon as possible?

   A. Miss out on company activities

   B. Miss out on employer-paid taxes and benefits

C. Miss out on being managed correctly

D. Miss out on potential training

143. A(n) _____ decides when, where, and how the work will be performed within broad guidelines. He or she can subcontract the work or parts of the project to others and can decide what tools to use and what work must be performed to complete the project.

A. Independent contractor

B. Flex-time worker

C. Temporary employee

D. Employee

144. Employers must pay _____ one-and-a-half times their regular rate of pay when they work more than 40 hours in a week.

A. Nonbenefit participating employees

B. Nonexempt employees

C. Temporary employees

D. Exempt employees

145. Which of the following is an FLSA exemption from overtime requirements?

A. Outside exemptions

B. Supply-chain exemption

C. White-collar exemption

D. Mandatory exemption

146. Fair Labor Standards Act's (FLSA's) current salary threshold for exemption from overtime pay is:

A. $30,000 per year

B. $23,660 per year

C. $24,500 per year

D. $27,500 per year

147. A qualification of the executive exemption under the FLSA would be:

A. The primary duty consists of performing office or nonmanual work directly related to the management or general business operations of the employer or the employer's customers.

B. The primary duty consists of managing the enterprise or a customarily recognized department or subdivision of the enterprise.

C. The primary duty consists of the performance of work requiring invention, imagination, originality, or talent in a recognized field of artistic or creative endeavor as opposed to routine mental, manual, mechanical, or physical work.

D. The primary duty consists of the application of system-analyst techniques and procedures, including consulting with users to determine hardware, software, or systems functional specifications.

148. To qualify for the learned professional exemption under the FLSA, one must:

   A. Have advanced knowledge in a field of science or learning

   B. Customarily and regularly be engaged away from the employer's place or places of business

   C. Customarily and regularly perform at least one of the exempt duties or responsibilities of the executive, professional, or administrative exemption

   D. Customarily and regularly direct the work of two or more full-time employees or their equivalents (for example, one full-time employee and two half-time employees)

149. Employers must pay _____ a predetermined amount of payment on a regularly set schedule.

   A. Flex-time employees

   B. Temporary employees

   C. Salaried exempt employees

   D. Nonexempt employees

150. Nonexempt employees are not required to be paid when attending training programs:

   A. If it is during normal work hours

   B. If attendance is voluntary

   C. If attendance is mandatory

   D. If other work is performed during the event

Objective 16   Job Analysis Methods and Job Description

151. Job descriptions at a company have been out of date for almost a decade. Recent hires have complained that the job they currently have is not what they thought they were applying for initially. As the HR manager, you want to keep employees informed of expectations but not disrupt daily operations. What planning process would you implement to achieve both goals?

   A. Conduct meetings with employees and direct supervisors to inform them of the expectations.

   B. A company-wide project to bring all job descriptions up to date starting immediately.

   C. A job analysis conducted annually and job descriptions revised accordingly.

   D. Conduct training with the staff weekly to bring them up to date on job expectations.

152. A new division needs to be fully staffed within six months. Which of the following would be the best first step in a comprehensive selection process?

   A. Determine who can staff the new division from internal applicants

   B. Determine hiring criteria

   C. Develop pre-employment skills testing for appropriate position

   D. Identify the qualifications necessary to do the jobs in the new division

153. A job description should include the following information about a job:

    A. Nonessential functions

    B. Essential functions

    C. Experience required

    D. All of the above

154. A job description should include the following information about a job except:

    A. Physical requirements

    B. Employee's disability status

    C. Mental requirements

    D. Approvals from management

155. What is the main reason it may be difficult to conduct a job analysis when the only employee who is at the company is a long-term employee?

    A. It can get difficult to separate what the employee brings to the job from the job's main purpose.

    B. The employee may have a bad attitude toward the position.

    C. The employee may misrepresent information about the job based on what he or she thinks is best.

    D. It's difficult to separate what the manager does versus what the employee does.

156. Each essential job function in a job description should consider:

    A. Pay level associated with it

    B. Level of complexity and frequency

    C. Education needed to complete the job function

    D. Work experience of past incumbents in the job

157. Job descriptions are also used for:

    A. Compensation purposes

    B. Proper classification of employees

    C. Benefit packages an employee receives

    D. Data for affirmative action reports

158. What is the purpose of job analysis?

    A. To define the organization's objectives

    B. To collect data for the affirmative action program

    C. To analyze EEO classifications

    D. To define a job so that it can be understood in the context of accomplishing organizational goals

159. Information can be collected during the job analysis process in several ways such as:

   A. Interviewing the incumbent

   B. Completing a task inventory

   C. Completing a structured questionnaire

   D. All of the above

160. Which of the following job competencies does someone in a manager's role need to possess?

   A. Developing subordinates

   B. Team work

   C. Communication

   D. Customer focus

Objective 17   Reporting Structure

161. Organizational structures were designed to:

   A. Provide a decentralized decision-making process

   B. Provide a framework for common requirements in the region that are different from other regions

   C. Provide a framework that keeps the information flowing from functions to employees who need to keep the organization moving

   D. Provide a formal and rigid process for businesses with a single product line

162. Functional structure is represented by the traditional:

   A. Matrix-shaped organizational type

   B. Product-based organizational type

   C. Pyramid-shape organizational type

   D. Seamless design organizational type

163. The most formal and rigid of all the organization structures is:

   A. Functional structure

   B. Matrix structure

   C. Divisional structure

   D. Product-based structure

164. When employees report to two managers, one for the product line and one for the functional line, it's an example of which type of structure?

   A. Product-based structure

   B. Functional structure

   C. Geographic structure

   D. Matrix structure

165. Which of the following is a horizontal organization connected by networks?

    A. Divisional organization

    B. Geographic organization

    C. Matrix organization

    D. Seamless organization

166. What is the main purpose of a seamless organization?

    A. To be on "best places to work" lists.

    B. To get millennials to work there.

    C. To enhance communication and creativity.

    D. It's easier for managers to manage people.

167. In a _____ structure, executives of regional areas are responsible for their business functions.

    A. Geographic

    B. Divisional

    C. Product-based

    D. Matrix-based

168. What is the disadvantage of a functional organizational structure?

    A. Divisions may be competing for the same customers.

    B. People are in specialized "silos" and often fail to coordinate or communicate with other departments.

    C. Employees with similar technical career paths have less interaction.

    D. It can result in a loss of efficiency and a duplication of effort because each division needs to acquire the same resources.

169. What is the main advantage of a matrix organizational structure?

    A. Ability to leverage all employees' talents.

    B. Faster response to market changes.

    C. It creates a functional and divisional partnership and focuses on the work more than on the people.

    D. Enhanced cooperation and information sharing among functions, divisions, and staff.

170. What is the disadvantage of a matrix organizational structure?

    A. The dual chain of command requires cooperation between two direct supervisors to determine an employee's work priorities, work assignments, and performance standards.

    B. Potential lack of trust between organizations.

    C. Potential lack of organizational identification among employees.

    D. Need for increased communication.

Objective 18   Types of External Providers of HR Services

171. An HR business process outcome (BPO) is an arrangement:

    A. Where payroll and benefit administration are entirely outsourced

    B. Where employees are leased to an outsourcing company

    C. Where employees are staffed by external recruitment agencies

    D. Where benefits are outsourced only to an external provider

172. In a professional employer organization (PEO) relationship, the PEO becomes the:

    A. Employer of choice

    B. Employer of record

    C. Source of full-time workers

    D. Source of temp workers

173. In human resources outsourcers (HROs), all the following functions are outsourced, except:

    A. Payroll

    B. Benefits

    C. Human resources

    D. Temp workers

174. Typically, a headhunter is used to help find _____.

    A. Temp workers

    B. Upper management

    C. HR staff

    D. Contingent workforce

175. What is the main benefit of using a benefit broker?

    A. Lower-cost benefit options.

    B. Can waive ACA regulations.

    C. They sell for multiple companies and typically can provide more options.

    D. They can sell for one company.

176. The following are all disadvantages of using a professional employer organization (PEO) except which one?

    A. Loss of control of essential processes and people

    B. An outside company's influence on your culture

    C. Your diminished value as an internal HR professional

    D. Higher benefit costs

177. All the following are disadvantages of using a third-party recruiter except which one?

   A. Higher costs

   B. Lack of control

   C. Indirect candidate access

   D. Longer time to fill position

178. All the following are examples of the advantage of using a benefit broker except which one?

   A. Potential tax breaks

   B. In-person assistance

   C. Saves time on buying plans

   D. Cheaper healthcare

179. Which of the following is an advantage of using a staffing organization?

   A. The employer shares the liability of employees with the staffing agency.

   B. Lower cost per employee.

   C. Lower costs on benefits.

   D. The employer shares the cost of the employee.

180. Prior to contacting a temporary employee agency, HR should determine all of the following except:

   A. The typical length of time you need a temporary worker

   B. The hours needed to work

   C. The skills usually needed

   D. Health insurance needed

Objective 19 Communication Techniques

181. Which of the following is the discovery and communication of meaningful patterns in data?

   A. Andragogy

   B. Analytics

   C. Aging

   D. ADDIE

182. Which of the following is a communication style that relies heavily on explicit and direct language?

   A. Heavy retention efforts

   B. Heavy employee engagement

   C. Low-context culture

   D. High-context culture

183. The following unresolved issues can cause interpersonal tension conflict and emotional stress for employees except?

A. Absenteeism

B. Turnover

C. Litigation

D. Higher performance review scores

184. Which of the following is the easiest way to recognize passive-aggressive communication in the workplace?

A. Lack of assertiveness and directness

B. Employees who have higher seniority

C. Talking too much in meetings

D. High absenteeism rates

185. Which of the following behaviors is *not* an example of passive-aggressive communication?

A. Yelling at co-workers in the workplace

B. Letting a problem escalate

C. Temporary compliance

D. Intentional inefficiency

186. Which of the following is a highly effective method of accessing direct feedback in a written format?

A. E-mail

B. Asking the employee their opinions of the workplace

C. Employee survey

D. Gathering data at the end of a performance review

187. When someone exhibits a pattern of not expressing their opinions or feelings, protecting their rights, or identifying and meeting their needs, it is an example of what type of communication?

A. Passive-aggressive

B. Assertive

C. Aggressive

D. Passive

188. Appearing passive on the surface but acting out anger in a subtle, indirect, or behind-the-scenes way is an example of what type of communication?

A. Passive-aggressive

B. Assertive

C. Aggressive

D. Passive

189. When a person expresses their feelings and opinions and advocates for their needs in a way that violates the rights of others, what is that an example of?

A. Passive-aggressive

B. Assertive

C. Aggressive

D. Passive

190. Stating opinions and feelings and firmly advocating for their rights and needs without violating the rights of others is an example of what type of behavior?

A. Passive-aggressive

B. Assertive

C. Aggressive

D. Passive

1. D	33. C	65. C
2. A	34. D	66. B
3. B	35. A	67. D
4. B	36. D	68. A
5. C	37. A	69. B
6. D	38. B	70. B
7. A	39. C	71. C
8. C	40. B	72. A
9. B	41. A	73. B
10. A	42. D	74. B
11. C	43. C	75. C
12. C	44. A	76. B
13. B	45. C	77. D
14. A	46. B	78. A
15. D	47. A	79. B
16. B	48. B	80. D
17. C	49. C	81. A
18. A	50. D	82. C
19. D	51. C	83. C
20. B	52. B	84. B
21. C	53. B	85. C
22. A	54. D	86. A
23. A	55. C	87. D
24. A	56. A	88. B
25. C	57. C	89. A
26. B	58. C	90. B
27. D	59. D	91. D
28. C	60. B	92. B
29. D	61. D	93. A
30. D	62. A	94. D
31. A	63. A	95. A
32. B	64. C	96. C

97. B	129. C	161. C
98. B	130. A	162. C
99. D	131. B	163. A
100. C	132. C	164. D
101. A	133. A	165. D
102. A	134. B	166. C
103. B	135. A	167. A
104. D	136. C	168. B
105. A	137. B	169. C
106. A	138. C	170. A
107. B	139. B	171. A
108. C	140. D	172. B
109. B	141. A	173. D
110. C	142. B	174. B
111. A	143. A	175. C
112. D	144. B	176. D
113. B	145. C	177. D
114. B	146. B	178. D
115. D	147. B	179. A
116. C	148. A	180. D
117. C	149. C	181. B
118. A	150. B	182. C
119. C	151. C	183. D
120. B	152. D	184. A
121. B	153. D	185. A
122. C	154. B	186. C
123. A	155. A	187. D
124. C	156. B	188. A
125. D	157. C	189. C
126. A	158. D	190. B
127. B	159. D	
128. D	160. A	

1. ☑ **D.** The definition of strategic planning is indeed the process by which key stakeholders of an organization envision its future and develop a mission, objectives, and procedures to achieve that future.

   ☒ **A, B,** and **C** are incorrect. **A** is incorrect because establishing goals is a result of the larger planning process. **B** is incorrect because although it is true that the larger planning process may require looking into the future, that is only part of the process. Although succession planning is an action that may result from the larger planning process, **C** is incorrect because succession planning is not the term describing the overall planning process.

2. ☑ **A.** Human resource planning involves analyzing and identifying the organization's labor pool needs. From there human resources forms its strategy in recruiting and retaining labor skills necessary for the organization to achieve its objectives.

   ☒ **B, C,** and **D** are incorrect. **B** is incorrect because a recruitment requisition is only part of the process. It is a process or form that hiring managers and recruiters use to communicate with one another about an open position need. **C** is incorrect because while it's true the intention of this process is to reach objectives, this is not the correct term used. **D** is incorrect because a training needs assessment is used to identify an organization's workforce skill needs.

3. ☑ **B.** An organization's core competency is a capability that distinguishes it from its competitors. It is the capability that an organization does exceptionally and uniquely well.

   ☒ **A, C,** and **D** are incorrect. **A** is incorrect because research and development is a function within an organization that is responsible for creating new products and services and is not necessarily a core competency of an organization. **C** is not the best answer because creating cheaper products does not necessarily make an organization competitive. Plus, it is not the product itself that creates a core competency but rather what an organization does collectively very well that makes it rise above competition. **D** is incorrect because while quickly hiring talent is important, it is really the type of talent that may contribute to the organization's core competency and enable it to be competitive.

4. ☑ **B.** A vision statement describes what the future of an organization looks like in concise terms.

   ☒ **A, C,** and **D** are incorrect. **A** is incorrect because a purpose statement is a sentence that summarizes the topic or goals of a particular document. **C** is incorrect because a financial statement is a collection of reports that describes an organization's financial activity such as a balance sheet, cash flow statement, or income statement. **D** is incorrect because a benefit statement, also called a *total compensation statement,* provides employees with a true picture of what they earn above and beyond their base pay.

5. ☑ **C.** A mission statement describes how an organization is going to achieve its vision.

   ☒ **A, B,** and **D** are incorrect. **A** is incorrect because a job description describes a job's responsibilities and qualifications that are required for success. **B** is incorrect because a purpose statement is a sentence that summarizes the topic or goals of a particular document. **D** is incorrect because a summary plan description communicates a health or retirement plan's eligibility requirements, obligations, and specific benefits available for employees and their dependents.

6. ☑ **D**. The values statement communicates to customers and employees what the organization's priorities are. An effective values statement is embraced by leadership and provides guidance in key decision-making requirements.

   ☒ **A, B**, and **C** are incorrect. They all represent different internal operational documents that may exist in an organization that do not necessarily communicate with the customer as to what are the overall priorities.

7. ☑ **A**. The statement "We aspire to be the best widget maker in America" is an example of a vision statement. A vision statement describes the ideal future state of an organization.

   ☒ **B, C**, and **D** are incorrect. **B** is incorrect because a financial statement describes an organization's financial activity, **C** is incorrect because a mission statement describes how an organization intends to accomplish the vision, and **D** is incorrect because a values statement describes the priorities of an organization.

8. ☑ **C**. The SWOT analysis evaluates the internal strengths, internal weaknesses, external opportunities, and external threats of an organization. The SWOT is designed to enable leaders to evaluate internally and externally what can help or hinder the organization's success in meeting its vision and mission.

   ☒ **A, B**, and **D** are incorrect. None of these options represents the SWOT analysis of strengths, weaknesses, opportunities, and threats of an organization.

9. ☑ **B**. Michael Porter's five forces analysis evaluates these five forces: political/legal, economic, social, technology, and competition. These forces are seen as primary influencers on an organization's ability to compete in the marketplace.

   ☒ **A, C**, and **D** are incorrect. None of these options represents Michael Porter's five forces analysis.

10. ☑ **A**. Goal alignment is how an organization works to ensure its employees see the overall direction and how they fit into the big picture of the organization's vision and mission. Human resources can often take the lead in goal alignment and influences employee engagement and connection to the overall direction of an organization.

    ☒ **B, C**, and **D** are incorrect. None is the best answer in terms of ensuring how employees are connected to the overall mission and vision of an organization.

11. ☑ **C**. Organizational culture is a shared understanding of values, beliefs, and norms. These are usually unwritten common understandings for all who work in any organization. Organizational culture is not something easily captured in a written document. Instead, organizational culture consists of shared values, beliefs, and norms that are widely embraced by employees and leadership.

    ☒ **A, B**, and **D** are incorrect. **A** is incorrect because vision, mission, and values are examples of statements that describe the objectives and priorities of an organization. **B** is incorrect because structure, systems, and people are internal components that make up an organization, and **D** is incorrect because finance, marketing, and operations are examples of functions within an organization.

12. ☑ **C**. Norms are unwritten expectations or informal guidelines of how one should behave in a group or organization. Norms are derived from values. Community participation, customer story sharing, and the unspoken expectation that everyone must work late in evenings to be successful are all examples of norms.

☒ **A**, **B**, and **D** are incorrect. **A** is not the best answer because norms are derived from values. Norms are external actions taken, while values are more of an abstract list of adjectives by which all agree to conduct business (i.e., integrity, respect, customer focused). **B** is incorrect because objectives are goals that are part of the overall strategic plan of an organization. **D** is incorrect because beliefs may shape norms and values. However, norms are actual external actions taken as a result of a belief system.

13. ☑ **B**. The leadership feeling like humor improves productivity is an example of a belief. Beliefs are assumptions and convictions that are believed to be true.

☒ **A**, **C**, and **D** are incorrect. **A** is incorrect because norms represent unwritten expectations of an organization. **C** is incorrect because directives are stated expectations, and **D** is incorrect because values are a list of adjectives used to describe the desired culture of an organization.

14. ☑ **A**. A values statement is typically used to guide decision-making within an organization. An example of a values statement is as follows:

Zappos Family Core Values

1. Deliver WOW Through Service
2. Embrace and Drive Change
3. Create Fun and a Little Weirdness
4. Be Adventurous, Creative, and Open-Minded
5. Pursue Growth and Learning
6. Build Open and Honest Relationships with Communication
7. Build a Positive Team and Family Spirit
8. Do More with Less
9. Be Passionate and Determined
10. Be Humble

☒ **B**, **C**, and **D** are incorrect. While each of these may provide operational information, none necessarily provides guidance with respect to overall purpose like a values statement does.

15. ☑ **D**. People will exhibit behaviors that are rewarded and recognized. Establishing a compensation program that encourages certain behaviors is an effective way to shape organizational culture. One common mistake is when an organization wants to change its culture but leaves the old compensation incentives in place that may run contrary to a new direction.

☒ **A**, **B**, and **C** are incorrect. **A** is incorrect because tracking internal human resource activities such as applications does nothing to shape organizational culture. **B** is incorrect because while returning phone calls is a good customer service tactic, it is not an effective method in shaping organizational culture. **C** is a superficial tactic that may not necessarily shape organizational culture.

16. ☑ **B**. Artifacts are a physical reminder or symbol of the organization's culture and what is important. Pictures, degrees, or certifications on walls, books, and gadgets are examples of artifacts.

☒ **A**, **C**, and **D** are incorrect. **A** is incorrect because rituals are celebrations or events held to signify something important in the organization. **C** is incorrect because a legend is an organizational hero that is exhibited in the form of storytelling that is passed on from one employee to another, and **D** is incorrect because beliefs are a set of understandings or assumptions.

17. ☑ **C**. A legend is an example of a cultural element that is exhibited in the form of storytelling that typically involves a villain and a hero ultimately saving the organization. Think of Facebook's CEO Mark Zuckerberg, for example. The story is that through his quick wit while a student at Harvard he was able to outwit colleagues and launch what we now know today as Facebook. In his organization he is known the cultural element, a legend. This is a story that is most likely shared from one employee to another.

☒ **A**, **B**, and **D** are incorrect. **A** is incorrect because rituals are events or celebrations held to signify something of importance to the organization. **B** is incorrect because artifacts are a physical element used to signify something of importance, and **D** is incorrect because beliefs are a set of unwritten assumptions.

18. ☑ **A**. Rituals are regular events or ceremonies that organizations engage in to celebrate, encourage, or educate certain desired behaviors. New-hire orientations, awards banquets, holiday parties, and annual training events are all examples of rituals.

☒ **B**, **C**, and **D** are incorrect. **B** is incorrect because artifacts are physical elements that signify something of importance. **C** is incorrect because legends are an organizational hero that is spoken of in the form of storytelling, and **D** is incorrect because beliefs are assumptions that are applied in the organization.

19. ☑ **D**. A change agent is a person who helps facilitate transformation within an organization. A change agent can be anyone external or internal that serves as a "champion of change." Often human resource staff are called upon to be change agents.

☒ **A**, **B**, and **C** are incorrect. While these all may have some role in the workplace, they may not necessarily serve as a facilitator of change.

20. ☑ **B**. A person's ability to be aware of and control one's own emotions and ultimately successfully handle interpersonal relationships is known as having emotional intelligence. Emotional intelligence is a fundamental component of human behavior not connected to a person's intellect.

☒ **A**, **C**, and **D** are incorrect. **A** is incorrect because anger management is the process of controlling one's inclination to easily become angry. While anger is an emotion, emotional intelligence encompasses all emotions. **C** is incorrect because human resource development refers to training and developing people in the workplace. This is not a relevant term for what we were looking for in emotional intelligence, and **D** is incorrect for the same reason in human resource development. These terms are used interchangeably and do not specifically define emotional intelligence.

21. ☑ **C.** The Fair Labor Standards Act (FLSA) of 1938 is the cornerstone wage and labor legislation. The FLSA established the 40-hour workweek, minimum wage, overtime guidelines and record-keeping, and child labor standards for both the private sector and governments.

    ☒ **A, B,** and **D** are incorrect. **A** and **B** are incorrect because the equitable treatment of all workers and fair wages for all workers are addressed in other legislation such as Title VII of the Civil Rights Act of 1964. **D** is incorrect because standards of conduct for supervisors are addressed both by employment legislation and by internal company policy; therefore, standards of conduct may vary from organization to organization.

22. ☑ **A.** The Labor Management Relations Act, or Taft-Hartley Act, provided that employees had the right to refrain from participating in union activities. The act also ensured that employees could not be forced to become part of a union as a condition of employment.

    ☒ **B, C,** and **D** are incorrect. These choices are all related to the employer whether private or government.

23. ☑ **A.** This is an example of a hot-cargo contract. A hot-cargo contract is a contract that the employer enters into with the union at the request of the union. The employer agrees that its employees will not handle the products or materials of another employer or that the employer itself will not deal with the other employer with whom the bargaining union considers unfair to organized labor. This is an unfair labor practice (ULP) on the part of the employer as defined by the National Labor Relations Act (NLRA).

    ☒ **B, C,** and **D** are incorrect. **B** is incorrect because featherbedding is a ULP on the part of the union where the union is requiring an employer to pay for services not rendered. For example, if an employer determines that, because of advances in technology, a position is no longer needed, then the union cannot force the employer to continue to employ someone in that position. **C** and **D** are incorrect because a yellow-dog or iron-clad contract is a contract where an employer requires an employer, as a condition of employment, to join a union. This was outlawed by the Norris-LaGuardia Act.

24. ☑ **A.** *Burlington Industries v. Ellerth* established that an employer can be held responsible for the unlawful acts of its employees. This is a legal concept known as vicarious liability.

    ☒ **B, C,** and **D** are incorrect. **B** and **C** are incorrect because the issue in both *Meritor Savings Bank v. Vinson* and *Harris v. Forklift Systems* is the existence of a hostile work environment of sexual harassment. **D** is incorrect because *Oncale v. Sundowner Offshore Services, Inc.* established the standard for same-sex sexual harassment.

25. ☑ **C.** The Supreme Court decision in *Vance v. Ball State University* established that a person is a supervisor for the purposes of vicarious liability in cases of unlawful harassment under Title VII only if that person can take tangible employment actions against the accuser. The Supreme Court rejected the guidance of the Equal Employment

Opportunity Commission (EEOC) that a supervisor may be an individual who has authority to direct an employee's daily work activities. However, the employee still maintains the right to sue the company for being negligent in preventing the harassment.

☒ **A, B,** and **D** are incorrect. **A** is incorrect because the assumption that Jasmine did not report the incidents is irrelevant. Also, the scenario does not indicate that she did not report, only that the sales director claims no knowledge of a report. Jasmine could have reported directly to HR or some other supervisory authority. **B** is incorrect because the *Ellerth* and *Faragher* cases, taken together, established that whether an employer is vicariously liable depends on what happened to the plaintiff and on whether the harassment resulted in tangible employment actions being taken. **D** is incorrect because the EEOC guidance is only guidance, but Title VII did not define "supervisor" for the purposes of unlawful harassment.

26. ☑ **B.** Following the reservist's application for reemployment, the employer must reinstate him promptly.

☒ **A, C,** and **D** are incorrect. The Uniformed Services Employment and Reemployment Rights Act (USERRA) of 1994 requires employers of reservists who have been on active duty for 181 or more days to reemploy them promptly after completing their service.

27. ☑ **D.** The Age Discrimination in Employment Act (ADEA) of 1967 provides protections in employment situations for employees 40 years or older. The act states that an employer cannot fail or refuse to hire or to discharge any individual or otherwise discriminate against any individual with respect to his compensation, terms, conditions, or privileges of employment because of such individual's age.

☒ **A, B,** and **C** are incorrect. **A** is incorrect because the Norris-LaGuardia Act is the legislation that banned yellow-dog contracts, which are pledges by workers to the potential employer not to join a union. **B** is incorrect because Title VII of the Civil Rights Act of 1964 provides protection for individuals who are discriminated against in employment situations on the basis of race, color, national origin, sex, and religion. Title VII applies to employers with at least 15 employees. **C** is incorrect because the Landrum-Griffith Act, or Labor Management Disclosure Act, is the legislation that regulates the relationship between unions and employers.

28. ☑ **C.** The Health Insurance Portability and Accountability Act is a privacy rule that regulates the security and confidentiality of patient information. The issue in this case is whether the employer did all it could to protect patient medical information.

☒ **A, B,** and **D** are incorrect. **A** is incorrect because the Federal Data Protection Act does protect consumer information but does not apply specifically to private medical information. **B** is incorrect because the Sarbanes-Oxley Act of 2002 does not apply to private medical information. **D** is incorrect because the Title 21 Code of Federal Regulations (21 CFR Part 11) does not apply to private patient medical information.

29. ☑ **D.** Identifying essential job functions and then identifying barriers to performance is the first step to determine whether a company can accommodate the disability.

☒ **A, B,** and **C** are incorrect. These are all later steps in the interactive process under the ADA.

30. ☑ **D**. COBRA is an amendment to ERISA. ERISA was passed in 1974 and set minimum standards for pension and health plans of private employers.

☒ **A, B,** and **C** are incorrect. **A** is incorrect because HIPAA is another amendment to ERISA. **B** is incorrect because USERRA is a law that protects the reemployment rights of armed service personnel when they return from a period of service. It has nothing to do with health insurance. **C** is incorrect because it is a separate law passed during the most recent administration. It works in conjunction with other healthcare-related statutes but is not an amendment to any prior statute such as ERISA.

31. ☑ **A**. The company is guilty of negligent hiring and should conduct complete background and reference checks, including a check of both state and FBI records going forward. Negligent hiring occurs when a company knew, or should have known, that a candidate is prone to be a danger to employees, customers, vendors, and anyone else the employee comes in contact with. If a thorough background check was done, including a search of the FBI database, it could have easily been uncovered that this employee was convicted and found guilty of battery.

☒ **B, C,** and **D** are incorrect. **B** is incorrect because, as it relates to HR, the FCRA requires that employers not use information obtained about an applicant's background in an adverse manner until certain criteria are met and that employers obtain consent prior to conducting any background check. **C** and **D** are incorrect because while it is negligent hiring, the Privacy Act of 1974 regulates how information collected is stored, requires that the candidate know what is being collected, and prevents information collected from being used for any purpose other than that which was intended. This does not apply in this case.

32. ☑ **B**. The Health Insurance Portability and Accountability Act (HIPAA) prohibits employers from disclosing confidential medical information to third parties and family members without the consent of the employee.

☒ **A, C,** and **D** are incorrect. There are few exceptions to HIPAA. If a person is injured and unable to give permission, a medical professional can share information with the people who are accompanying the injured if it seems as though this will be in the injured's best interest. However, the employer should not intentionally share information simply because it was deemed that the information could save a person's life.

33. ☑ **C**. If an employer can provide a legitimate business reason for monitoring an employee's electronic communications, the employer can do so with or without the employee's consent.

☒ **A, B,** and **D** are incorrect. An employer is prohibited from monitoring any electronic employee communication without the consent of the employee or a legitimate business purpose per the provisions of the ECPA.

34. ☑ **D**. Any surveillance system that a company is considering should be installed only if there is a legitimate business purpose, and the policy that accompanies the installation should be narrowly written to ensure employees' privacy rights are not violated. In addition, as in the NLRB ruling against Whole Foods in 2015, the policy cannot interfere with any union-organizing activity that both union and nonunion employees may legally participate in.

☒ **A**, **B**, and **C** are incorrect. HR's most important role in this scenario is to ensure that the policy has met the necessary legal standard. HR is best served if it is working with risk management and legal in crafting a policy that affects employee privacy expectations.

35. ☑ **A**. Under the federal Stored Communications Act (SCA), without authorization from an employee, an employer can't intentionally access a facility through which an electronic communication service is provided. This means an employer can review e-mails that an employee sends on the employer's server but can't access e-mails with a password that the employee saved on a company device.

☒ **B**, **C**, and **D** are incorrect. Employees do not have a right to privacy when accessing e-mail using an organization's server. However, the employer doesn't have the right to use any information stored on an employee's device whether there is a legitimate business reason. Whether an employee is allowed to store information on a company's server is a matter of company policy, not the law.

36. ☑ **D**. Latoya's carelessness in not deleting her personal e-mail account is not the same as giving the employer authorization to access her e-mail. In the legal case *Lazette v. Kulmatycki 2013*, the courts found the same in a similar case.

☒ **A**, **B**, and **C** are incorrect. While Latoya had no expectation of privacy, she was not giving implicit consent by forgetting to delete the account.

37. ☑ **A**. Privacy and confidentiality are closely related terms. Confidentiality refers to how information is treated. For example, if information is confidential, an organization does not have the right to share the information collected on an employee via a third party. Privacy refers to who has a right to an employee's information.

☒ **B**, **C**, and **D** are incorrect. While the two concepts are related, there is a difference between confidentiality and privacy. Confidentiality refers to how employee information is handled. Stated differently, confidentiality examines whether the organization has the right to share information about an employee. Privacy examines whether the organization or a person has the right to obtain the employee's information.

38. ☑ **B**. If an employee makes a disability claim, the employer must release health information to the insurer to assist in determining the merits of the claim.

☒ **A**, **C**, and **D** are incorrect. **A** is incorrect because health information should never be released to an employee's manager. If the information affects whether a person meets the minimum qualifications for a job transfer, then HR should review and share with the manager that the person is ineligible to transfer. Why an employee is ineligible is not important. **C** is incorrect because an employer should not accept verbal authorization when discussing health information. Releasing health records should be scrutinized and information released in the narrowest fashion allowed by law. **D** is incorrect because employers cannot share health information with a third party unless the employee authorizes such in writing.

39. ☑ **C**. Once Jackson disclosed his amphetamines prescription because of an underlying medical condition, the employer became aware of his potential disability. After the job offer was made, rather than firing him after receiving the positive drug screen, HR should have engaged Jackson in the interactive process to ensure that the type of accommodation needed to ensure his ability to execute his job function was in place.

✗ **A**, **B**, and **D** are incorrect. **A** is incorrect because the Drug-Free Workplace Act does not require pre-employment testing. The act only requires that certain employers maintain a drug-free workplace. **B** and **C** are incorrect because the ADEA is applicable only if Jackson was not hired or was released because of his age or because he is a member of a protected class. Neither was the basis of the employer's decision to terminate his employment.

40. ✓ **B**. In this case, the employer does not have to comply with the FCRA because the employer is not using a third party to collect the information. There are other privacy, ADA, and EEO regulations that the employer must adhere to, but specifically the FCRA is applicable only when utilizing a third party to conduct a background check and that third party meets the definition of a consumer reporting agency (CRA).

✗ **A**, **C**, and **D** are incorrect because all three are FCRA requirements that an employer must meet if utilizing a consumer reporting agency to conduct a background check.

41. ✓ **A**. A balanced scorecard is a strategic management system. It may include both nonfinancial measurements and traditional financial metrics. It is used to provide a concise picture of the organization's overall performance and includes performance metrics from four perspectives: financial, customers, learning/growth, and internal business processes.

✗ **B**, **C**, and **D** are incorrect. **B** is incorrect because benchmarking is part of an HR audit. Planning of the audit process, whether internal or external, requires that the auditor set points of reference against which areas to be audited can be compared. **C** is incorrect because an HR audit is another type of performance measure that is systematic and comprehensive. There are various types of HR audits whose purpose is to evaluate areas where the organization may be vulnerable to litigation. **D** is incorrect because Lean Six Sigma is a quality management methodology that systematically improves, optimizes, and stabilizes business processes and design by utilizing the Define, Measure, Analyze, Improve, and Control (DMAIC) model. The Lean Six Sigma methodology focuses largely on collaboration and team effort to accomplish the goal of better efficiencies in business processes.

42. ✓ **D**. All the choices listed are core business functions that an HR professional can expect to encounter in every organization. Core business functions that are found in every organization are sales and marketing, information technology, production/operations, finance and accounting, and research and development. The names of the functions vary depending on the industry and whether the organization is a private or public entity. For example, in a public school district, research and development may be the curriculum department, but at a pharmaceutical company, it may actually be called research and development. For an HR professional to display credibility and expertise, it is critical that there is a solid understanding of how each function executes their contribution to the organization.

✗ **A**, **B** and **C** are incorrect. They are all incorrect since "all of the above" is the correct answer.

43. ☑ **C.** Operations is the function that essentially makes the business go and brings it all together. Operations is responsible for developing, producing, and delivering products and services to the consumer. Marketing and research and development (R&D) defines a product/service, and sales figures out the best way to get consumers to buy the product/service.

☒ **A, B,** and **D** are incorrect. **A** is incorrect because marketing is responsible for positioning a product or service to the consumer. **B** is incorrect because finance is responsible for processing and documenting the financial resources of the company. **D** is incorrect because research and development is responsible for exploring and developing new products or services that will bring in future revenue for the company.

44. ☑ **A.** The best description of the differences between the two core functions are that the accounting team focuses on tracking the daily transactions or flow of money in and out of the business. Finance typically handles financial planning and modeling, which helps the organization's business leaders make decisions about new markets to enter, acquisitions, and divestures, as well as make a host of other strategic decisions.

☒ **B, C** and **D** are incorrect. **B** is incorrect because while accounting and finance departments are sometimes seen as one function led by a chief financial officer (CFO), depending on the size of the organization, they are not interchangeable terms. **C** is incorrect because it is true that an accounting duty is to track expenditures; finance is not primarily responsible for budgeting. In fact, HR, as well as the other core functional areas, bears some of responsibility for budgeting. **D** is incorrect because accounting tracks financial metrics such as the balance sheet, assets, liabilities, and so on.

45. ☑ **C.** With respect to the sales force, HR should work closely and collaboratively to adopt incentive programs that align with the culture and practices of the markets where the sales team is conducting business. This is a strategic function of HR.

☒ **A, B,** and **D** are incorrect. **A** is incorrect because managing costs is a cross-functional relationship HR has primarily with finance and accounting. **B** and **D** are incorrect because managing labor relations is primarily a cross-functional relationship of HR, and operations and staffing is a cross-functional relationship that HR has with all core business functions.

46. ☑ **B.** HR brings the most value to an organization when HR professionals are knowledgeable about all parts of the business. Functional leaders are able to leverage HR's knowledge of the business and how it impacts the people aspect to determine the best strategic direction for their areas and the company overall.

☒ **A, C,** and **D** are incorrect. **A** and **D** are incorrect because recruiting and training highly skilled talent is a function of HR, but these are not the only areas where HR contributes materially to the business. **C** is incorrect because an HR professional can't guarantee that a company will never be sued. HR must be ready to provide and interpret information in an employee's file and any investigations to third parties such as courts or government agencies.

47. ☑   **A.** HR's efforts to show how the department is a strategic partner is best expressed to upper management in terms of how HR can partner/support the entire organization at both the functional and strategic levels. It is best for HR employees to take a consultative approach by positioning themselves as subject-matter experts (SMEs) in the areas of workforce planning and retention, employee relations, and performance management, with the ultimate mission of supporting the creation and maintenance of an engaged workforce.

☒   **B, C,** and **D** are incorrect. They are all incorrect because while they are important components to the effective and efficient functioning of human resources, the focus on the needs of human resources during the strategic planning process should not be presented first in discussions. Often this causes an irreparable breakdown in communication between HR and functional leaders.

48. ☑   **B.** A decentralized structure is best for franchises or any organization with a wide geographic reach. The corporate office provides support in the form of product development and national marketing, but the franchise owner has the independence to make decisions based on knowledge of the local market.

☒   **A, C,** and **D** are incorrect. **A** is incorrect because a centralized structure is most appropriate for small businesses or companies with a small geographic reach. **C** is incorrect because matrix organizations are a combination of centralized and decentralized models where an employee may report to multiple supervisors or report into multiple divisions. This level of complexity is not best for a franchise. **D** is incorrect because a functional structure refers to a structure that is set up along business units or functional areas. This structure works best in companies that are not very agile and focus on a single product or service.

49. ☑   **C.** HR's strategic role varies depending on the organization's strategic orientation. To ensure that there is clarity regarding how HR can be of continual value to the organization, HR must advocate to be part all phases of the strategic planning and implementation process.

☒   **A, B,** and **D** are incorrect. All three choices are important but do not fully represent the reason why HR needs to be involved in all parts of the strategic planning process.

50. ☑   **D.** An HRIS is a human resource information system. This database not only stores employee information but synthesizes information that affects employees obtained from various functional areas. Several areas should be collaborated with to ensure that implementation of an HRIS is aligned to the company's strategic direction. For example, finance and accounting will be concerned with the cost of the software, and if those costs are projected to result in savings for the company, sales may be concerned with how the HRIS will track commissions earned.

☒   **A, B,** and **C** are incorrect. A decision that affects the entire employee population, such as the implementation of an HRIS, should never be made in a silo. At a minimum, a focus group or a survey that captures how all employees and functional areas will interact with the software is needed before decisions are finalized. All of these choices limit the involvement of functional areas that are not immediately obvious such as HR and IT.

51. ☑ **C.** Modified duty is the best description of what is applicable because the accommodation would be temporary.

☒ **A**, **B** and **D** are incorrect. **A** is incorrect because a reasonable accommodation is a permanent solution. Farough only requires an accommodation for a little less than 2 weeks. **B** is incorrect because a fit-for-duty exam is an appropriate and useful part of a return to work program but, in this case, it is already established that Farough can return to work shortly. The only question is how soon. **D** is incorrect because an interactive dialogue between the employee and the Return to Work Coordinator regarding the employee's fitness to return to work is something required by the American with Disabilities Act. However, carpal tunnel is not covered under ADA. It is a best practice for an employer to maintain an open dialogue with injured employees but it is not required in all cases.

52. ☑ **B.** Under the ADA, you have a disability if you have at least one of the following: a physical or mental impairment that substantially limits one or more major life activities, a record of such an impairment, or you are regarded as having such an impairment.

☒ **A**, **C**, and **D** are incorrect. They are incorrect because the impairment needs only one limit on major life activity.

53. ☑ **B.** In 1994, the ADA was amended to cover employers with 15 or more employees.

☒ **A**, **C**, and **D** are incorrect. They are all incorrect because only companies with 15 or more employees are required to comply with the ADA regulations.

54. ☑ **D.** All the options are correct. The ADA makes it unlawful to discriminate in all employment practices such as benefits, promotions, pay, recruitment, hiring, firing, job assignments, training, leave, lay-off, and all other employment-related activities.

☒ **A**, **B**, and **C** are incorrect. **D** is the best answer.

55. ☑ **C.** Affirmative action plans (AAPs) define an employer's standard for proactively recruiting, hiring, and promoting women, minorities, disabled individuals, and veterans. Affirmative action is deemed a moral and social obligation to amend historical wrongs and eliminate the present effects of past discrimination.

☒ **A**, **B**, and **D** are incorrect. **A** is incorrect because it is a remedy to assist wrongdoing, but an affirmative action plan is considered the foremost remedy to amend historical wrongdoings. **B** and **D** are incorrect. They are reporting requirements under separate laws.

56. ☑ **A.** Federal contracts exceeding $50,000 and companies that have more than 50 employees are required to have an affirmative action plan.

☒ **B**, **C**, and **D** are incorrect. They are all incorrect because the dollar threshold for affirmative action plans is a contract of $50,000 or more.

57. ☑ **C.** All private employers that are subject to Title VII and have 100 or more employees need to file an EEO-1 report.

☒ **A**, **B**, and **D** are incorrect. The correct number is 100 employees. Federal contractors with 50 or more employees are required to file the EEO-1 report. This includes all private employers that are subject to Title VII of the Civil Rights Act of 1964 (as amended by the Equal Employment Opportunity Act of 1972) with 100 or more employees, *excluding* state and local governments, primary and secondary school systems, institutions of higher education, Indian tribes, and tax-exempt private membership clubs other than labor organizations. This also includes all federal contractors (private employers) that are not exempt as provided for by 41 CFR 60-1.5; have 50 or more employees; are prime contractors or first-tier subcontractors; have a contract, subcontract, or purchase order amounting to $50,000 or more; serve as a depository of government funds in any amount; or are a financial institution that is an issuing and paying agent for U.S. Savings Bonds and Notes.

58. ☑ **C.** The first step in a progressive discipline process is an oral/verbal warning.

☒ **A, B,** and **D** are incorrect. **A** is incorrect because a performance improvement plan could possibly be issued after a verbal warning was given to an employee to help the employee with performance for a variety of reasons. **B** is incorrect because this would be outside of the formal employer process. **D** is incorrect because that would typically be the second step of the process.

59. ☑ **D.** Treating employees fairly in order to cultivate a positive corporate culture would be the main reason.

☒ **A, B,** and **C** are incorrect. Although they may be factors, none of these are the main reason for a company wanting to implement a progressive disciplinary policy.

60. ☑ **B.** Progressive discipline generally includes a series of increasingly severe penalties for repeated offenses, typically beginning with counseling or a verbal warning.

☒ **A, C,** and **D** are incorrect. A series of increasingly severe penalties for repeated offenses is called a progressive discipline policy.

61. ☑ **D.** As Ralph's HR business partner, you will need to help him explore more than just the turnover ratio. His concern is that he is losing staff during a time when he needs employees for a major deliverable. The turnover ratio will help him figure out how frequent turnover really happens and why. The number of grievances will help him figure out, with your help, if the loss in staff is because of a growing displeasure with working conditions, and the cost per hire ratio will help him understand what the true cost of replacing each lost employee is to the organization.

☒ **A, B,** and **C** are incorrect. They take into account only one aspect of Ralph's concerns. As his HR business partner, it is your role to help him interpret and draw some conclusions about what may be the cause of the increase in turnover and the best staffing strategy forward.

62. ☑ **A.** Tracking referral sources is a typical talent acquisition/recruiting activity. Applicants are asked to identify how they heard of a particular job opportunity. If the company web site is frequently identified as the origin, the talent acquisition team may make the decision to invest more in web site promotion; conversely, if the web site isn't consistently identified as a referral source for candidates, perhaps talent acquisition decides to divert time and money advertising elsewhere.

☒ **B, C,** and **D** are incorrect. They are all incorrect because tracking fans, followers, and retweets are social metrics that an organization can use to know its reach in order to make decisions about where and when to market products and services.

63. ☑ **A.** A ratio of offers to acceptances measures the company's ability to hire. If a large number of top talent declines a company's offer to work for competitors, that is a sign that the compensation, benefits, or overall company reputation is not competitive.

☒ **B**, **C**, and **D** are incorrect. **B** is incorrect because regrettable voluntary turnover measures retention. It does not necessarily measure how competitive a company is at attracting top talent. **C** is incorrect because hires as a percentage of total employees is measured based on recruitment activity. It does not necessarily reflect the ability to attract top talent. **D** is incorrect because voluntary turnover within 90 days reflects retention. It does not reflect the company's ability to attract top talent.

64. ☑ **C**. Revenue per employee would be a good place to capture how effective each employee is in completing sales.

☒ **A**, **B**, and **D** are incorrect. **A** is incorrect because customers per employee measures the quantity of customers each employee manages. It does not measure how effective an employee is in closing sales. **B** is incorrect because expenses per employee measures how much is spent per employee. It does not measure how effective an employee is in closing sales. **D** is incorrect because labor cost per employee measures how much a company spends on wages and benefits per employee. It does not measure employee effectiveness.

65. ☑ **C**. Retiree benefit cost as a percentage of expense will provide insight into the cost of retirement benefits in relation to overall expenses.

☒ **A**, **B**, and **D** are incorrect. **A** is incorrect because benefit costs as a percentage of revenue measure health, dental, and vision and do not necessarily narrow in on retirement costs. **B** is incorrect because benefit costs as a percentage of expense, as in option **A**, include all things related to benefits. It does not narrow in on retirement costs. **D** is incorrect because compensation as a percentage of expense does not measure retirement costs.

66. ☑ **B**. Organizations use the basic compensation ratio of an employee's pay rates divided by the pay range midpoint to determine whether employee salaries are competitive in the marketplace when compared to employees of comparable skills and experience.

☒ **A**, **C**, and **D** are incorrect. **A** is incorrect because pay compression, which occurs when employees with less experience are paid almost as much as those with significantly more experience, is determined by comparing the salaries of senior employees to junior employees. **C** is incorrect because the company's overall cost per employee is determined by adding all salaries (includes overtime), benefits, and bonuses and by dividing that by the total amount spent on all employees in the organization.

67. ☑ **D**. Native Americans and African-Americans would experience adverse impact in this case. To calculate adverse impact, first divide the number of new hires by the number of applicants in that particular group to determine the selection rate. Then multiply the highest selection rate by 80 percent (the four-fifths rule). The selection rate for African-Americans is 10 percent, and for Native Americans it is 9 percent. The highest selection rate is for Caucasians at 29 percent. Four-fifths of 29 percent is 23 percent. The selection rate for Asians is 27 percent, which is above the 23 percent benchmark.

☒ **A**, **B**, and **C** are incorrect. When applying the four-fifths rule, neither Asians nor Caucasians are adversely impacted. All three of these answers include either Asians or Caucasians as a choice.

68. ☑ **A.** To calculate the yield ratio of qualified applicants to job offers made, divide 10 (number of offers) by 50 (qualified job applicants). Yield can be calculated throughout the recruiting process to help talent acquisition determine the effectiveness of various recruiting initiatives.

☒ **B, C,** and **D** are incorrect. **B** is incorrect because it's the ratio of offers to total applicants. **C** is incorrect because it's the ratio of qualified applicants to total applicants. **D** is incorrect because it's simply an incorrect calculation.

69. ☑ **B.** Talent acquisition must balance the desire to fill positions quickly with the cost to engage in aggressive recruiting tactics, as well as with the quality of the applicants. Losing focus on all three measures may decrease quality and lengthen the recruiting process.

☒ **A, C,** and **D** are incorrect. **A** is incorrect because the length that a position is open does not necessarily increase the likelihood that it will go unfilled. **C** and **D** are incorrect because both are recommended strategies to address hiring needs that companies might determine are best given the company's unique situation.

70. ☑ **B.** Absentee rate and workers' compensation incidence rates are good ways to measure the effectiveness of employee engagement initiatives. Higher absenteeism typically means lower engagement. Additionally, more workplace injuries can also highlight lowered engagement. For example, employees in a factory may be distracted because of lowered morale and therefore handle machinery more carelessly.

☒ **A, C,** and **D** are incorrect. **A** is incorrect because by tracking total revenue at any point without comparing revenue with several other business factors, it will be difficult to determine whether change in revenue truly correlates to change in employee engagement. **C** and **D** are incorrect because cost per hire is a talent acquisition metric. It is the total cost a company incurs to attract talent.

71. ☑ **C.** A spreadsheet is computer software such as Excel or Lotus that simulates a worksheet used to tabulate data and create graphs based on data entered. HR will often use spreadsheets to calculate compensation, employee scheduling, recruitment candidate tracking, checklists, and so on.

☒ **A, B,** and **D** are incorrect. None of them represents spreadsheet software that calculates data and creates graphs.

72. ☑ **A.** A database holds an extensive amount of information and is often used to store and track employee data. Access is a common tool that is often used in HR for task management, training and class tracking, and employee information storage and tracking.

☒ **B, C,** and **D** are incorrect. Graphs and software may contain information, but a database stores an extensive amount of information that can be used to track certain components of a business. Cells connect a row and a column in a spreadsheet.

73. ☑ **B.** An enterprise resource planning (ERP) system is a collection of integrated applications that manage business processes. An ERP, when implemented correctly, can automate many tactical functions such as data entry, manual communication between HR and payroll, vacation requests, and so on.

☒ **A**, **C**, and **D** are incorrect. **A** is incorrect because an applicant tracking system (ATS) is a system that stores and tracks applicants for a recruitment process. Typically this type of system can be isolated as a stand-alone system or can be integrated into a wider ERP system. **C** is incorrect because a time and attendance (TAA) system tracks when people work, when they start and end shifts, and when they are absent from work. Like an ATS, a TAA can also function as a stand-alone system or be integrated into a wider ERP. **D** is incorrect because a learning management system (LMS) tracks the delivery of electronic educational courses or training programs (also called *e-learning*). An LMS can function as a stand-alone system or be integrated into a wider ERP system.

74. ☑ **B**. A query is a request for information from a database or a series of tables. Often HR will query data from an information system that may give insights on turnover, employee demographics, compensation and benefits information, and so on.

    ☒ **A**, **C**, and **D** are incorrect. They are not the best answers because they do not meet the definition of a query. They do not extract information from a database.

75. ☑ **C**. A spreadsheet is used to track and display nonrelational data that is used to calculate or draw statistical comparisons. In other words, a spreadsheet will hold data such as employee names, job title, department, and compensation compa-ratio to determine whose pay is closest to market.

    ☒ **A**, **B**, and **D** are incorrect. **A** is incorrect because a presentation is a vague term and does not track data. **B** is incorrect because a database tracks relational data in terms of tables. **D** is not the best answer because a report is something printed from a spreadsheet or database but not what we are looking for in an application or software capability.

76. ☑ **B**. Multiple people who can produce complex queries can use a database.

    ☒ **A**, **C**, and **D** are incorrect. While they all have different levels of information, they do not produce at the capacity of a database. Some of these are static or can be used by only one person at a time such as a spreadsheet or report.

77. ☑ **D**. A vlookup is a function in a spreadsheet that enables someone to combine two lists into a single list. This function filters through large volumes of data and selects information based on a set of conditions.

    ☒ **A**, **B**, and **C** are incorrect. They do not reflect the function of combining two lists in a spreadsheet.

78. ☑ **A**. A pivot table can automatically sort, count, total, or average data and display it. This is a function that is often used to rapidly summarize data into a compact, understandable format.

    ☒ **B**, **C**, and **D** are incorrect. These may have some role in sharing information, but they do not necessarily serve as a specific function of sorting and counting data.

79. ☑ **B**. A dashboard displays at a high level a series of important HR metrics. From an organizational perspective, that data can be pulled into a larger multidisciplinary (i.e., production, marketing) dashboard often called a *balanced scorecard*.

    ☒ **A**, **C**, and **D** are incorrect. None is the best answer. A spreadsheet, presentation, or report shares information at a detailed level. A dashboard provides a high-level summary.

80. ☑ **D.** A statistical analysis tool that gives an overview of variables that tend to go up and down together and in a specific direction is a correlation study or matrix. This statistical analysis tool can provide insights into how one variable can impact another.

☒ **A, B,** and **C** are incorrect. These are all tools that may not directly provide a correlation of variables. It depends on how the spreadsheet or database is set up to display information.

81. ☑ **A.** Conducting employee surveys helps an organization understand what is on the hearts and minds of employees. Ultimately, employee survey information can enable an organization to stay competitive in driving employee motivation, retention, and productivity.

☒ **B, C,** and **D** are incorrect. None of them is the best reason for why an organization would conduct an employee survey.

82. ☑ **C.** Utilizing random protected passwords, using third-party administration, and establishing a good communication plan are best practices for helping employees overcome privacy fears.

☒ **A, B,** and **D** are incorrect. These are not the best methods for helping employees feel comfortable sharing information through a survey. Great care needs to take place, and a strong communication plan about the steps taken to secure privacy is the best approach.

83. ☑ **C.** Conducting focus group sessions is a great way to gain further insights in otherwise confusing survey results. A focus group is when a group of people is asked about their perceptions, opinions, beliefs, and attitudes toward a topic, concept, or idea.

☒ **A, B,** and **D** are incorrect. They are not the best way to validate confusing results. Resurveying employees can cause survey fatigue, and often employees will grow complacent in providing any useful information over time. In addition, employees may not want to be identified individually because they may be reluctant to provide honest feedback. Taking great care and utilizing surveys effectively, an organization will yield benefits from insights already provided by employees.

84. ☑ **B.** A targeted selection interview is a type of interview that depends on job analysis to identify critical job requirements such as competencies for each position by focusing on what the person has done in previous situations.

☒ **A, C,** and **D** are incorrect. They do not meet the definition of a targeted selection interview. While they are types of interviews, they may not be based on a specific set of critical job requirements.

85. ☑ **C.** A patterned interview is a structured interview in which the interviewer asks a series of predetermined questions. This method ensures that answers can be reliably aggregated and that comparisons between surveys or interviews can be made with confidence.

☒ **A, B,** and **D** are incorrect. **A** is incorrect because a panel interview is when a candidate or participant is asked a series of questions by a group of people. **B** is incorrect because a targeted selection interview is based on a predetermined set of competencies and asks how a participant acts in certain situations. **D** is incorrect because an observation method of interview is to simply watch how a participant performs.

86. ☑ **A.** A panel interview is a format in which one participant is interviewed by a group of interviewers at one time. For example, an organization will set up a series of panel interviews for a candidate. Function, level, or department teams determine how the people are grouped. The rationale for using this interviewing type is to minimize individual bias and increase accuracy.

☒ **B, C,** and **D** are incorrect. They are all incorrect because they do not represent a group of interviews. We are looking for a panel interview as the definition.

87. ☑ **D.** Validity is when a test or a survey effectively measures what it is supposed to measure. The validity of a test describes the degree to which you can make specific conclusions or predictions about people based on how they score.

☒ **A, B,** and **C** are incorrect. They do not represent the best definition of a valid test. Validity, or content validity, is the best formal answer.

88. ☑ **B.** When a test or survey consistently measures what it is supposed to, it is known to be reliable. For example, test-retest reliability is a form of measure that is obtained by administering the same test twice over a period of time to a group of individuals.

☒ **A, C,** and **D** are incorrect. They do not best represent the formal answer to a survey that consistently measures what it is supposed to measure.

89. ☑ **A.** Collecting and analyzing work samplings or reviewing employee logs is an example of an observation method to data collection. For example, this method is helpful when analyzing specifically what tasks or duties a particular job requires.

☒ **B, C,** and **D** are incorrect. They are incorrect because panel, structured, and semi-structured are all interviewing methods that may follow the observation method.

90. ☑ **B.** An interview in which the interviewer determines the major questions beforehand but allows sufficient flexibility to probe further is known as a semi-structured interview. The benefit of using this data collection method is it allows new ideas to surface from comments made by the participant.

☒ **A, C,** and **D** are incorrect. **A** is incorrect because a structured interview is strictly the use of predetermined questions. This method does not allow flexibility to probe other ideas. **C** is incorrect because the observation method doesn't ask formal questions; rather, it involves watching certain tasks to be performed. **D** is not the best answer because a panel interview consists of a group of people who interviews a single candidate at one time. The panel interview may be structured or semi-structured.

91. ☑ **D.** An executive summary is a short document, or section of a document, that provides a brief overview of a longer report, proposal, or business plan. In other words, an executive summary provides a concise summary of key points in a longer, more detailed report. This is a popular feature of any report when presenting information to a busy C-suite executive.

☒ **A, B,** and **C** are incorrect. They are incorrect because an analysis, a problem statement, and recommendations are typically parts of the executive summary and the larger report.

92. ☑ **B.** A histogram is a graphical representation of data using bars, often in different heights, depending on the distribution of numerical data. For example, a histogram may be used to display employee distribution by years of service, by age, or by salary.

☒ **A, C,** and **D** are incorrect. They are incorrect because a pie chart, a scatter graph, and a line graph display data other than in a bar format.

93. ☑ **A.** A pie chart is a type of graph in which a circular shape is divided into sections that each represents a proportion of the whole. For example, HR may use a pie chart to show a visual representation of head count percent per department or head count by location.

☒ **B, C,** and **D** are incorrect. They are incorrect because a histogram, scatter, or line graph is not circular in format.

94. ☑ **D.** A line graph is used to visualize the value or trend of something over time. For example, HR may use a line graph to display monthly or yearly turnover trends.

☒ **A, B** and **C** are incorrect. They are not the best answers because pie charts, histograms, and frequency distributions do not plot a trend over time.

95. ☑ **A.** The difference between a histogram and a bar chart is that a histogram plots quantitative data and a bar chart plots categorical data. Quantitative data is about numbers. Categorical data represents types of data that can be organized in groups by race, age, and educational level.

☒ **B, C,** and **D** are incorrect. They are incorrect because they don't accurately represent the difference between a histogram and a bar graph.

96. ☑ **C.** Benchmarking is comparison of an organization's performance against the best practices of other leading companies. For example, HR will often seek best-practice information in recruitment, employee engagement and retention, and HR strategies in helping organizations to achieve the desired business results.

☒ **A, B,** and **D** are incorrect. They are incorrect because while competition, metrics, and analytics may be part of benchmarking, they do not individually adequately define the seeking and comparing of best practices.

97. ☑ **B.** A balanced scorecard consists of performance metrics used in strategic management to identify, report, and improve various internal functions of a business. The balance scorecard typically is inclusive of measures representing multidisciplinary areas such as financial, customer, business process, and learning and growth measures. In other words, the balanced scorecard translates strategy into four perspectives, thus "balanced" between internal/external measures and objective/subjective measures.

☒ **B, C,** and **D** are incorrect. Benchmarking, performance evaluation, and business intelligence do not adequately represent what we were looking for in a balanced scorecard definition. These answers represent one aspect of measurement or are too vague.

98. ☑ **B.** Forecasting is the estimation of the likelihood of an event becoming a reality in the future, based on available data from the past. HR may forecast both short- and long-term staffing needs based on projected sales, new service lines, and attrition, which all affect a company's need for skills.

☒ **A, B,** and **D** are incorrect. Benchmarking, metrics, and executive summary are indicators of the "here and now" and do not adequately represent what we were looking for in terms of predicting the future.

99. ☑ **D.** A trend analysis is creating statistical models that predict demand for the next year, given relatively objective statistics from the previous year. HR may create a trend analysis of turnover from the previous year to predict labor needs in the next year. A trend analysis feeds forecasting decisions.

☒ **A**, **B**, and **C** are incorrect. They are not the best answers because graphs, metrics, and benchmarking are too vague. A trend analysis may utilize graphs or metrics to display data, but these items do not necessarily indicate a trend that can be used to predict the future.

100. ☑ **C**. It is business intelligence that provides insight into business trends and patterns and helps improve decisions. For HR, business intelligence is displayed as metrics, analytics, or dashboards.

☒ **A**, **B**, and **D** are incorrect. They are incorrect because pie charts, histograms, and executive summaries are part of business intelligence. They may not individually provide meaningful insights into business trends.

101. ☑ **A**. Biometric screening can be a threat to employee privacy and result in identity theft because these measures allow the employer to collect a significant amount of demographic information and, in the case of retinal scans, medical information. If the employer doesn't house this information in a secure and encrypted database, then an employee could have his or her information stolen and used by an enterprising hacker.

☒ **B**, **C**, and **D** are incorrect. **B** and **C** are incorrect for similar reasons. As long as employees are made aware of the new security procedures and the hospital management is cooperative with the police if there are unwelcomed visitors, there is no "threat." **D** is incorrect because the advocates of the new policy have indicated that this heightened level of security is desired by the residents of the maternity ward.

102. ☑ **A**. Employers benefit from the wide reach the Internet provides. However, with that larger audience for open positions comes an increase in unqualified candidates because of the ease of applying for open positions. It becomes challenging for employers to sift through these additional candidates, and, at times, qualified candidates get lost in the sheer volume. Many employers utilize recruiting software like Taleo to do keyword searches in hopes of increasing the chance that qualified candidates make it through the initial applicant screen.

☒ **B**, **C**, and **D** are incorrect. The ability to target specialized skills, improve candidate mapping, and increase the candidate pool are all benefits of e-recruiting.

103. ☑ **B**. A good social media policy details what types of communication, both on and off the job made via social media, are acceptable. A company with a policy like this in place that was signed or acknowledged by employees helps to negate or discourage undesirable employee behavior with regard to social media.

☒ **A**, **C**, and **D** are incorrect. **A** is incorrect because ECPA makes no mention of social media. The act establishes that employers can monitor the creation of electronic communication prior to it being sent or after its receipt if it occurs during the course of business and employees have consented. **C** is incorrect because the Privacy Act of 1974 is not applicable in this scenario. It governs the collection and use of personally identifiable information. It provides that employees can request their records and have to be granted access to their records and given the opportunity to request a correction to those records. **D** is incorrect because an Internet use policy addresses how an employee accesses the Internet on company time.

104. ☑ **D.** Predictive analytics can help HR professionals evaluate several employment risks. For example, HR can use predictive analytics, which is the use of statistics to evaluate historical data and use that data as a predictor of future behavior, to determine whether the implementation of a new time management system will improve overtime expense management based on how new time management systems have affected overtime usage in the past.

☒ **A, B,** and **C** are incorrect. **A** and **B** are incorrect because identifying more potential consumers and improving sales forecasts are benefits of big data to the marketing and sales function of a company. **C** is incorrect because big data has no impact on the ease of access to employee information.

105. ☑ **A.** A policy prohibits the sharing of passwords and the utilization of monitoring software that tracks and blocks the attempted download of phishing programs or malware.

☒ **B, C,** and **D** are incorrect. Protecting data integrity focuses on the corruption of company information assets. Examples include downloading malware and becoming a victim of a social engineer. Social networking sites, the potential release of copyright information, and sending e-mails from work have no effect on the corruption of electronically stored data.

106. ☑ **A.** Hacking was used to describe exploring technology through trial and error. Today it has grown to mean the act of deliberately accessing another person's computer without their permission.

☒ **B, C,** and **D** are incorrect. **B** is incorrect because phishing is specifically the use of e-mails, phone calls, texts, or instant messages masked as originating from a legitimate source with the intent of enticing you to reveal your passwords in order to gain access to your computer and accounts. **C** is incorrect because an e-card usually references an online greeting card delivered via e-mail. Within the context of technological security, an e-card usually appears like a legitimate greeting or job announcement, but when the user opens it, a harmful program is released that could damage your computer. **D** is incorrect because a security alert is an e-mail or pop-up alerting you that your computer has been comprised and purports that clicking the link provided will run a program that will fix the problem. With respect to security risks, this e-mail is fake and will run a program that will infect your computer.

107. ☑ **B.** Software as a service (SaaS), sometimes referred to as *software on demand*, is a system where software is delivered over the Internet to customers on a pay-per-use basis. Customers are charged only for the users and bandwidth they use.

☒ **A, C,** and **D** are incorrect. **A** is incorrect because cloud computing is an all-encompassing description of IT solutions delivered as a service using Internet technologies. SaaS is an example of cloud computing. **C** is incorrect because an application service provider (ASP) is similar to SaaS but is best considered a precursor or first generation of SaaS. This is mainly because with ASP computer-based services are delivered to the client via a network versus the Internet. Customization is more complex and costly. **D** is incorrect because service level agreements (SLAs) are service contracts that detail the delivery of an IT solution.

108. ☑ **C.** An effective communication policy will include that a company has the right to monitor all technology use to and from company equipment. Typically, an organization would not have a separate technology policy but rather capture all technology-related guidelines as part of a larger communications policy.

☒ **A, B,** and **D** are incorrect. **A** is incorrect because HR policies do not have to be ISO 9000 compliant. Seeking the ISO 9000 designation is an organization decision rather than a legal requirement. **B** is incorrect because an effective communication policy will state that an employee may be held responsible for online posts even if they are anonymous. **D** is incorrect because it is not necessary to list all available technologies in a policy. Simply stating "all company equipment" or a similar statement suffices.

109. ☑ **B.** An effective social media policy will detail who is allowed to create, maintain, and post to the company blog.

☒ **A, C,** and **D** are incorrect. They are incorrect because the blog design and the purpose of the blog are all important considerations for the business but have little effect on policy development.

110. ☑ **C.** Telepresence provides users with an almost in-person experience. Video images and audio are near-life-like.

☒ **A, B,** and **D** are incorrect. **A** is incorrect because a web conference is not interactive. **B** is incorrect because multifaceted groupware is a collaboration platform that allows participants to be interactive, but the images and audio are not the same degree of quality as that of a telepresence platform. **D** is incorrect because videoconferencing uses cameras and other software to simulate face-to-face communication, but, again, the technology is not of the same quality as a telepresence platform.

111. ☑ **A.** Retention and destruction timeline expectations are an important part of any employee record policy or procedure. Federal, state, and local laws and regulations require that specific employee records and documents, whether stored electronically or on paper, be kept for a specified period of time, even extending beyond the employee's termination date.

☒ **B, C,** and **D** are incorrect. **B** is incorrect because how large an employee file is irrelevant given record retention and destruction legal requirements. **C** is incorrect because medical records should never be kept with the general file documents because of privacy requirements, and **D** is incorrect because HR office hours are irrelevant given record retention and destruction legal requirements.

112. ☑ **D.** The best reason to maintain security protocols over employee records is to prevent discrimination, identity theft, and privacy breaches. Often employee records contain information such as the employee's Social Security number, birth dates, private addresses, and salary information. Especially in an era of cyber hacking, this information in the wrong hands can damage an employee's identity, economic, and private standing. Further, those records may also contain race, age, national origin, and other EEO-protected information. If the records are mishandled or unfortunate employment decisions are made based on EEO-protected information, the employer may face discrimination charges. Employers should take employee record security very seriously and take great care in protecting employee information to prevent harm to employees and public relation nightmares.

☒ **A**, **B**, and **C** are incorrect. These reasons do not rise to the "best" reason to protect employee records. As stated, it is critical to take great care in protecting private employee information.

113. ☑ **B**. The hiring manager should have access to applications, résumés, and reference check results in order to make reasonable and job-related hiring decisions.

☒ **A**, **C**, and **D** are incorrect. **A** is incorrect because drug test details contain private medical information. The only thing the hiring manager needs to know is if the candidate passed or failed the drug test. **C** is incorrect because background check results also contain private information such as Social Security numbers, credit, or other non–job-related information. Like the drug test, the only thing the hiring manager needs to know is if the candidate passed or failed the background check. **D** is incorrect because the I-9 form contains EEO-protected information such as race or national origin. It is discriminatory to base hiring decisions on race or national origin information. The hiring manager doesn't need to see the I-9 form to make reasonable and job-related hiring decisions.

114. ☑ **B**. An employer is required to retain I-9 forms for 3 years from the date of hire or 1 year following termination of employment, whichever is later. Savvy HR professionals will keep a record with expiration dates for each form. Further, when auditing the forms, it is best to randomly select forms or audit 100 percent of the forms as opposed to selecting only certain national origins to audit to avoid discrimination charges.

☒ **A**, **C**, and **D** are incorrect. None is the best answer because there is only one regulatory answer to how long I-9 forms should be retained.

115. ☑ **D**. The Office of Federal Contract Compliance Programs (OFCCP) require that any employment record made or kept by the contractor be retained by the employer for a period of 2 years from the date of creating the record or the record requiring a personnel action, whichever occurs later.

☒ **A**, **B**, and **C** are incorrect. They are incorrect because there is only one right answer in this case. Sometimes retention requirements may differ depending on the size of the organization. For example, if a federal contractor has fewer than 150 employees or less than $150,000 in contracts, the timeline required to retain employment records is 1 year.

116. ☑ **C**. Concerning an EEOC charge, all records must be kept until the final disposition of the charge regardless of whether the employee is with the organization or not.

☒ **A**, **B**, and **D** are incorrect. All other answers simply do not satisfy legal requirements. Once a charge is filed, making records available for agency viewing is required regardless of previous timeline requirement or policies.

117. ☑ **C**. The Equal Employment Opportunity Commission (EEOC) regulations require employers to retain records for an employee who has been involuntarily terminated for 1 year.

☒ **A**, **B**, and **D** are incorrect. There is only one correct answer in this case. While the EEOC has only a 1-year requirement, other agency regulations or laws may contradict the 1-year requirement. In that case, it is best to identify the longest required timeframe and apply it to your policy.

118.   ☑   **A.** The Federal Labor Standards Act (FLSA) requires employers to retain payroll records for 3 years.

☒   **B, C,** and **D** are incorrect. There is only one answer to this question. Payroll records must also be retained in case there are any disputes with pay or a need to produce records upon agency request.

119.   ☑   **C.** The Occupational Safety and Health Administration (OSHA) requires the OSHA 300 log to be retained by the employer for 5 years following the end of the calendar year in which the record occurs. Further, the OSHA 300 log must be updated during the 5-year period if newly recordable injuries or illnesses information was discovered.

☒   **A, B,** and **D** are incorrect. None is the best answer because again in this regulatory sense there is only one answer. All other options are simply not correct.

120.   ☑   **B.** Destroying paper copies after they are converted to an electronic format is an efficient and effective record standard for a couple of reasons. First, keeping records neat and tidy and removing any potential for security breaches is a good idea. Second, if an organization should keep records longer than required regardless if in paper or electronic format, it winds up establishing a record retention precedence in the eyes of regulatory agencies, and the employer could be required to maintain records longer than necessary.

☒   **A, C,** and **D** are incorrect. They are all incorrect because the reasons listed are irrelevant and not important to employee record retention standards.

121.   ☑   **B.** The Employee Retirement Income Security Act (ERISA) requires employers to file Form 5500 annual reports on employee benefits offered. Retirement and health benefit plans must file the Form 5500 to report their financial condition, investments, and operations. The due date for the Form 5500 reports is the last day of the seventh month after the plan year ends.

☒   **A, C,** and **D** are incorrect. All these options are irrelevant to ERISA reporting requirements.

122.   ☑   **C.** Under Title VII, employers must file an EEO-1 indicating numbers of employees by specific covered protected categories. Those protected categories include race, ethnic origin, and sex.

☒   **A, B,** and **D** are incorrect. They are incorrect because all of these forms or reports indicate other types of information required for different reasons having nothing to do with protected categories.

123.   ☑   **A.** The Patient Protection and Affordable Care Act (PPACA) requires employers with a self-insured health plan to complete and file Forms 1095-B and 1094-B with the IRS, as well as provide employees with a copy of Form 1095-B. These forms report certain information to the IRS and to taxpayers about individuals who are covered by minimum essential benefit coverage. These forms exempt individuals from having to pay a fine, also known as the individual shared responsibility payment.

☒   **B, C,** and **D** are incorrect. None of those agencies has an interest in self-insured health plan required reporting.

124. ☑ **C.** The Patient Protection and Affordable Care Act (PPACA), or also known as the ACA, reporting requirements apply to employers that employ 50 or more full-time employees on average.

⊠ **A**, **B**, and **D** are incorrect. They are not the best answers because none is relevant or applicable to the ACA reporting requirements.

125. ☑ **D.** Employers with 100 or more employees and federal contractors with 50 or more employees are required to submit the EEO-1 report annually.

⊠ **A**, **B**, and **C** are incorrect. None of these answers is applicable to the EEO-1 reporting requirement.

126. ☑ **A.** The EEO-1 report includes employees' race, ethnicity, and sex. New regulations will require employers to also report pay ranges per these specific categories if the regulations are not overturned with new federal administration changes. Savvy HR professionals will pay close attention to any new federal or state regulatory changes.

⊠ **B**, **C**, and **D** are incorrect. They are incorrect because these categories are not applicable to the EEO-1 required report.

127. ☑ **B.** Employers are required to report all workplace fatalities to the Occupational Safety and Health Administration (OSHA) within 8 hours of learning of the event.

⊠ **A**, **C**, and **D** are incorrect. They are not relevant to OSHA. Employers must act quickly to report unfortunate events such as a workplace fatality to OSHA.

128. ☑ **D.** For any employee inpatient hospitalization, amputation, or eye loss that occurs within 24 hours of a work-related incident, an employer must report it to OSHA within 24 hours of learning of the event.

⊠ **B**, **C**, and **D** are incorrect. There is only one answer in this case.

129. ☑ **C.** Employers may have to file Form 1099-MISC to the Internal Revenue Service (IRS) if someone who was not an employee was paid at least $600 for services, also called an *independent contractor*.

⊠ **A**, **B**, and **D** are incorrect. They are not the best answer because again in this regulatory sense there is only one answer. All other options have no interest or are not applicable to independent contractor reporting requirements.

130. ☑ **A.** Employers must file copies of employees' W-2s with the Social Security Administration (SSA) by the end of February of every year. Providing a copy of a W-2 to each employee by January 31 is also an annual requirement.

⊠ **B**, **C**, and **D** are incorrect. All other agencies have no interest and are not applicable to the W-2 reporting requirement.

131. ☑ **B.** A human resource information system (HRIS) is able to handle data collection and reporting for all HR functional areas. It is left to the HR professional to interpret the raw data for management to aid in decision-making.

⊠ **A**, **C**, and **D** are incorrect. They are incorrect because they describe limited HRIS capability.

132. ☑ **C.** It would be cost effective and efficient to customize an off-the-shelf solution in this case. While the company does have the expertise in-house, the IT staff is of more value focusing on the many new accounts the company has acquired because of their skill. Also, since the needs for the HRIS are relatively standard, an off-the-shelf solution will meet the company's needs, and the areas that need a bit of customization can be handled by the company's IT staff.

☒ **A, B,** and **D** are incorrect. **A** is incorrect because outsourcing would be best if there was a high degree of specialization or customization needed to fit the company's needs. Outsourcing is also costlier than an off-the-shelf solution. **B** and **D** are incorrect because while the company has a highly skilled IT staff that could take on this project, that staff is already stretched thin with the number of projects related to newly acquired business. Also, since the company needs are relatively standard, there are multiple off-the-shelf solutions that will meet its needs.

133. ☑ **A.** In this case, scalability is central to the selection of an HRIS. The organization is expecting rapid growth, so any IT solution has to be able to grow efficiently and economically along with the organization.

☒ **B, C,** and **D** are incorrect. They are incorrect because they are all considerations that need to be weighed when making a decision regarding the selection of an HRIS but are not primary for this company whose biggest challenge is the rate of growth.

134. ☑ **B.** The primary benefit of continuous or waterfall integration is that most bugs or other workflow issues can be identified and fixed as they manifest themselves, as opposed to the "big bang" approach where it is more difficult to trace system failures because all components were integrated at once.

☒ **A, C,** and **D** are incorrect. **A** and **C** are incorrect because they are descriptive of a "big bang" approach to systems integration. **D** is incorrect because bugs or other system failures are mostly eliminated during testing, but most systems implementations or integrations tend to reveal some workflow or other technical issues after they are live.

135. ☑ **A.** A best-of-breed HRIS solution is the use of several smaller systems, each responsible for managing a different HR function. These systems are quicker to implement because they are not as complex as an integrated solution.

☒ **B, C,** and **D** are incorrect. **B** is incorrect because vendor management is a disadvantage of a best-of-breed solution. **C** is incorrect because ease of data integration is an advantage of an integrated solution. **D** is incorrect because an integrated solution is less expensive per application than multiple solutions like with the best-of-breed option.

136. ☑ **C.** Generating reports that will be referenced as part of a strategic planning session is an example of decision-maker access to the HRIS. Decision-makers may use dashboards to view real-time data in aggregate that can help inform various business decisions.

☒ **A, B,** and **D** are incorrect. **A** is incorrect because changing tax withholdings is an example of employee self-service. **B** is incorrect because approving paid time off is an example of manager self-service. **D** is incorrect because applying for an internal job posting is an example of an employee-driven activity that may take place through an HRIS or another recruiting platform.

137. ☑ **B.** Encryption is the conversion of data into a format that protects or hides its natural presentation.

☒ **A, C,** and **D** are incorrect. **A** is incorrect because data mining involves collecting, searching, and analyzing large amounts of data to discover relationships. **C** is incorrect because Hypertext Transfer Protocol (HTTP) is a computer formatting language used by web browsers. **D** is incorrect because a database management system (DBMS) is a software application system that stores electronic data.

138. ☑ **C.** When an organization has unique business needs and both the technical and functional knowledge in-house, it is recommended that the company develop its own HRIS. If the needs are unique but there is not an abundance of technical and functional knowledge, it is more cost effective for the organization to outsource the development of the HRIS.

☒ **A, B,** and **D** are incorrect. **A** is incorrect because when a robust customized solution is needed and there is not sufficient technical and functional knowledge in-house, organizations should outsource. **B** and **D** are incorrect because off-the-shelf systems are best when the business needs are standard.

139. ☑ **B.** A hosted approach is when a company has software installed on its equipment but IT support services are provided by an external staff.

☒ **A, C,** and **D** are incorrect. **A** is incorrect because this is a feature of both the hosted approach and the on-premise approach. On-premise means that the software is installed on internal machines and managed by an internal IT department. **C** is incorrect because a subscription service describes software as a service (SaaS). With SaaS, the company doesn't purchase or support the software on-site. The organization, rather, pays a periodic fee to subscribe to the software that is deployed through a web browser. **D** is incorrect because with the hosted approach IT support is provided off-site.

140. ☑ **D.** Since all components are integrated simultaneously, if there are system failures, it is difficult and time consuming for developers to locate the root cause of the failure.

☒ **A, B,** and **C** are incorrect. **A** is incorrect because simultaneous integration is a feature, not a disadvantage, of the "big bang" approach. **B** is incorrect because in the "big bang" approach testing is done in a test environment once all components are implemented. In the continuous integration approach, testing is done in a working environment. **C** is incorrect because it is a feature of the continuous integration (waterfall) approach to implement components incrementally.

141. ☑ **A.** This is the only one that is not a factor when determining whether there is an employment relationship.

☒ **B, C,** and **D** are incorrect. These are all factors when determining an employment relationship.

142. ☑ **B.** The employee and the government would miss out on company-paid taxes and insurance.

☒ **A, C,** and **D** are incorrect. Although they may be factors, none of these would be the main reason why you would want to properly classify workers correctly.

143. ☑ **A.** An independent contractor decides when, where, and how the work will be performed within broad guidelines. The contractor can subcontract the work or parts of the project to others and can decide what tools to use and what work must be performed to complete the project.

 ☒ **B**, **C**, and **D** are incorrect. An employee would still be told when and where the work needed to be completed.

144. ☑ **B.** Employers must pay nonexempt employees one-and-a-half times their regular rate of pay when they work more than 40 hours in a week.

 ☒ **A**, **C**, and **D** are incorrect. **A** is incorrect because it is not the main answer or obvious choice; however, if the job the person occupies is classified as nonexempt, the employee does have to be paid overtime pay. **C** is incorrect because through an agency or on the employer's payroll, an employer can employ individuals for a finite period of time; this is a temporary employee. If a person works in a job that is classified as nonexempt, the person has to be paid overtime. **D** is incorrect because exempt employees are not required to be paid overtime for hours more than 40 per week.

145. ☑ **C.** A white-collar exemption is an actual exemption under the Fair Labor Standards Act.

 ☒ **A**, **B**, and **D** are incorrect. None of these is an actual exemption under the Fair Labor Standards Act.

146. ☑ **B** is correct because the Fair Labor Standards Act (FLSA) current salary threshold for exemption from overtime pay is $23,660 per year.

 ☒ **A**, **C**, and **D** are incorrect. They are incorrect because $23,660 is the salary threshold for exemption from overtime pay.

147. ☑ **B.** The primary duty under the executive exemption is to manage the enterprise.

 ☒ **A**, **C**, and **D** are incorrect. **A** is incorrect because this would be the primary duty under administrative exemption. **C** is incorrect because this would be a primary duty under the computer exemption. **D** is incorrect because this would be a primary duty under the computer exemption.

148. ☑ **A.** Having advanced knowledge in a field of science or learning is a requirement of the learned professional exemption under the FLSA.

 ☒ **B**, **C**, and **D** are incorrect. **B** is incorrect because it would be a qualification of an outside salesperson. **C** is incorrect because it would be a qualification of a highly compensated employee. **D** is incorrect because it would be a qualification of an executive exemption.

149. ☑ **C.** Employers must pay salaried exempt employees a predetermined amount of payment on a regularly set schedule.

 ☒ **A**, **B**, and **D** are incorrect. **A** and **B** are incorrect because a flex-time employee or temporary employee could be exempt or nonexempt. **D** is incorrect because nonexempt employees are paid on an hourly basis and are eligible for overtime.

150. ☑ **B.** Nonexempt employees are not required to be paid when the training attendance is voluntary.

 ☒ **A**, **C**, and **D** are incorrect. These are correct requirements for someone to be paid.

151. ☑ **C.** A job analysis done on a regular cycle such as once per year will cause little interruption to daily operations while keeping descriptions current.

 ☒ **A, B,** and **D** are incorrect. **A** is incorrect because conducting meetings with the employees would not be the ideal method. **B** is incorrect because an immediate company-wide project to update job descriptions through the job analysis process would be disruptive for business. An effective job analysis includes interviewing supervisors, co-workers, and incumbents; creating a task list; and so on. **D** is incorrect because providing weekly staff meeting updates is not an effective way to maintain a current catalog of job descriptions.

152. ☑ **D.** Identifying the qualifications to do the jobs in the new division is the best first step because this is equivalent to conducting a job analysis. There has to be a job analysis from which to build a job description, which, in turn, helps HR to make the best job-to-person fit.

 ☒ **A, B,** and **C** are incorrect. **A** is incorrect because selecting from a pool of internal applicants occurs before completing the job analysis. **B** and **C** are incorrect because both developing pre-employment tests and hiring criteria take place after the job analysis. The components of both are built from the information compiled through the job analysis.

153. ☑ **D.** All these elements should be included in a job description.

 ☒ **A, B,** and **C** are incorrect. "All of the above" is the best answer.

154. ☑ **B** is correct because disability status of an employee should never be listed on a description.

 ☒ **A, C,** and **D** are incorrect. **A** and **C** are incorrect because they are job-related criteria often required to perform the essential job functions as defined in the ADA. They should be included in job descriptions. **D** is incorrect because management approvals should be listed on job descriptions.

155. ☑ **A.** It can be difficult to separate what the employee brings to the job from the job's main purpose.

 ☒ **B, C,** and **D** are incorrect. Although these may play a small part in why it's difficult, they are not the main reason.

156. ☑ **B.** Frequency and complexity should be considered when determining essential job functions.

 ☒ **A, C,** and **D** are incorrect. They are not relevant to the essential job functions.

157. ☑ **C.** A job description would not be that useful in determining a benefit package for an employee.

 ☒ **A, B,** and **D** are incorrect. These would be another use for a job description.

158. ☑ **D.** The primary purpose of job analysis is to identify and describe what is happening in jobs in the organization.

 ☒ **A, B,** and **C** are incorrect. **A** is incorrect because the job analysis would not be helpful in defining organizational objectives. **B** is incorrect because it would not be its main purpose. **C** is incorrect because analyzing EEO data would not be part of this process.

159. ☑ **D**. All of the above are methods to collect data for the job analysis.

☒ **A**, **B**, and **C** are incorrect. All these options are indeed ways that information can be collected during the job analysis, so "All of the above" is the correct choice.

160. ☑ **A**. Developing subordinates would be a specific job competency for a management role.

☒ **B**, **C**, and **D** are incorrect. These are examples of core competencies that everyone in an organization might share.

161. ☑ **C**. Providing a framework keeps the information flowing from functions to employees who need to keep the organization moving.

☒ **A**, **B**, and **D** are incorrect. **A** is incorrect because this is an example of a functional structure. **B** is incorrect because this is an example of a geographic structure. **D** is incorrect because this is an example of a divisional structure.

162. ☑ **C**. The functional structure is represented by the traditional pyramid-shape organizational type.

☒ **A**, **B**, and **D** are incorrect. **A** is incorrect because the matrix-shape organizational type is where employees report to two managers, one for the product line and the other for the functional responsibility. **B** is incorrect because the product-based organizational type is organized by product line and is appropriate when the company has well-defined product lines that are clearly separate from each other. **D** is incorrect because a seamless structure is one in which the traditional hierarchies do not exist.

163. ☑ **A**. The most formal and rigid of all the organization structures is the functional structure.

☒ **B**, **C**, and **D** are incorrect. These options are not as rigid or formal.

164. ☑ **D**. A matrix structure is where employees report to two managers, one for the product line and one for the functional line.

☒ **A**, **B**, and **C** are incorrect. These options do not reflect a dual reporting relationship.

165. ☑ **D**. A horizontal (flat) organization connected by networks is a seamless organization.

☒ **A**, **B**, and **C** are all incorrect. These options would be reflected by a hierarchical structure.

166. ☑ **C**. The main purpose of a seamless organization is to foster creativity and communication.

☒ **A**, **B**, and **D** are incorrect. These may be other reasons, but they are not the main reason.

167. ☑ **A**. In a geographic structure, executives of regional areas are responsible for their business functions.

☒ **B**, **C**, and **D** are incorrect. **B** is incorrect because in a divisional structure, criteria other than marketing or industry are applicable. **C** and **D** are incorrect because they do not describe a geographic structure.

168. ☑ **B**. The main disadvantage of a functional organizational structure is that people are in specialized "silos" and often fail to coordinate or communicate with other departments.

☒ **A**, **C**, and **D** are incorrect. These are all examples of the disadvantages of a divisional organizational structure.

169. ☑ **C.** A matrix organizational structure creates a functional and divisional partnership and focuses on the work more than on the people.

☒ **A**, **B**, and **D** are incorrect. All these options are examples of the advantages of a boundary-less organization.

170. ☑ **A.** The main disadvantage of a matrix organizational structure is because the dual chain of command requires cooperation between two direct supervisors to determine an employee's work priorities, work assignments, and performance standards.

☒ **B**, **C**, and **D** are incorrect because these are examples of the disadvantages of a virtual organization.

171. ☑ **A.** A business process outcome (BPO) is an arrangement where payroll and benefit administration is entirely outsourced.

☒ **B**, **C**, and **D** are incorrect. **B** is incorrect because this is an example of a professional employer organization (PEO). **C** and **D** are incorrect because they are not examples of a BPO.

172. ☑ **B.** In a professional employer organization (PEO), the PEO becomes the employer of record, and the employees are leased back to them.

☒ **B**, **C**, and **D** are incorrect. **A** is incorrect because employer of choice is not a type of relationship. **C** and **D** are incorrect because they are used to provide staff to an organization.

173. ☑ **D.** In an HRO relationship, payroll, benefits, and HR could all be outsourced, but temporary workers would not be part of that relationship.

☒ **A**, **B**, and **C** are incorrect. They are all part of an HRO relationship.

174. ☑ **B.** A headhunter is used to help find upper-management positions typically because of the high costs associated with this service.

☒ **A**, **C**, and **D** are incorrect. **A** and **C** are incorrect because other types of staffing firms may be used to find employees at this level. **D** is incorrect because organizations don't directly employ contingent workers.

175. ☑ **C.** They sell for multiple companies and typically can provide more options.

☒ **A**, **B**, and **D** are incorrect. They are untrue of a benefit broker.

176. ☑ **D.** Having a PEO could actually save money on benefit costs.

☒ **A**, **B**, and **C** are incorrect because these are true disadvantages of a PEO.

177. ☑ **D.** The time to fill a position can actually be quicker.

☒ **A**, **B**, and **C** are incorrect. These are all disadvantages of using a third-party recruiter.

178. ☑ **D.** The costs are usually the same as other benefit options.

☒ **A**, **B**, and **C** are incorrect. These are all examples of advantages of using benefit brokers.

179. ☑ **A.** An advantage of using a staffing organization is that the employer and staffing agency share the burden and liability of employees.

☒ **B**, **C**, and **D** are incorrect. **B** and **C** are incorrect because they would not reduce the costs or benefits. **D** is incorrect because sharing the cost of an employee is not an advantage.

180. ☑ **D.** Prior to contacting a temporary employee agency, HR should determine all the options except what health insurance is needed because health insurance is typically not offered to temporary employees.

☒ **A**, **B**, and **C** are incorrect. These are things HR should determine before contacting a staffing agency.

181. ☑ **B.** Analytics is the discovery and communication of meaningful patterns in data.

☒ **A**, **C**, and **D** are incorrect. **A** is incorrect because andragogy is the art and science of teaching adults. **B** is incorrect because aging is an inappropriate answer. **D** is incorrect because ADDIE is an acronym that describes the elements of instructional design: Analysis, Design, Development, Implementation, Evaluation.

182. ☑ **C.** A low-context culture is a communication style that relies heavily on explicit and direct language.

☒ **A**, **B**, and **D** are incorrect. A low-context culture is the correct answer.

183. ☑ **D.** For employees, unresolved issues of interpersonal tension and conflict can create emotional stress and absenteeism, litigation, and turnover, but performance problems would not be created by this.

☒ **A**, **B**, and **C** are incorrect. Unresolved tension could cause these to happen.

184. ☑ **A.** The easiest way to recognize passive-aggressive employees is a lack of assertiveness or directness in forms of communication.

☒ **B**, **C**, and **D** are incorrect. They are not ways to recognize passive-aggressive behavior. They could potentially be factors, but not the easiest or most direct way to recognize passive-aggressive employees.

185. ☑ **A.** Yelling at an employee would be an example of an aggressive behavior, not passive-aggressive behavior.

☒ **B**, **C**, and **D** are incorrect. These would be examples of passive-aggressive behavior.

186. ☑ **C.** A highly effective method of accessing direct feedback in a written format is an employee survey.

☒ **A**, **B**, and **D** are incorrect. **A** is incorrect because although written, an employee survey would be more effective. **B** and **D** are incorrect because these are examples of oral communication.

187. ☑ **D.** This would be an example of a passive communication.

☒ **A**, **B**, and **C** are incorrect. **A** is incorrect because passive-aggressive communication is when individuals appear passive on the surface but are really acting out anger in a subtle, indirect, or behind-the-scenes way. **B** is incorrect because an assertive communication style would be a style in which individuals clearly state their opinions and feelings and firmly advocate for their rights and needs without violating the rights of others. **C** is incorrect because an aggressive communication style is when individuals express their feelings and opinions and advocate for their needs in a way that violates the rights of others.

188. ☑ **A.** Appearing passive on the surface but really acting out anger in a subtle, indirect, or behind-the-scenes way is a passive-aggressive communication style.

☒ **B, C,** and **D** are incorrect. **B** is incorrect because assertive communication would be when individuals clearly state their opinions and feelings and firmly advocate for their rights and needs without violating the rights of others. **C** is incorrect because aggressive communication would be when individuals express their feelings and opinions and advocate for their needs in a way that violates the rights of others. **D** is incorrect because passive communication is when someone exhibits a pattern of not expressing their opinions or feelings, protecting their rights, or identifying and meeting their needs.

189. ☑ **C.** Expressing their feelings and opinions and advocating for their needs in a way that violates the rights of others are examples of aggressive communication.

☒ **A, B,** and **D** are incorrect. **A** is incorrect because passive-aggressive behavior appears passive on the surface, but it's really acting out anger in a subtle, indirect, or behind-the-scenes way. **B** is incorrect because assertive communication is when individuals clearly state their opinions and feelings and firmly advocate for their rights and needs without violating the rights of others. **D** is incorrect because passive communication is when someone exhibits a pattern of not expressing their opinions or feelings, protecting their rights, or identifying and meeting their needs.

190. ☑ **B.** Stating opinions and feelings and firmly advocating for their rights and needs without violating the rights of others are examples of assertive communication.

☒ **A, C,** and **D** are incorrect. **A** is incorrect because passive-aggressive is when individuals appear passive on the surface but are really acting out anger in a subtle, indirect, or behind-the-scenes way. **C** is incorrect because expressing their feelings and opinions and advocating for their needs in a way that violates the rights of others is an example of aggressive communication. **D** is incorrect because passive communication would be when someone exhibits a pattern of not expressing their opinions or feelings, protecting their rights, or identifying and meeting their needs.

3

Recruitment and Selection

This functional area includes coverage of the following responsibilities and knowledge objectives:

- **01**   Applicable laws and regulations related to recruitment and selection, such as nondiscrimination, accommodation, and work authorization (for example, Title VII, ADA, EEOC Uniform Guidelines on Employee Selection Procedures, Immigration Reform and Control Act)

- **02**   Applicant databases

- **03**   Recruitment sources (for example, employee referral, social networking/ social media)

- **04**   Recruitment methods (for example, advertising, job fairs)

- **05**   Alternative staffing practices (for example, recruitment process outsourcing, job sharing, phased retirement)

- **06**   Interviewing techniques (for example, behavioral, situational, panel)

- **07**   Post-offer activities (for example, drug testing, background checks, medical exams)

Human resource (HR) professionals are tasked now more than ever with finding the best candidate for the job. In this economy of intellectual skill and innovation, competition is at a high for the right hire. It is the HR professional's responsibility to carefully design the job description, the skills necessary to do the job, and the legal aspects of recruitment. An effective recruitment and selection process can also help reduce organizational turnover.

The recruitment and selection process consists of identifying a candidate who has the experience and aptitude to do the job that you are looking to fill. It is also equally important to find someone who shares and endorses your company's core values. Recruitment is the process of having the right person in the right place at the right time. Recruitment and selection is also tasked with ensuring diversity standards and relevant legislation regarding hiring within an organization.

Recruitment and Selection accounts for 15 percent of the HR Certification Institute (HRCI) Associate Professional in Human Resources (aPHR) exam. This chapter focuses on the hiring process, including regulatory requirements, sourcing of applicants, formal interviewing, the selection process, and the onboarding of a new hire. Also included in this chapter is an emphasis on applicant databases, recruitment sources, alternative staffing practices, and post-offer activities.

Use this chapter to gauge your knowledge of Recruitment and Selection.

Objective 01 Applicable Laws and Regulations Related to Recruitment and Selection

1. An African-American female candidate was interviewed for an IT manager position at a company. After the first interview, the recruiter told her that she was the top candidate but there was concern about her professional appearance. The recruiter advised her to cut her hair, which was styled in "locs," before meeting with the CTO. She refused to cut her hair, citing religious reasons, and was told the day after the second interview that she would not be hired because they were looking for someone with more current IT knowledge. The company hired a white male for the position two months later. The candidate files a complaint with the EEOC. What steps should the HR director take to eliminate future potential discriminatory hiring practices?

   A. The HR director should train staff on Title VII of the Civil Rights Act of 1964 and as amended in 1972, 1978, and 1991.

   B. The HR director should terminate the recruiter who made such an obvious error.

   C. The HR director should just respond to any requests by the EEOC with the confidence that this case has no merit given that the reason for the decision not to hire had nothing do with race.

   D. The HR director should contact the candidate and apologize for any misunderstanding on behalf of the recruiter.

2. A local government is recruiting police officers. The advertisement states that an applicant must be 21 to 50 years old and a high-school graduate. Norman applies. He is 51 and a college graduate and was not called for an interview. Does Norman have a viable discrimination complaint?

   A. Yes, because according to the Age Discrimination in Employment Act, a company or municipality can't set an age requirement for candidates.

   B. No, because the requirement of being 21 to 50 years old may be a bona fide occupational qualification (BFOQ) given the nature of the work.

   C. No, because the hiring of police officers is a specific exception of the Age Discrimination in Employment Act.

   D. Yes, because all employers must adhere to Title VII.

3. A company is recruiting for a coastal scientist. The position requires a PhD in physics. There are no Hispanic candidates. As the HR director, what would concern you the most about this scenario?

   A. Potential disparate treatment of Hispanic candidates.

   B. Discriminatory access to training for Hispanic candidates.

   C. Ineffective recruiting strategies as it relates to Hispanic candidates.

   D. Potential disparate impact on Hispanic candidates.

4. Which of the following statements best describes the Older Worker Benefit Protection Act (OWBPA)?

   A. It is applicable only to public employers.

   B. Older workers can waive ADEA rights if they are given at least 10 business days to consider their options.

   C. It prevents hiring discrimination on the basis of age.

   D. It's unlawful to target older workers during a reduction in force (RIF).

5. A restaurant hires only blonde women who are 18 to 25 years old as hostesses. What might this be an example of?

   A. Disparate impact

   B. Sexual harassment

   C. Disparate treatment

   D. Bona-fide occupational qualification (BFOQ)

6. Which of the following is not specifically mentioned in Title VII of the Civil Rights Act of 1964 but has been interpreted by courts to be inclusive of this protection?

   A. Race

   B. Sex

   C. Gender identity

   D. National origin

7. The Immigration Control and Reform Act requires that all new hires prove their eligibility to work in the United States at the time of hire. What documents should you request to prove legal status to work in the United States?

   A. Driver's license and Social Security card.

   B. It's the new hire's choice based on the choices listed on the I-9.

   C. Passport.

   D. State ID or driver's license.

8. What is the primary provision of the amended Civil Rights Act of 1991?

   A. That punitive damages can be awarded

   B. Gender identity discrimination protections

   C. Established that discrimination claims had to be arbitrated first

   D. Provided protections for transgender Americans

9. Which of the following is a provision of the Pregnancy Discrimination Act (PDA)?

   A. Pregnant women accrue seniority while on leave though other disabled employees do not.

   B. Pregnant women can't be forced to leave work if they are ready, willing, and able to perform their job.

   C. Hiring preference must be given to pregnant women if they are competing against someone of similar qualifications.

   D. The 80 percent rule has to be applied when interviewing pregnant women.

10. What is the purpose of the Uniform Guidelines on Employee Selection Procedures (UGESP)?

    A. To provide detail on Title VII exemptions

    B. To help employers administer affirmative action programs

    C. To help govern the interviewing behaviors of employers

    D. To help employers comply with Title VII

11. Why was the Equal Employment Opportunity Commission (EEOC) established?

    A. To mediate discrimination cases

    B. To arbitrate discrimination cases

    C. To litigate discrimination cases

    D. To enforce antidiscrimination provisions of Title VII

Objective 02   Applicant Databases

12. An automated method for keeping track of job applicants is formally called a(n):

   A. Human resource information system (HRIS)

   B. Applicant tracking system (ATS)

   C. Learning management system (LMS)

   D. Affirmative action plan (AAP)

13. Which of the following criteria fits the definition of an Internet applicant according to the Office of Federal Contract Compliance Programs (OFCCP)?

   A. The individual's expression of interest indicates the individual possesses the basic objective qualifications for the position.

   B. The individual applies for a job through the Internet, uploads their résumé, and later voluntarily withdraws from consideration.

   C. The individual applies by filling out a paper application and mails it in to the organization's human resource department.

   D. The organization meets an individual at a career fair whose qualifications match the job requirements.

14. As a federal contractor, the applicant tracking system must track which of the following elements?

   A. All publications and social networks where job ads are run and how many individuals apply from those ads

   B. Career fair dates and locations and number of individuals who visit the organization's career fair booth.

   C. Applications, résumés, job posting, job descriptions with basic qualifications, EEO data, and applicant flow data

   D. Individual's name, address, phone number, e-mail address, association memberships, and social networks

15. Which of the following is an example of hiring discrimination?

   A. The applicant tracking system asks a person to disclose his or her race, sex, color, religion, national origin, or age.

   B. The applicant tracking system fails to collect genetic and medical history information from all individuals.

   C. The applicant tracking system fails to process applications for those who have self-disclosed their disability status.

   D. The applicant tracking system requires individuals to take a test related to the position they are interested in.

16. How can an applicant tracking system best be used to increase diversity within specific job classifications?

    A. Delete all applications received by individuals who do not fall into a protected EEO group.

    B. Attend only those career fairs that focus on recruiting diverse individuals who fall into a protected EEO group.

    C. Post the job with a disclaimer that only those in minority groups should apply for the open position.

    D. Search the applicant database by specific EEO categories and invite identified qualified candidates to apply.

17. Applicant tracking systems can miss out on a large talent pool today if it lacks what functionality?

    A. Quality of hire tracking

    B. Ad placement tracking

    C. Cost per hire tracking

    D. Mobile access

18. In the sex discrimination lawsuits *EEOC v. LA Pure Weight Loss* and *EEOC v. Outback Steakhouse Florida, LLC*, what was one of the key settlements required of the companies?

    A. Both companies were required to post jobs internally for 10 days.

    B. Both companies were required to implement applicant tracking systems.

    C. Both companies were required to implement staffing quotas.

    D. Both companies were required to hire human resource professionals.

19. A web site where employers can go to advertise their open positions and job seekers can go to search and apply for open positions is known as a(n):

    A. Job board

    B. Application

    C. Billboard

    D. Bulletin board

20. A database of job seeker contact information and applications used by recruitment professionals to match job openings to available applicants is called:

    A. A job board

    B. An applicant pool

    C. A software database

    D. Job posts

21. Which of the following best applies to federal employers and private and public employers subject to Title VII (i.e., those with 15 or more employees) and intends to help employers avoid adverse impact and suggest that applicant tracking records are to be kept only by sex, race, and national origin?

 A. Uniform Guidelines on Employee Selection Procedures (UGESP)

 B. The organization's mission, vision, and values

 C. The organization's policies and standard operating procedures

 D. Office of Federal Contract Compliance Programs (OFCCP)

22. What is the best way to utilize an applicant tracking database to engage passive candidates in the applicant pool?

 A. Insist that every applicant drop off a paper cover letter and résumé.

 B. Delete applicants who haven't been active for at least 12 months.

 C. They've lost interest; there is no need to try to engage passive candidates.

 D. Encourage candidates to update their knowledge, skills, and abilities.

Objective 03   Recruitment Sources

23. What are the advantages and disadvantages of internal-only recruitment sources?

 A. It is always a good idea to recruit only from outside the organization.

 B. They are low cost but not familiar with organizational culture and expectations.

 C. They are low cost and familiar with organizational culture but limited in supply.

 D. There is plenty of supply in the talent pool, but they are high in cost and will lower morale.

24. What are the advantages and disadvantages of using advertisements for open positions?

 A. Can target large groups of people but can generate unqualified candidates

 B. Can generate a large group of qualified candidates but result in high costs

 C. Can be low in cost but can annoy candidates with ads they do not care to see

 D. Can generate lots of interest in the organization but be high in costs

25. An internal recruitment method employed by organizations to identify potential candidates from their existing employees is known as:

 A. Independent contractors

 B. Temporary agencies

 C. Job posting

 D. Employee referral

26. What are the advantages and disadvantages of utilizing an employee referral program?

    A. May target large groups of people but be high in financial costs

    B. Produces the best candidates but may lack in organizational diversity

    C. May target large groups but not be effective in finding quality candidates

    D. Low in cost but effective only when utilizing social media

27. Companies dedicated to match the employment needs of an employer with a candidate having the required knowledge, skills, and abilities is known as:

    A. Employment agencies

    B. Employee referrals

    C. Independent contractors

    D. External consultants

28. Attending career fairs and conducting information sessions on campuses to speak with students about the benefits of working for the organization is called:

    A. Advertising

    B. Open house

    C. Employee referral

    D. College recruiting

29. Recruiting candidates by using social platforms as talent databases or for advertising is known as:

    A. Applicant tracking

    B. Social recruiting

    C. Employee referral

    D. Open house

30. Social recruiting may utilize what type of recruitment tools to attract talented candidates?

    A. Since it's virtual, no tools are necessary.

    B. Hiring manager, interviewing, and job offer.

    C. Internet sites, blogs, and social media profiles.

    D. Job posting, paper applications, and résumés.

31. A place where multiple organizations and candidates meet to discuss employment opportunities is called:

    A. A job posting

    B. Advertising

    C. Job fairs

    D. Employee referrals

32. People who apply for a job based on a sign on an organization's premises is called:

   A. Employee referrals

   B. Job fairs

   C. Social recruiting

   D. Walk-ins

33. Searching the Internet to locate passive job seekers with the characteristics and qualifications needed for a position is known as:

   A. Internet data mining

   B. Job fairs

   C. College recruiting

   D. Employee referrals

Objective 04   Recruitment Methods

34. All of the following can be used for a social media recruitment tool except which one?

   A. Twitter

   B. LinkedIn

   C. Facebook

   D. Myspace

35. What is the main benefit of a job fair?

   A. Employers can quickly meet hundreds of job applicants.

   B. They are cost effective.

   C. Managers do not need to be present.

   D. Employers can pay employees less when recruiting from a job fair.

36. What is the main reason a potential employee would want to attend a job fair?

   A. Applicants could potentially meet the hiring manager and learn about the company.

   B. Applicants can sign up to learn more information about the company.

   C. Applicants can skip the background check process.

   D. Applicants do not need to fill out an application for a position.

37. Which of the following would be included in a job posting?

   A. Brief description of competencies, responsibilities, and company profits

   B. Brief description of competencies, responsibilities, and stock prices

   C. Brief description of competencies, responsibilities, and pay frequency

   D. Brief description of competencies, responsibilities, and company mission and vision

38. Advertising jobs on the radio can be effective when:

    A. A company is having a hard time filling a position

    B. A company is trying to fill a large number of positions

    C. A company is looking for only a certain minority group

    D. A company is experiencing too many applicants

39. Television ads are helpful when a company is trying to:

    A. Attract applicants and explain company vision

    B. Attract applicants and explain company mission

    C. Attract applicants and raise the stock price

    D. Attract applicants and solicit customers

40. What step should an employer take after attending a job fair?

    A. Add all business cards received to the applicant tracking system

    B. Collect résumés and respond to applicants

    C. Make hiring decisions

    D. Decide on pay rates based on the type of applicants

41. In preparing for a job fair, how many company representatives should attend the job fair booth?

    A. Two to four

    B. One

    C. Five to seven

    D. Four to five

42. Company representatives should bring all of the following with them to a job fair except which one?

    A. Company information

    B. Business cards

    C. Benefit information

    D. Assessment tests

43. Company representatives should bring all the following with them to a job fair except which one?

    A. I-9

    B. Application

    C. Company mission and vision

    D. Description of benefit programs

44. When are employment web sites best used for recruiting?

    A. Large company with a good reputation

    B. Small company in a rural area

    C. Large company with many openings

    D. Startup company

Objective 05   Alternative Staffing Practices

45. Job sharing is an alternative where:

    A. Workers get called only when work is needed

    B. Two people with complementary skills share a full-time position

    C. Employees share benefits

    D. An agency refers the workers

46. A worker who is self-employed is commonly referred to as a(n):

    A. Independent contractor

    B. Temporary worker

    C. Contingent contractor

    D. Seasonal help

47. Which of the following employee types would help a company if they needed particular skills but not on a full-time basis?

    A. Job sharing employees

    B. Contingent workers

    C. Interns

    D. Part-time employees

48. Payrolling allows an organization to:

    A. Use an agency for people they want to hire and the agency provides payroll and tax services

    B. Hire college students with specific skills

    C. Hire only during the season in which the work is heavy

    D. Outsource the payroll, benefit, and HR function to an outside company

49. _____ workers are hired only at times of the year when the workload increases.

    A. On-call

    B. Contingent

    C. Seasonal

    D. Temporary

50. _____ are self-employed individuals who work on a project or fee basis with multiple customers or clients.

   A. Contingent workers

   B. Independent contractors

   C. Part-time workers

   D. Temporary workers

51. What is the main reason why an employer would want to use caution when deciding whether a worker is an independent contractor or an employee?

   A. Low employee morale

   B. Substantial fines by the government

   C. Less work getting accomplished

   D. Performance reviews not accurate

52. Which of the following is *not* an advantage of using telecommuting as an alternative staffing method?

   A. It reduces energy and overhead costs.

   B. They are ready to work only when the work is needed.

   C. It reduces consumption and traffic congestion.

   D. Employees may have valid reasons for wanting to work from home.

53. The IRS has guidelines for determining whether an individual is an independent contractor or employee. Which option is not one of those guidelines?

   A. Behavioral controls

   B. Financial controls

   C. The type of relationship that exists between parties

   D. Pay rate controls

54. What is giganomics?

   A. On-call workers being called in at the last minute for a job

   B. The creation of employment through the piecing together of several projects or gigs

   C. Temporary workers working on one project

   D. Recruiting for gigs only

55. A(n) _____ worker is a worker who is employed for a particular performance or a defined time.

   A. Full-time

   B. Independent contractor

   C. Gig worker

   D. Part-time

Objective 06   Interviewing Techniques

56. Which type of interview uses past performance as a predictor of future behavior?

    A. Structured

    B. Competency-based

    C. Behavioral

    D. Stress

57. What is a pre-employment test that tests a candidate's capacity to learn a new skill?

    A. Cognitive ability

    B. Aptitude

    C. Assessment center

    D. Psychomotor

58. Kayla is interviewing at a customer service call center. She is scheduled to spend 2 hours shadowing a current call center representative. What is Kayla experiencing?

    A. Realistic job preview

    B. Panel interview

    C. Group interview

    D. Job assessment

59. A school bus driver completes a series of pre-employment tests of his physical ability. Which substantive assessment method is described here?

    A. Medical screening exam

    B. Drug test

    C. Assessment center

    D. Psychomotor test

60. Burt is interviewing for the director of research and development position at Affinity Group International. He is interviewed by the functional head of each division in the company at the same time. What type of interview is Burt part of?

    A. Team interview

    B. Multirater interview

    C. Unstructured interview

    D. Panel interview

61. An interview where the candidate is asked to respond to how they would handle a particular set of events whether from past experiences or hypothetically is what type of interview?

    A. Structured

    B. Behavior-based

    C. Situational

    D. Competency-based

62. Which of the following choices are characteristics of a prescreening interview?

    A. 15 to 20 minutes long

    B. Conducted by management

    C. Divided into several smaller interviews

    D. Interview with colleagues and line managers

63. The sales manager is preparing to interview candidates for account representative positions at a pharmaceutical sales company. He wants to ask a mixture of situational and behavioral questions. As the HR director, what would be the best source from which to develop these types of questions?

    A. List of job competencies

    B. List of essential functions

    C. List of job specifications

    D. List of job duties

64. A new career college campus will be in need of admissions representatives. The campus president knows a few talented salespeople from a past employer and wants to interview them ASAP. HR will post the position in one week, and standard procedure for interested candidates is to complete an online application. As the HR director, what would you suggest the campus president do next?

    A. Set up interviews with the salespeople ASAP so she doesn't lose good candidates.

    B. Contact the salespeople and tell them to submit résumés directly.

    C. Contact the salespeople and tell them to complete online applications when the position posts.

    D. Set up phone screens with the salespeople ASAP so she doesn't lose good candidates.

65. At the conclusion of interviews for a new financial analyst, a member of the interview team rates one of the candidates poorly but could not articulate why. The other three members of the interview team have a different view of the same candidate. Which of the following best describes the kind of interviewer bias displayed in this case?

    A. Horn effect

    B. Negative emphasis

C. First impression

D. Stereotyping

66. The pre-employment tests for administrative assistants measure typing speed and accuracy. The current company need for administrative support is in the area of competency with computer software programs such as Microsoft Office and payroll/finance software. The new supervisor decides to develop a test and administer it after each interview. As the HR director, what would concern you the most about this scenario?

   A. The tests should be given only after an offer of employment is made.

   B. The tests have not been proven to be reliable and valid predictors of job success.

   C. The tests were administered without prior approval from HR.

   D. The physical space that the test was administered in wasn't adequate.

Objective 07   Post-Offer Activities

67. A drug test should be completed in what phase of recruitment and selection?

   A. At one year of employment

   B. Pre-offer

   C. Post-offer

   D. In the interview

68. What is the main reason why an employer would want to institute post-offer drug testing?

   A. Reasonable suspicion based on performance and conduct indicators

   B. To impress investors

   C. To comply with ethics standards

   D. To reduce workers' compensation costs

69. Pre-offer drug testing could violate which act?

   A. Family Medical Leave Act

   B. Americans with Disabilities Act

   C. Age Discrimination in Employment Act

   D. Title VII of the Civil Rights Act

70. What is the main reason why off-site drug testing is ideal?

   A. Protects employees' confidentiality

   B. Less chance employees will threaten to sue

   C. Employees feel safer in doing so

   D. Defensible in litigation

71. What is the recommended practice an employer should do before starting a drug testing program?

    A. Include temporary workers in the program

    B. Survey employees on their views before instituting

    C. Clearly establish a policy

    D. Test applicants before starting

72. Employers may make medical inquiries or require medical examinations of newly hired or existing employees only if:

    A. The employer believes the health or safety of the individual or others is at risk

    B. The employer thinks the individual will not be able to be successful at the job

    C. The employer thinks the individual will not get along with the other staff

    D. The employer thinks that the worker may not stay long at the company

73. When should an employer conduct a background check?

    A. Pre-offer

    B. Post-offer

    C. During the application process

    D. After 60 days of employment

74. All of these are reasons why an employer would want to perform a background check, except which one?

    A. To protect the employer's business through financial loss or image and reputational issues

    B. To protect other employees by sexual harassment or workplace violence

    C. To protect an organization's customers by, for example, sexual assault on business premises

    D. To protect the neighborhood in which the employer resides

75. What is the main reason why an employer would want to conduct a reference check?

    A. Because past performance is a strong indicator of future performance

    B. To save the company money

    C. To perform a background check

    D. To gather past education and experience information

76. All of the following are factors why organizations are trending toward completing more reference checks except which one?

    A. Security issues in a post–September 11 world.

    B. Employees are looking to work in safe organizations.

C. Technological advances make background investigations faster and more economical.

D. Increased awareness of the various risks of failure to conduct adequate background checks.

77. An employer can legally ask which of the following questions before an offer of employment is made?

A. "Do you have any disabilities?"

B. "Can you tell me the nature of your disabilities?"

C. "Can you perform the essential functions of the job?"

D. "Can you take a medical exam?"

1. A	27. A	53. D
2. C	28. D	54. B
3. D	29. B	55. C
4. D	30. C	56. C
5. C	31. C	57. B
6. C	32. D	58. A
7. B	33. A	59. D
8. A	34. D	60. D
9. B	35. A	61. C
10. D	36. A	62. A
11. D	37. D	63. A
12. B	38. B	64. C
13. A	39. D	65. D
14. C	40. B	66. B
15. C	41. A	67. C
16. D	42. D	68. A
17. D	43. A	69. B
18. B	44. A	70. D
19. A	45. B	71. C
20. B	46. A	72. A
21. A	47. D	73. B
22. D	48. A	74. D
23. C	49. C	75. A
24. A	50. B	76. B
25. D	51. B	77. C
26. B	52. B	

1. ☑ **A.** It is clear that, at a minimum, training and clarification are needed by all the individuals involved in the hiring process. Title VII of the Civil Rights Act of 1964, and as amended in 1972, 1978, and 1991, prohibits discriminatory recruiting, selection, and hiring on the basis of race whereby race is a protected class. "Locs" are a culturally specific hairstyle most naturally worn by people of African descent. Requiring that "locs" be cut as a prerequisite to obtaining employment may be deemed discriminatory.

   ☒ **B, C,** and **D** are incorrect. **B** is incorrect because terminating the recruiter doesn't solve a possible systemic problem. The hiring manager (CTO) may also have a similar misunderstanding as to what is an appropriate action during the selection process. Further, there is no evidence to support that the recruiter really did say these things. **C** is incorrect because it would be irresponsible on the HR director's part not to take the allegation seriously. The director is not in a position to draw conclusions on the merits of the case. That is the responsibility of the EEOC. A forward-thinking HR director should recognize this unfortunate incident as an opportunity to further educate staff and streamline processes. **D** is incorrect because neither the HR director nor anyone involved in preparing responses to the complaint should have direct contact with the candidate. All contact should be directly to the EEOC or through the company's attorneys to the EEOC. Direct contact with the candidate presents litigation risks for the company.

2. ☑ **C.** The Age Discrimination in Employment Act specifies certain exceptions. The hiring of firefighters and police officers is an exception.

   ☒ **A, B,** and **D** are incorrect. They are all incorrect because a municipality can set an age requirement when hiring firefighters and police officers; the age requirement is not a BFOQ, but it is a separate exception, and all employers do not have to adhere to Title VII if their situation is covered by one of the exceptions.

3. ☑ **D.** The HR director should be most concerned with disparate impact. Disparate impact is an unlawful practice where a practice seems fair on its face but has an adverse impact on a protected group. Adverse impact is illegal unless justified by job-related business necessity. In this case, there may be a very valid reason why the position requires a PhD in physics but the fact that there is not a single Hispanic applicant is something the HR director should take a closer look at, modifying recruiting practices if necessary.

   ☒ **A, B,** and **C** are incorrect because disparate treatment is when an employer intentionally treats one group of candidates differently than another. **B** is incorrect because this example does not offer up enough information to indicate that Hispanics have less access to training, and access to training is usually an issue after a candidate becomes an employee. **C** is incorrect because while it is possible that a recruiting strategy that focuses on increasing Hispanic candidates for these positions is necessary, the HR director in this case should focus immediately on the potential ramifications of engaging in an unlawful hiring practice.

4. ☑ **D**. The OWBPA amends the Age Discrimination in Employment Act (ADEA) to provide additional protections to older workers. One of those protections is that during a reduction in force, older workers can't be targeted for early retirement.

☒ **A**, **B**, and **C** are incorrect. **A** is incorrect because the OWBPA is applicable to public and private employers. **B** is incorrect because older workers can't waive ADEA rights unless they are given 21 days to consider or 45 days when there is a group termination or a voluntary retirement program is under consideration. **C** is incorrect because the OWBPA does not provide guidelines related to hiring. The overarching legislation, the ADEA, does.

5. ☑ **C**. Disparate treatment exists. The restaurant management screens out other applicants in favor of *only* blonde women between the ages of 18 and 25. Therefore, management is treating this group of applicants differently than others.

☒ **A**, **B**, and **D** are incorrect. **A** is incorrect because disparate impact happens unintentionally. **B** is incorrect because there is no evidence of sexual harassment in the information provided. **D** is incorrect because a BFOQ is something that an applicant must possess in order to reasonably carry out the duties of a job. For example, being Jewish would be a BFOQ for a rabbi. There is no BFOQ present in hiring a hostess as stated in the question.

6. ☑ **C**. Gender identity, a person's internal sense of masculinity or femininity, is covered under Title VII due to court decisions but was not specifically included in the act. Title VII refers to sex discrimination, which the EEOC has interpreted to include gender and gender identity.

☒ **A**, **B**, and **D** are incorrect. They are all incorrect because race, sex, and national origin are all specifically named in Title VII.

7. ☑ **B**. HR should never tell new employees what documents to provide to prove their eligibility to work. It is the person's choice based on what documents are listed on the form. The Immigration Control and Reform Act prevents employers from discriminating against employees on the basis of national origin and assigns penalties to employers who knowingly hire undocumented people.

☒ **A**, **C**, and **D** are incorrect. All the choices specify documents to present, which is illegal per the ICRA.

8. ☑ **A**. The Civil Rights Act of 1991 further clarified the protections and rights of protected classes. Primarily the act established that employees who win discrimination cases could be awarded compensatory (out-of-pocket expenses) and punitive (awarded when the defendant's acts are egregious and willful) damages.

☒ **B**, **C**, and **D** are incorrect. **B** and **D** are incorrect because gender identity protections are covered under sex discrimination under Title VII. **C** is incorrect because there is no federal legal requirement that discrimination claims be arbitrated before a lawsuit can be considered.

9. ☑ **B**. A provision of the PDA is that pregnant women can work as long as they choose to as long as they are ready, willing, and able to perform their job.

☒ **A**, **C**, and **D** are incorrect. **A** is incorrect because an employer does not have to accrue seniority for a pregnant woman on leave if that isn't the practice for other employees absent from work because of a disability. **C** is incorrect because preference does not have to be given to pregnant women. The protection is that pregnant women can't be denied a job offer solely because they are pregnant. **D** is incorrect because the 80 percent rule is applicable to measuring disparate (adverse) impact.

10. ☑ **D**. The UGESP is a set of procedures helping employers comply with Title VII.
    ☒ **A**, **B**, and **C** are incorrect. All these choices are not reflective of the Uniform Guidelines on Employee Selection Procedures (UGESP).

11. ☑ **D**. The EEOC was established in 1964 to enforce Title VII. In 1972 the Equal Employment Opportunity Act granted the EEOC the power to conduct enforcement litigation.
    ☒ **A**, **B**, and **C** are incorrect. They are all incorrect because meditating, arbitrating, and litigating discrimination cases were not the original vision for the EEOC.

12. ☑ **B**. An automated method for keeping track of job applicants is formally called an applicant tracking system (ATS). These tracking systems may also be called candidate management systems, talent management systems, or job applicant systems.
    ☒ **A**, **C**, and **D** are incorrect. **A** is incorrect because a human resource information system (HRIS) is too broad and includes the tracking of all components of human resources, including benefits, compensation, and payroll. **C** is incorrect because a learning management system (LMS) tracks and delivers training. **D** is incorrect because an affirmative action plan (AAP) directs a federal contractor's diversity efforts and measures success or failure in recruiting and promoting minority groups into leadership positions.

13. ☑ **A**. The individual's expression of interest indicates the individual possesses the basic objective qualifications for the position, and this is one of the criteria that fits the definition of an Internet applicant according to the Office of Federal Contract Compliance Programs (OFCCP). Other criteria include the following:

    • The contractor considered the individual for employment in a particular position.

    • The individual, at no point in the contractor's selection process prior to receiving an offer of employment from the contractor, removed himself or herself from further consideration or otherwise indicated that he or she was no longer interested in the position.

    ☒ **B**, **C**, and **D** are incorrect. These choices are not the criteria set by the Office of Federal Contract Compliance Programs (OFCCP).

14. ☑ **C**. Applications, résumés, job posting, job descriptions with basic qualifications, EEO data, and applicant flow data are all elements that as a federal contractor the applicant tracking system must track and produce upon an OFCCP request.
    ☒ **A**, **B**, and **D** are incorrect. None of these elements is mandated to track and produce.

15. ☑ **C**. When the applicant tracking system fails to process applications for those who have self-disclosed their disability status, this is discrimination. This would be considered disparate impact if it has a disproportionate "adverse impact" against any group based on race, national origin, color, religion, sex, familial status, or disability when there is no legitimate, nondiscriminatory business need for the practice. This is true even when there is an accidental system glitch that causes the disparity.

    ☒ **A**, **B**, and **D** are incorrect. None of these is the best answer because none of these answers is an example of discrimination.

16. ☑ **D**. An applicant tracking system is best used to increase diversity within specific job classifications by searching the applicant database by EEO category and job classification and inviting individuals or their friends to apply.

    ☒ **A**, **B**, and **C** are incorrect. None of these answers effectively leverages an applicant tracking system to source and recruit a diverse workforce.

17. ☑ **D**. Applicant tracking systems can miss out on a large talent pool today if it lacks mobile access functionality. Statistics show a growing majority of talent utilizes smart phones and tablets. Utilizing an applicant tracking database that enables the applicant to apply for jobs from their smart phone gives an organization a competitive advantage in attracting top talent.

    ☒ **A**, **B**, and **C** are incorrect. None of these answers is a hiring metric. They are not of interest to potential applicants.

18. ☑ **B**. In the sex discrimination lawsuits *EEOC v. LA Pure Weight Loss* and *EEOC v. Outback Steakhouse Florida, LLC,* both companies were required to implement applicant tracking systems. This is a remarkable outcome of these cases because the courts are seen as viewing applicant tracking systems as a way of ensuring the use of objective hiring practices, ultimately minimizing discrimination.

    ☒ **A**, **C**, and **D** are incorrect. None of these answers is a requirement of these key court cases.

19. ☑ **A**. A job board is a web site where employers can go to advertise their open positions and job seekers can go to search and apply for open positions.

    ☒ **B**, **C**, and **D** are incorrect. While all of these choices may be tools used to manage the recruitment and hiring process, they are not a web site where employers can go to advertise their open positions and where job seekers can apply.

20. ☑ **B**. A database of job seeker contact information and applications used by recruitment professionals to match job openings to available applicants is called an applicant pool. This is also called a talent or candidate pool.

    ☒ **A**, **C**, and **D** are incorrect. None of these choices is the best answer. They are either too broad or not specific to a database that contains job seeker information and applications.

21. ☑ **A.** Uniform Guidelines on Employee Selection Procedures (UGESP) are guidelines for federal employers and private and public employers subject to Title VII (i.e., those with 15 or more employees) intending to help employers avoid adverse impact and suggest that applicant tracking records are to be kept only by sex, race, and national origin. These are guidelines and not laws. However, courts use these guidelines to determine good practices in hiring and tracking processes. Some theorize that if an organization follows these guidelines, it should be in good shape should it face any lawsuit.

   ☒ **B**, **C**, and **D** are incorrect. The choices are not reflective of the Uniform Guidelines on Employee Selection Procedures (UGESP).

22. ☑ **D.** The best way to utilize an applicant tracking database to engage passive candidates in the applicant pool is to periodically ask them to update their knowledge, skills, and abilities. This is a good way to see whether they are still interested in working for an organization.

   ☒ **A**, **B**, and **C** are incorrect. All these answers are not reflective of the best answer to engage passive job candidates.

23. ☑ **C.** The advantage of internal recruitment efforts is that they are low in cost and that the employee is already familiar with organizational culture. Often promoting from within raises morale. The disadvantage is that there is a limited supply in talent internally. Most organizations recruit externally in order to tap into an unlimited supply of talent.

   ☒ **A**, **B**, and **D** are incorrect. **A** is incorrect because it doesn't accurately describe the advantages and disadvantages of an internal recruitment source. Also, options with words like *always* are usually incorrect. **B** is incorrect because while internal referrals may be low in cost, the second part of this answer choice is not correct. Internal referrals are employees who already know the organizational culture and are familiar with processes. **D** is incorrect because no part of the option is correct because it relates to utilizing an internal referral recruitment strategy. The talent supply internally may be limited in supply. Further, it is a low-cost, not high-cost, strategy. Finally, an internal recruitment strategy raises employee morale as it sends the message the organization values its existing employees.

24. ☑ **A.** The advantage of job advertising is that it can target large groups of people. But the disadvantage is that it can generate a large group of unqualified candidates.

   ☒ **B**, **C**, and **D** are incorrect. **B** is incorrect because while job advertising can generate a large group of candidates, they are not necessarily qualified candidates. An uncertain economy with slow recovery rendered many people unemployed. Oftentimes in this reality people will apply for advertised jobs whether they are qualified or not in the hope of finding employment. **C** is incorrect because today online advertising has become quite sophisticated. Social networks enable employers to run ads that are targeted to specific groups of people who very well may be interested and not annoyed with the ad they see, and **D** is incorrect because while it's true the advertisement can generate lots of interest in the organization, it may not necessarily be high in costs. Again, with social network/Internet job advertising, often there are plans in place where the employer pays per click, meaning they pay only when a candidate clicks the ad.

25. ☑ **D**. An internal recruitment method employed by organizations to identify potential candidates from their existing employees is known as an employee referral. The employee referral recruitment method is thought of as one of the most effective methods of recruiting talented people to an organization.

☒ **A**, **B**, and **C** are incorrect. **A** is incorrect because an independent contractor is someone from outside the organization to do work. **B** is incorrect because temporary agencies are an external agency that fills job openings temporarily for an organization, and **C** is incorrect because a job posting is not an accurate definition of an employee referral program.

26. ☑ **B**. The advantage of an employee referral program is that it can produce the best candidates. Often the employee who exhibits the best work ethic and needed skills will most likely know others like him or her. The disadvantage of utilizing an employee referral program is that a company may lack in hiring a diverse workforce.

☒ **A**, **C**, and **D** are incorrect. **A** is incorrect because an employee referral program may not be high in costs. It depends on the referral bonus offered if there is one. **C** is incorrect because an employee referral program can indeed help an organization find qualified candidates. In fact, the common thought is that skilled and talented people hang out with other skilled and talented people. Or they may know how to contact others with the top qualifications and will refer only those who the referring employee would feel proud to work with. **D** is not the best answer because social media does not have to be the only tool used in an employee referral program. The truth is to implement a successful program, communicating it effectively internally to employees is what is key.

27. ☑ **A**. Companies that are dedicated to matching the employment needs of an employer with candidates having the required knowledge, skills, and abilities are known as employment agencies. They are also called temporary, staffing, or job agencies. Often organizations will utilize this method to recruit new people because they can see what the temporary employee is capable of and the temporary employee can determine whether they like the employer and the work required. Another benefit is that if employers deal with fluctuating work volumes, they can flex the temporary staff up or down without laying off employees.

☒ **B**, **C**, and **D** are incorrect. **B** is incorrect because an employee referral is an internal recruitment source and does not represent companies that are dedicated to filling open positions for an organization. **C** is incorrect because an independent contractor is an individual who is hired to perform certain tasks or projects. **D** is incorrect because external consultants are similar to independent contractors, but they may work for a larger firm.

28. ☑ **D**. Attending career fairs and conducting information sessions on campuses to speak with students about the benefits of working for the organization is called college recruiting. It is also called on-campus recruiting.

⊠ **A**, **B**, and **C** are incorrect. **A** is incorrect because advertising is too broad of a term for what we are looking for in this answer. **B** is incorrect because an open house refers to a recruitment event on an organization's premises, and **C** is incorrect because an employee referral is an internal recruitment program having nothing to do with going to college campuses to recruit new graduate students.

29. ☑ **B.** Recruiting candidates by using social platforms as talent databases or for advertising is known as social recruiting. This is a relatively new recruitment method that involves reaching out to qualified candidates through social network platforms. The advantage to this method is that organizations can post videos of their own employees talking about what it's like to work there; in addition, it's low in cost.

⊠ **A**, **C**, and **D** are incorrect. **A** is incorrect because applicant tracking is too broad of a term in this case and is not relevant to what we are looking for in social recruiting. **C** is incorrect because an employee referral is an internal recruitment program, and **D** is incorrect because an open house is a program that may or may not utilize social platforms to recruit candidates.

30. ☑ **C.** Social recruiting may utilize Internet sites, blogs, and social media profiles to attract talented candidates.

⊠ **A**, **B**, and **D** are incorrect. **A** is incorrect because tools are necessary to recruit candidates regardless of whether they're virtual or not. Candidates won't learn about an organization's opportunities unless they get the word out through the use of blogs, Internet sites, and social media platforms. **B** is incorrect because the hiring manager, interviewing, and job offer may ultimately be involved in the process; these are not what is used to attract candidates through social recruitment methods. **D** is incorrect because often social recruiting involves an electronic application process.

31. ☑ **C.** A place where multiple organizations and candidates meet to discuss employment opportunities is called a job fair. Colleges, cities, counties, or private recruitment firms may host job fairs to draw out many people to come to a signal location to meet one another.

⊠ **A**, **B**, and **D** are incorrect. **A** is incorrect because a job posting is a position announcement and is not an adequate definition of a job fair. **B** is incorrect because advertising is too broad of a term in this case and does not define a job fair, and **D** is not correct because an employee referral is an internal recruitment program that does not require a job fair event.

32. ☑ **D.** People who apply for a job based on a sign on an organization's premises are called walk-ins.

⊠ **A**, **B**, and **C** are incorrect. **A** is incorrect because an employee referral is an internal recruitment program that does not entail a sign to be posted on an organization's premises. **B** is incorrect because job fairs are located away from the employer's premises, and **C** is incorrect because social recruitment is on a virtual platform and does not occur physically on the employer's premises.

33. ☑ **A.** Searching the Internet to locate passive job seekers with the characteristics and qualifications needed for a position is known as Internet data mining. Social platforms or online recruitment sources such as Indeed.com or Monster.com enable employers to search a database of résumés.

☒ **B, C,** and **D** are incorrect. **B** is incorrect because job fairs are located at a physical location and don't include the option of searching a database full of résumés. **C** is incorrect because college recruiting is not relevant to searching the Internet for résumés, and **D** is incorrect because an employee referral is an internal recruitment program really having nothing to do with Internet data mining.

34. ☑ **D.** Myspace is no longer a social media tool.

☒ **A, B,** and **C** are incorrect. These are all current social media methods of recruitment.

35. ☑ **A.** Employers can quickly meet hundreds of job applicants at a job fair.

☒ **B, C,** and **D** are incorrect. These are not factors of a job fair. Managers would still need to be present, employers would still need to pay fair wages, and typically a job fair is not a low-cost strategy.

36. ☑ **A.** Applicants can meet the hiring manager and learn about the company.

☒ **B, C,** and **D** are incorrect. **B** is incorrect because applicants can learn more information about the company, but this would not be the main reason. **C** and **D** are incorrect because they are not applicable in a job fair setting.

37. ☑ **D.** A brief description of competencies, responsibilities, and company mission and vision would be included on a job posting.

☒ **A, B,** and **C** are incorrect. These would typically not be listed on a job posting but would rather be told to the employee once they start at the company.

38. ☑ **B.** If a company is trying to fill a large number of positions, a radio ad would be able to reach a wide variety and number of people quickly.

☒ **A, C,** and **D** are incorrect. **A** is incorrect because this method would not be that helpful; a more targeted advertising method would be more useful. **C** is incorrect because looking for just a certain minority group would be unlawful and not an HR best practice. **D** is incorrect because this method would just lead to an influx of even more applicants, which would make the recruiting process worse.

39. ☑ **D.** Television ads are helpful when a company is trying to attract applicants and solicit customers at the same time.

☒ **A, B,** and **C** are incorrect. A TV ad would not be the way to accomplish these goals.

40. ☑ **B.** Collecting résumés and responding to applicants are the next best steps for the employer after attending a job fair.

☒ **A, C,** and **D** are incorrect. These all would be done later in the hiring process.

41. ☑ **A.** Having two to four company representatives attend a job fair is ideal.

☒ **B, C,** and **D** are incorrect. One is not enough, and any more than 4 could be overwhelming for the applicant.

42. ☑ **D.** An assessment test would be used later in the hiring process.

☒ **A, B,** and **C** are incorrect. These items would all be useful to bring to the job fair.

43. ☑ **A.** An I-9 would need to be filled out after an offer of employment has been made.
    ☒ **B, C,** and **D** are incorrect. These are all items an employer would want to bring to a job fair.

44. ☑ **A.** Employment web sites are best used for recruiting when it's for a big company that has a good reputation because it is already getting visitors to the site for other reasons.
    ☒ **B, C,** and **D** are incorrect. All these answers are not reflective of the best answer for when an employment web site is most applicable.

45. ☑ **B.** Job sharing allows two people with complementary skills to share a full-time job.
    ☒ **A, C,** and **D** are incorrect. **A** is incorrect because it is an example of on-call workers. **C** is incorrect because employees are not allowed to share benefits. **D** is incorrect because it is an example of a temporary employee.

46. ☑ **A.** A worker who is self-employed is commonly referred to as an independent contractor.
    ☒ **B, C,** and **D** are incorrect. **B** is incorrect because a temporary worker works for a company only on a temporary basis and could be referred by an agency. **C** is incorrect because it is an incorrect term. **D** is incorrect because a seasonal worker would work only during one time period per year or season when the company is busiest.

47. ☑ **D.** The employee type that would help a company if it needs particular skills but not on a full-time basis is a part-time employee.
    ☒ **A, B,** and **C** are incorrect. **A** is incorrect because job sharing is when two people share the job duties of one person. **B** is incorrect because a contingent worker is the best answer; that term refers to many different types of nontraditional workers. **C** is incorrect because interns are hired to give students educational opportunities.

48. ☑ **A.** Payrolling allows an organization to refer to an agency for people it wants to hire, and the agency provides payroll and tax services.
    ☒ **B, C,** and **D** are incorrect. **B** is incorrect because this describes an internship. **C** is incorrect because this describes a seasonal worker. **D** is incorrect because this describes a professional employer organization (PEO).

49. ☑ **C.** Workers who are hired only at times of the year when the workload increases are seasonal workers.
    ☒ **A, B,** and **D** are incorrect. **A** is incorrect because an on-call worker can be called in to work at any point during the year. **B** is incorrect because a contingent worker refers to many different types of nontraditional workers. **D** is incorrect because a temporary worker could also work at any time of year when needed.

50. ☑ **B.** Independent contractors are self-employed individuals who work on a project or fee basis with multiple customers or clients.
    ☒ **A, C,** and **D** are incorrect. **A** is incorrect because contingent worker refers to many different types of nontraditional workers. **C** is incorrect because part-time workers don't work on a project or fee basis but rather a reduced schedule per week. **D** is incorrect because a temporary worker works any time on a temporary basis.

51. ☑ **B.** The main reason why an employer would want to use caution when deciding whether a worker is an independent contractor or an employee is that the government could impose substantial fines and penalties for making the wrong determination.

☒ **A, C,** and **D** are incorrect. Although these all could be a possibility, none would be the main reason.

52. ☑ **B.** This is an example of an on-call worker.

☒ **A, C,** and **D** are incorrect. They are all advantages of telecommuting.

53. ☑ **D.** The IRS has guidelines for determining whether an individual is an independent contractor or employee, and pay rate controls are not one of those guidelines.

☒ **A, B,** and **C** are incorrect. **A** is not correct because behavioral controls such as the right to direct tasks is a guideline. **B** is not correct because financial control such as whether the organization controls the business aspect is a guideline. **C** is incorrect because the type of relationship that exists between parties such as contracts, health insurance, and so on, is a guideline.

54. ☑ **B.** Giganomics is the creation of employment through the piecing together of several projects or gigs.

☒ **A, C,** and **D** are incorrect. **A** is incorrect because on-call workers being called in at the last minute for a job would be classified as an on-call worker. **C** and **D** are incorrect because they are not accurate terms.

55. ☑ **C.** A gig worker is a worker who is employed for a particular performance or a defined time.

☒ **A, B,** and **D** are incorrect. **A** and **D** are incorrect because they are not hired for a particular time only. **B** is incorrect because they are usually hired on a project basis.

56. ☑ **C.** Behavioral interviews include questions such as, "Tell me about a time…" or "Describe a situation…." These questions are designed to get the candidate to describe situations they have encountered in the past and explain how they handled the final outcome. The idea is that past behavior will help interviewers predict future behavior.

☒ **A, B,** and **D** are incorrect. **A** is incorrect because a structured interview means that the interviewer asks the same questions of every candidate. **B** is incorrect because a competency-based interview occurs when an interviewer asks questions based on the competencies required for success in the role and candidates are asked to demonstrate an example of the competency. **D** is incorrect because a stress interview is one where a candidate is purposely asked questions to place them on the defensive. The goal of the interview is to analyze how a candidate reacts under pressure. Stress interviews may be used in jobs such as EMT or 911 operators where the candidate will encounter several high-pressure situations on a regular basis.

57. ☑ **B.** An aptitude test measures a person's ability to acquire new skills.

☒ **A, C,** and **D** are incorrect. **A** is incorrect because a cognitive ability test assesses skills already learned. **C** is incorrect because an assessment center is a battery of simulated exercises designed to assess readiness for higher-level managerial competencies. **D** is incorrect because a psychomotor test is used to determine physical dexterity.

58. ☑ **A.** A realistic job preview provides candidates with an honest experience of the work environment.

☒ **B, C,** and **D** are incorrect. **B** and **C** are incorrect because panel interviews are a type of group interview where there are interviewers present from varying disciplines in the company. They take turns asking questions that are usually aligned with their area of expertise. **D** is incorrect because a job assessment is a process for gathering information on the interests, skills, and abilities of candidates.

59. ☑ **D.** A psychomotor test may be used to test a candidate's physical dexterity as a measure of the physical fitness necessary to perform the essential functions of a job.

☒ **A, B,** and **C** are incorrect. **A** and **B** are incorrect because medical screening and drug tests are contingent assessment methods used to identify those who abuse drugs or who may have health risks that make them not fit for the job. **C** is incorrect because an assessment center is a battery of simulated exercises designed to assess readiness for higher-level managerial competencies.

60. ☑ **D.** A panel interview is an interview where there are interviewers present from varying disciplines in the company. They take turns asking questions that are usually aligned with their area of expertise.

☒ **A, B,** and **C** are incorrect. **A** is incorrect because a team interview includes subordinates, peers, and management from the same team as interviewers. **B** is incorrect because this is not an interview type. **C** is incorrect because an unstructured interview may be group or individual. Unstructured interviews are characterized by the lack of formality.

61. ☑ **C.** A situational interview is similar to a behavior-based interview, but a candidate can draw on prior experiences or use hypothetical examples to respond to how they would handle the situation presented to them.

☒ **A, B,** and **D** are incorrect. **A** is incorrect because a structured interview is an interview where the interviewer asks the same questions of every candidate. **B** is incorrect because a behavior-based interview is an interview where candidates are asked questions designed to generate answers about how the candidate has handled past situations. The premise of the behavior-based interview is that past behaviors are predictors of future behavior. **D** is incorrect because a competency-based interview occurs when an interviewer asks questions based on the competencies required for success in the role and candidates are asked to demonstrate an example of the competency.

62. ☑ **A.** A prescreen interview usually lasts 15 to 20 minutes and is handled by an HR representative.

☒ **B, C,** and **D** are incorrect. All these choices represent characteristics of in-depth interviews.

63. ☑ **A.** Job competencies guide interviewers in that they help them formulate questions that seek feedback from the candidate that is more expansive. Responses to questions developed from job competencies help to determine how well a candidate fits the overall culture and not just whether they are able to perform the tasks associated with a job. An example would be hiring a campus director for a small school that is experiencing rapid growth. This person would have to display a job competency of adaptability and flexibility.

⊠ **B**, **C**, and **D** are incorrect. **B** is incorrect because lists of essential functions aren't the best source for developing behavioral and situational questions. Essential functions are the barest minimum tasks required to perform a job. The sales manager, in this example, is seeking to identify behaviors, both past and present, that will help her determine a candidate's overall fit for an account representative job. **C** and **D** are incorrect because job specifications are simply a detailed listing of work to be done or job duties coupled with minimum qualifications such as education, certifications, and so on.

64. ☑ **C.** The campus president should contact these salespeople and make them aware of the upcoming opening. It is a smart move to get them engaged. Posting a position and then interviewing applicants is an orderly and systematic way to consider applicants, and it is in accordance with the principles of the Uniform Guidelines on Employee Selection Procedures (UGESP). The UGESP was developed by the Equal Employment Opportunity Commission (EEOC), the Civil Service Commission (CSC), the Office of Federal Contract Compliance Programs (OFCCP), and the Department of Justice (DOJ). The purpose of the UGESP is to give employers a guide to ensure compliance with Title VII, Executive Order 11246, and related employment legislation.

⊠ **A**, **B**, and **D** are incorrect. **A** is incorrect because interviews should never be set before a position is posted. A component of the applicant tracking process for Internet applicants is for the employer to "act" to fill a position. The normal procedure for this school is to post positions online and then interested candidates apply and set interviews accordingly. Posting the position online, in this case, is the employer "acting" to fill the position. **B** is incorrect because direct résumé submission is not the school's normal process. Another component of the applicant tracking process related to Internet applicants is that the individual follows the employer's normal process for applying. **D** is incorrect because setting up phone screens is the same as setting up in-person interviews, which should not happen prior to posting the position.

65. ☑ **D.** This is stereotyping. This interviewer is drawing a conclusion based on intuition without any facts to support his opinion of the candidate. Stereotyping is forming a generalized opinion about how people of a particular gender, religion, or race appear, think, act, feel, or respond.

⊠ **A**, **B**, and **C** are incorrect. **A** is incorrect because the horn effect occurs when the interviewer draws a conclusion based on one negative trait of the candidate. **B** is incorrect because negative emphasis happens when the interviewer uses a small amount of negative information to draw an unfavorable opinion of the candidate. **C** is incorrect because first-impression bias occurs when the interviewer determines an opinion of the candidate, whether negative or positive, from the first impression.

66. ☑ **B.** It is a requirement of the UGESP that any pre-employment test be both valid and reliable.

⊠ **A**, **C**, and **D** are incorrect. **A** is incorrect because a pre-employment test can be given before an offer of employment is made. **C** and **D** are incorrect because neither of these is most concerning about the scenario presented. It is true that no pre-employment test should be administered without being thoroughly vetted by HR, and the physical space within which any test is administered matters to the reliability of the test. However, these tests have already been administered, which may have affected the hiring decision made in regard to some of the candidates. At this point, as the HR director, it would be best to remove the tests from use immediately, review the scores of the candidates who may have been affected, and take corrective action as necessary to protect the company from liability.

67. ☑ **C**. A drug test should be completed in the phase of post-offer.

   ☒ **A**, **B**, and **D** are incorrect. It could be unlawful to do a drug test during these phases.

68. ☑ **A**. The main reason why an employer would want to institute drug testing is because reasonable suspicion based on performance could indicate drug use on the job.

   ☒ **B**, **C**, and **D** are incorrect. None of these options is the best reason why an employer would institute drug testing. They are factors and would be a by-product of drug testing but would not be the main reason.

69. ☑ **B**. Doing pre-offer drugs tests could violate the Americans with Disabilities Act.

   ☒ **A**, **C**, and **D** are incorrect. **A** is incorrect because the Family Medical Leave Act requires covered employers to provide employees with job protection and unpaid leave for qualified medical and family reasons. **C** is incorrect because the Age Discrimination in Employment Act protects workers older than 40 against discrimination. **D** is incorrect because the Title VII of the Civil Rights Act prohibits employment discrimination based on race, color, religion, sex, and national origin.

70. ☑ **D**. The main reason why off-site drug testing is ideal is because is it could hold up in court as a third-party neutral source.

   ☒ **A**, **B**, and **C** are incorrect. These may be true some of the time but would not be the main reason why.

71. ☑ **C**. The recommended practice an employer should do before starting a drug testing program is to clearly establish a policy.

   ☒ **A**, **B**, and **D** are incorrect. They would not be the best answer or a proper best practice.

72. ☑ **A**. Employers may make medical inquiries or require medical examinations of newly hired or existing employees only if they feel the health or safety of the individual or others is at risk.

   ☒ **B**, **C**, and **D** are incorrect. They would not be valid reasons to make medical inquires or require medical examinations and could possibly violate the Americans with Disabilities Act.

73. ☑ **B**. An employer should conduct a background check at the post-offer time frame.

   ☒ **A**, **C**, and **D** are incorrect. **A** and **C** are incorrect because neither would be a HR best practice as it could be unlawful to conduct the background check before an offer is made. **D** is incorrect because it would be ideal to conduct the check after the offer and before someone actually starts on the job. If they are allowed to work for 60 days and then they fail the background check, then you have to terminate their employment, which is harder to do than simply not let the work begin.

74. ☑ **D**. Conducting a background check would not necessarily protect the neighborhood.

    ☒ **A**, **B**, and **C** are incorrect. They are all reasons why an employer would want to do background checks.

75. ☑ **A**. The main reason why an employer would want to conduct a reference check is that past performance is a strong indicator of future performance.

    ☒ **B**, **C**, and **D** are incorrect. **B** and **D** are incorrect because they may play a factor but would not be the main reason. **C** is incorrect because a background check would not be a reason to conduct a reference check.

76. ☑ **B**. Employees looking to work in safe organizations is not a factor in why there is an increase in reference checks completed.

    ☒ **A**, **C**, and **D** are incorrect. **A** is incorrect because security issues in a post–September 11 world have employers thinking more about security issues in the workplace. **C** is incorrect because technological advances make background investigations faster and more economical and therefore easier for employers to complete. **D** is incorrect because there is increased awareness of the various risks of failure to conduct adequate background checks that are published and discussed in many areas of business.

77. ☑ **C**. An employer may ask if the candidate can perform the essential functions of the job before an offer of employment is made.

    ☒ **A**, **B**, and **D** are incorrect. These options would be unlawful to ask prior to the offer of employment and could possibly violate the Americans with Disabilities Act.

CHAPTER 4

Compensation and Benefits

This functional area includes coverage of the following responsibilities and knowledge objectives:

- **01** Applicable laws and regulations related to compensation and benefits, such as monetary and nonmonetary entitlement, wage and hour, and privacy (for example, ERISA, COBRA, FLSA, USERRA, HIPAA, PPACA, tax treatment)

- **02** Pay structures and programs (for example, variable, merit, bonus, incentives, noncash compensation, pay scales/grades)

- **03** Total rewards statements

- **04** Benefit programs (for example, healthcare plans, flexible benefits, retirement plans, wellness programs)

- **05** Payroll processes (for example, pay schedule leave, time-off allowances)

- **06** Uses for salary and benefits surveys

- **07** Claims processing requirements (for example, workers' compensation, disability benefits)

- **08** Work-life balance practices (for example, flexibility of hours, telecommuting, sabbatical)

QUESTIONS

Benefits and compensation include all forms of financial and nonfinancial components of an employee's overall compensation, including base salary, company contributions to retirement plans, and company-paid medical insurance. A well-designed compensation package is used to attract and retain top talent. A poorly managed or noncompetitive compensation package may negatively impact employee morale, decrease productivity, and increase absenteeism. Other less obvious forms of temporary compensation that provide partial income replacement include workers' compensation and disability insurance. In this chapter, you will review the knowledge you have gained throughout your studies about laws applicable to compensation, designing pay structures, and various work-life balance structures.

Objective 01 Applicable Laws and Regulations Related to Compensation and Benefits

1. Which of the following laws states that the statute of limitations on pay discrimination lawsuits resets as each alleged discriminatory paycheck is issued?

   A. Lily Ledbetter Fair Pay Act

   B. Equal Pay Act

   C. Davis-Bacon Act

   D. Copeland "Anti- Kickback" Act

2. What federal law sets uniform minimum standards to ensure that employee benefit plans are established and maintained in a fair and financially sound manner?

   A. Fair Labor Standards Act (FLSA)

   B. Securities Exchange Act (SEC)

   C. Employee Retirement Income Security Act (ERISA)

   D. Patient Protection and Affordable Care Act (PPACA)

3. What is an example of required communication that HR must provide to employees?

   A. Personalized benefit statements

   B. COBRA rates when the employee first starts with an organization

   C. Notification of Continuation of Benefits under COBRA

   D. Benefit manuals

4. Marlene, a senior project manager and a captain in the Air National Guard, asks to be excused from work to attend a weeklong military training session. Which of the following defines Marlene's responsibilities to her employer?

   A. COBRA

   B. USSERA

C. PPACA

D. ERISA

5. You have decided to conduct an exempt versus nonexempt audit based on the Federal Labor Standards Act (FLSA). Which of the following is most likely to be considered nonexempt?

   A. An employee who is paid $25,000 per year ($481 per week)

   B. A manager who supervises two or more employees

   C. An employee who functions as the employer's attorney

   D. An employee who regularly performs routine or clerical duties

6. Which of the following amends COBRA and establishes that a person's preexisting condition can't prevent the person from qualifying for health insurance if there is less than a 63-day break in coverage?

   A. Military Caregiver Leave

   B. FMLA

   C. HIPAA

   D. ERISA

7. Dana is a delivery driver for Shipping and Packaging, LLC. Which amendment to the Fair Labor Standards Act (FLSA) defines how Dana should be paid when he makes deliveries for the company on the way home from work?

   A. The Portal to Portal Act

   B. The Fair Pay Act

   C. The Equal Pay Act

   D. The Fair Wage Act

8. Which of the following is characteristic of an independent contractor?

   A. Uses company equipment but works remotely

   B. Maintains employer pay records on an ongoing basis

   C. Attends sales training provided by employer

   D. Always uses personal computer, printer, and paper to produce reports

9. What organizations must comply with the FLSA?

   A. Private employers that earn at least $250,000 annually

   B. Private employers that engage in interstate commerce

   C. Public and private employers that handle at least $250,000 in business annually

   D. Public and private employers that handle at least $500,000 in business annually

Objective 02   Pay Structures and Programs

10. The established pay range at a company for customer service representatives is $10 to $12 an hour. Which of the following is an example of a red circle rate?

    A. An employee earns $15 an hour.

    B. An employee earns $9 an hour.

    C. An employee earns $10 an hour.

    D. An employee earns $12 an hour.

11. Sandra and Pete are both senior financial analysts. Sandra started at Dozier Financial 20 years ago as an accounting clerk and has consistently been promoted. She currently earns $88,000 per year. Pete started with the company 1.5 years ago. He earns $$90,000 per year. Comparing both of their salaries, what is this an example of?

    A. Pay compression

    B. Pay regression

    C. Pay adjustment

    D. Seniority increase

12. Which of the following identifies a pay adjustment that is given to all employees regardless of employee performance or the organization's financial health?

    A. Differential pay

    B. Market-based increase

    C. Cost-of-living adjustment

    D. Lump-sum increase

13. Which of the following describes a typical executive remuneration plan that allows an executive to purchase company stock at a predetermined price?

    A. Phantom stock

    B. Stock purchase plan

    C. Stock option

    D. Restricted stock grant

14. What is the most appropriate compensation plan for a sales professional when the company's first priority is increasing sales even at the risk of poor customer service?

    A. Low base salary plus commission

    B. Commission only

    C. High base salary plus commission

    D. Base salary only

15. Which choice describes a base pay system that pays every employee performing the same job regardless of seniority or performance?

   A. Performance-based

   B. Step-rate

   C. Flat-rate

   D. Merit

16. What is a drawback of using pay-for-performance (P4P) systems?

   A. Raises are a permanent increase in payroll costs.

   B. Performance improvement is not incentivized.

   C. Senior employees feel undervalued because they are paid the same as junior employees.

   D. Scheduled incremental pay increases don't keep pace with inflation.

17. Lancelot receives $1 for each pair of pants he hems up to 50 pants. If Lancelot reaches this goal in 2 days instead of the average of 5 days, he will receive $3 per pant hemmed for the remaining 3 days of the workweek. What type of pay system does this represent?

   A. Person-based

   B. Differential piece-rate system

   C. Piece-rate system

   D. Competency-based

18. Amar is paid $27 an hour when he works from 8 a.m. to 5 p.m. On the days when he works 4 p.m. to 12 a.m., he is paid $32 per hour. What kind of pay structure is described?

   A. Time-based differential pay

   B. Incentive pay

   C. COLA

   D. Pay adjustment

Objective 03   Total Rewards Statements

19. A total rewards statement provides what type of information?

   A. A balance sheet that reports on company assets, liability, and owners' equity

   B. A personalized document that provides the overall value of tangible rewards

   C. A formal summary of the objectives and values of an organization

   D. A statement that identifies what an organization would like to be in the future

20. What is a key purpose for employers to produce a total rewards statement?

    A. The Equal Employment Opportunity Commission (EEOC) requires it.

    B. To communicate to employees the cost of their wages.

    C. To increase the productivity of the human resource department.

    D. To increase employee engagement, ultimately driving business results.

21. Typically, a total rewards statement would include what key elements?

    A. Years of experience, date of hire, and benefits enrollment date

    B. Benefits enrollment date, benefits selected, and dependents information

    C. The value of wages, benefits, allowances, holidays, and voluntary benefits

    D. Job title, job classification, status, wages, and employee name

22. To maximize the value of a total rewards statement, what steps are important?

    A. Personalize it as much as possible and ensure the contents are accurate.

    B. There are no extra steps necessary because employees will be grateful.

    C. Ensure that every total rewards statement is signed by the employees.

    D. Give every employee a raise before the total reward statements come out.

23. Which of the following is an example of an intangible reward?

    A. A thank-you letter

    B. A bonus check

    C. A gift card

    D. A wage raise

24. Which of the following is an example of a tangible reward?

    A. Pat on the back

    B. Public thank-you

    C. Fringe benefits

    D. Development coaching

25. Many employers choose to try to include perks in the total rewards statement. Which of the following is considered a perk?

    A. Health benefits

    B. Pension plan

    C. Paycheck

    D. Company car

26. To ensure employees have the opportunity to fully understand the total rewards statement, an employer may want to take which of the following steps?

   A. Do nothing; there is no way to thoroughly understand the statement.

   B. Create an interactive platform such as a company forum.

   C. Send all statements out in paper format to employees' homes.

   D. Make the statement as generic as you can so questions are not necessary.

27. The Affordable Care Act (ACA) requires applicable large employers that offer health insurance to provide employees with which of the following?

   A. 1095-C form

   B. EEO-1 report

   C. I-9 form

   D. 5500 form

Objective 04 Benefit Programs

28. An owner of a midsize organization wants to retire. The owner would like to fund his retirement without having to sell the company to outsiders. What would be a viable alternative to selling the organization to outside investors?

   A. Establish a 401(k) retirement plan for all employees.

   B. Convince relatives of the owner to take over the organization.

   C. Establish an employee stock option plan (ESOP).

   D. There are no other alternatives to selling the organization.

29. What is the main disadvantage to an employee when using a flexible spending account (FSA)?

   A. Employees risk losing their money at the end of year if funds are not used by the year-end deadline.

   B. There are too many restrictions on what is a qualified health expense.

   C. It's difficult to keep receipts for qualified health expenses.

   D. It's difficult to predict future health expenses.

30. An individual (or individuals) who has discretionary decision-making over a group's health plan carries what specific role and responsibility according to the Department of Labor, specifically the Employee Retirement Income Security Act (ERISA)?

   A. A profitability responsibility

   B. A fiduciary responsibility

   C. A recruitment responsibility

   D. A talent satisfaction responsibility

31. Which of the following is a health and welfare program where an employee may receive incentives to complete a smoking cessation program?

   A. Wellness

   B. Employee assistance program (EAP)

   C. Disability

   D. Workers' compensation

32. An employee at International Financial Consultants has been diagnosed with terminal cancer. The employee is enrolled in both the short-term and long-term disability plans at the time of diagnosis. The employee has already exhausted the benefits under the short-term disability plan. What is the next step the HR manager should take to help this employee with benefits coverage?

   A. Advise the employee to apply for life insurance

   B. Advise the employee to apply for long-term disability and to coordinate with Social Security to avoid duplication of coverage

   C. Advise the employee to draft a will

   D. Advise the employee to pick a richer medical plan to cover the high costs associated with cancer

33. When conducting a benefit needs assessment, which of the following describes the final step in the process?

   A. Gap analysis

   B. Organizational strategy review

   C. Organizational philosophy review

   D. Analysis of design and utilization data

34. What is the main purpose of international Social Security agreements?

   A. To eliminate government interference into an expatriate compensation agreement

   B. To eliminate an employer from having to pay Social Security on the employee's behalf

   C. To eliminate any additional work for the employer and the employee

   D. To eliminate dual Social Security taxation, which occurs when a worker from one country works in another country where workers are required to pay Social Security taxes on the same wages

35. Which of the following describes a mandatory feature of a high-deductible health plan?

   A. Option to enroll in a vision plan

   B. Option to enroll in a dental plan

   C. Health reimbursement arrangement (HRA)

   D. Health savings account (HSA)

36. Which of the following identifies a qualified expense when utilizing funds of a dependent-care flexible spending account?

    A. Babysitting

    B. Elder care while employee is at work

    C. Nursing home expenses

    D. After-school soccer lessons

Objective 05   Payroll Processes

37. A bank of hours in which the employer provides time that employees use for illness, vacation, and holidays is known as:

    A. Vacation time off

    B. Personal time off

    C. Sick time off

    D. Paid time off

38. When an employer provides paid time off for employees who are summoned to participate in a judicial proceeding, it is called:

    A. Sick time

    B. Jury duty

    C. Family medical leave

    D. Military leave

39. When an employer wants to grant an employee optional time off for purposes that are unrelated to sick, vacation, or holiday, they are granting what type of leave?

    A. Family medical leave

    B. Sick leave

    C. Personal leave

    D. Military leave

40. The lowest amount an employer can pay an employee mandated under federal and state laws is called:

    A. Annual salary

    B. Base rate pay

    C. Overtime pay

    D. Minimum wage

41. Additional pay given to a prospective employment candidate to entice them to work for an employer is called:

   A. A sign-on bonus

   B. Overtime pay

   C. Base rate pay

   D. Annual salary

42. Employees who are eligible for overtime as mandated by the Federal Labor Standards Act (FLSA) are categorized as:

   A. Managerial

   B. Technical

   C. Nonexempt

   D. Salaried

43. When determining the regular rate of pay, which of the following pay elements is included in the calculation?

   A. Overtime

   B. Base earnings

   C. Bonuses

   D. Stock options

44. A set of pay rates that is defined by minimum, midpoint, and maximum rates of pay and is assigned to any job is called:

   A. Bonuses

   B. Pay range

   C. Base rate

   D. Overtime

45. Incentive pay that is connected to a percentage of sales achieved by an employee is called:

   A. Regular rate

   B. Overtime

   C. Differential pay

   D. Commissions

Objective 06   Uses for Salary and Benefits Surveys

46. The main purpose why employers conduct salary surveys is to:

   A. Keep HR busy

   B. Ignore market trends

C. Set competitive wages

D. Compress pay

47. Which of the following laws prohibits price fixing among employers?

    A. Sherman Antitrust Act of 1890

    B. Americans with Disabilities Act 1990

    C. Affordable Care Act 2010

    D. Fair Labor Standards Act 1938

48. Compensation and benefits survey data results are usually organized in what following way?

    A. By how many products and services are produced

    B. By how many policies an organization has

    C. By industries and geographical regions

    D. By Equal Employment Opportunity (EEO) classifications

49. To ensure an accurate comparison of the organization's jobs to the survey data, which of the following is an important step?

    A. Create random jobs to compare to the survey data

    B. Delete jobs so to not have to compare to survey data

    C. Just take a guess because there is no certainty in survey data

    D. Ensure the employer job profile matches the market job profile

50. If an organization chooses to focus on the 75th percentile of the market, what type of pay philosophy has it adopted?

    A. Market leader

    B. Lag-lead

    C. Matching the market

    D. Market lag

51. If an organization chooses to focus on the 25th percentile of the market, what type of pay philosophy has it adopted?

    A. Market leader

    B. Lag-lead

    C. Matching the market

    D. Market lag

52. If an organization chooses to focus on the 25th percentile of the market for the beginning of the year and then catch up to the 75th percentile in the second half of the year, what type of pay philosophy has it adopted?

   A. Market leader

   B. Lag-lead

   C. Matching the market

   D. Market lag

53. What is the benefit of utilizing multiple data sources to obtain market information?

   A. To confuse managers.

   B. To find numbers that fit a budget.

   C. To cross-validate data.

   D. There is no benefit.

54. When an employer can't afford to purchase a wage survey every year, the employer may utilize what method to obtain new data?

   A. Aging the old data

   B. Searching the Internet for wage information

   C. Using the old data

   D. Asking competitors what they are paying

Objective 07 Claims Processing Requirements

55. The definition of disability is detailed in which of the following acts?

   A. Title VII of the Civil Rights Act

   B. Americans with Disabilities Act

   C. Age Discrimination in Employment Act

   D. Family Medical Leave Act

56. Which is the correct definition of a disability under the Americans with Disabilities Act?

   A. Physical or mental impairment that causes substantial limitation to a major life activity

   B. A medical condition causing a doctor's care

   C. A chronic condition that requires regular medication

   D. A condition that the employer has diagnosed

57. What does short- and long-term disability protect?

   A. Employer from loss of profits

   B. Employees from loss of wages

   C. Employee's family in the event of death

   D. Employee's family in the event of dismemberment

58. Once short-term disability ends, long-term disability could last until:

    A. 5 years from the date of illness or injury

    B. 10 years from the date of illness or injury

    C. Age 60

    D. Age 65

59. When paying a workers' compensation claim, _____ is decided before paying a monetary value.

    A. Where the injury took place

    B. Seriousness of the injury

    C. What state the injury took place in

    D. If the employee was impaired

60. What is it called when a state pays the total cost of any injuries or illnesses when they occur instead of paying insurance premiums for workers' compensation?

    A. Workers' comp lost wages pool

    B. Workers and companies unite

    C. Self-funded

    D. Risk management

61. Workers' compensation is regulated by:

    A. Each company

    B. Federal government

    C. Each individual state

    D. City ordinances

62. A 43-year-old man has been accidently killed in a warehouse explosion while at work. What benefits would the man's family be entitled to?

    A. Workers' compensation

    B. Short-term disability

    C. Long-term disability

    D. Family Medical Leave Act

63. Under workers' compensation plans, which of the following assumes all costs of injuries regardless of who is to blame?

    A. Employees

    B. Employers

    C. The state

    D. The federal government

Objective 08   Work-Life Balance Practices

64. Because of advances in _____, this allows employees more telecommuting options.

    A. HRIS systems

    B. Gross domestic product

    C. Performance review systems

    D. Technology

65. Which of the following is an example of a compressed workweek?

    A. Working from home

    B. Sharing job responsibilities with another colleague

    C. Working four 10-hour days

    D. Working 20 hours a week

66. An employee who comes into work at 10 a.m. to miss heavy traffic and take her children to school is utilizing which type of work-life balance program?

    A. Compressed workweek

    B. Job sharing

    C. Flex time

    D. Telecommuting

67. Which of the following is typically true of a sabbatical?

    A. Time off is granted with no pay.

    B. Time off is granted with pay.

    C. Time off is granted with a reduced rate of pay.

    D. No time is given, but a new publication is required.

68. Where are sabbaticals most commonly found?

    A. Educational institutions

    B. Startup companies

    C. Public companies

    D. Private companies

69. Which of the following is not an example of a flex work arrangement?

    A. An employee works 10 hours per workday, reducing the workweek to 4 days a week.

    B. Employees start later in the day and work into the evening.

    C. An employee works 9-hour workdays Monday through Thursday and 4 hours each Friday.

    D. Two part-time employees are assigned to the same job, equivalent to one full-time employee.

70. Which of the following is *not* a reason a company would institute a flex work arrangement?

    A. To improve recruitment

    B. To save costs

    C. To increase performance review scores

    D. To improve attendance

71. Which of the following is *not* a challenge of telecommuting?

    A. A heightened feeling of being "owned" by the organization, in that the company now has a virtual presence in the employee's home

    B. Loss of productivity

    C. A negative impact on career advancement and perception that employees away from the office are not as available as those working in a traditional office setting

    D. Distraction by spouse, children, pets, and others in the workspace

72. Which of the following is true of hoteling?

    A. Having telecommuters reserve an office or workstation for their in-office days in lieu of assigning them a permanent workspace

    B. Offering a hotel to employees who work more than 50 miles from the office

    C. Offering a hotel to employees who work more than 75 miles from the office

    D. Offering a hotel to an employee who is required to go out of town on business

1. A	25. D	49. D
2. C	26. B	50. A
3. C	27. A	51. D
4. B	28. C	52. B
5. D	29. A	53. C
6. C	30. B	54. A
7. A	31. A	55. B
8. D	32. B	56. A
9. D	33. A	57. B
10. A	34. D	58. D
11. A	35. D	59. B
12. C	36. B	60. C
13. C	37. D	61. C
14. B	38. B	62. A
15. C	39. C	63. B
16. A	40. D	64. D
17. B	41. A	65. C
18. A	42. C	66. C
19. B	43. B	67. B
20. D	44. B	68. A
21. C	45. D	69. D
22. A	46. C	70. C
23. A	47. A	71. B
24. C	48. C	72. A

1. ☑ **A.** This is the main tenet of the Lily Ledbetter Fair Pay Act.

   ☒ **B, C,** and **D** are incorrect. **B** is incorrect because the Equal Pay Act prohibits wage discrimination by requiring equal pay for equal work. **C** is incorrect because this refers to establishing prevailing wage and benefit requirements for contractors on federally funded projects. **D** is incorrect because this refers to precluding a federal contractor or subcontractor from inducing an employee to give up any part of the compensation to which the employee is entitled.

2. ☑ **C.** The Employee Retirement Income Security Act (ERISA) sets uniform minimum standards to ensure retirement plans are established and maintained in a fair and financially sound manner.

   ☒ **A, B,** and **D** are incorrect. **A** is incorrect because the Fair Labor Standards Act (FLSA) establishes standards for wages and hours. **B** is incorrect because the Securities Exchange Act (SEC) is responsible for the enforcement of U.S. federal securities law. It protects investors by requiring accurate disclosure of financial statements. **D** is incorrect because the Patient Protection and Affordable Care Act (PPACA) is a law that relates to widening the health insurance market.

3. ☑ **C.** An organization is required by federal law to provide employees with a notification of continuation of benefits under the Consolidated Omnibus Budget Reconciliation Act (COBRA).

   ☒ **A, B,** and **D** are incorrect. **A** and **D** are incorrect because employers are not required to provide benefit statements or benefit manuals to employees. **B** is incorrect because COBRA rates are applicable only when an employee is terminated.

4. ☑ **B.** The Uniformed Services Employment and Reemployment Rights Act (USERRA) is a federal law that details the employment rights of armed services personnel. The act defines the employee's responsibility to notify the employer of the need to be absent from work for a reason covered by USERRA.

   ☒ **A, C,** and **D** are incorrect. **A** is incorrect because the Consolidated Omnibus Budget Reconciliation Act (COBRA) is an amendment to ERISA that contains provisions that gives certain former employees and their dependents continued temporary medical coverage. **C** is incorrect because the Patient Protection and Affordable Care Act (PPACA) is a law that relates to widening the health insurance market. **D** is incorrect because the Employee Retirement Income Security Act (ERISA) is a federal law that protects retirement assets and ensures that employee benefit plans are established and maintained in a fair manner.

5. ☑ **D.** There are various exceptions to overtime eligibility. However, an employee who regularly performs routine or clerical duties generally would be considered nonexempt and eligible for overtime pay.

   ☒ **A, B,** and **C** are incorrect. An outside salesperson, a manager who supervises two or more employees, and an employee who functions as the employer's attorney are considered exempt and not eligible for overtime pay.

6. ☑ **C**. The Health Insurance Portability and Accountability Act (HIPAA) of 1996 is an amendment to COBRA. One of the amendments ensures that if an individual was covered under an employer-sponsored health plan, their preexisting condition does not bar them from obtaining new health insurance if the lapse in coverage was less than 63 days.

   ☒ **A, B**, and **D** are incorrect. **A** is incorrect because Military Caregiver Leave is a provision of the Family Medical Leave Act (FMLA). **B** is incorrect because FMLA is the federal law that provides job-protected leave to eligible employees for the care of their own medical condition or to be a caregiver for a family member with a medical condition. **C** is incorrect because the Employee Retirement Income Security Act (ERISA) is a federal law that protects retirement assets.

7. ☑ **A**. The Portal to Portal Act of 1947 amended the FLSA by further defining how employees are paid for hours worked. Delivering a package on the way home may be considered a concluding activity for which Dana would be paid.

   ☒ **B, C**, and **D** are incorrect. **B** is incorrect because the Lily Ledbetter Fair Pay Act is the law that established that the statute of limitations on pay discrimination lawsuits resets as each alleged discriminatory paycheck is issued. **C** is incorrect because the Equal Pay Act prohibits wage discrimination by requiring equal pay for equal work. **D** is incorrect because there is not a law that is referred to as the Fair Wage Act.

8. ☑ **D**. Independent contractors provide their own tools and equipment to complete work for clients.

   ☒ **A, B**, and **C** are incorrect. **A** is incorrect because an employee would typically use the company's equipment to complete work whether on-site or remotely. **B** is incorrect because this choice describes an employee who has an ongoing relationship with the employer. An independent contractor's relationship with a client is usually project-based as opposed to ongoing. **C** is incorrect because attending employer-provided training is a characteristic of an employee rather than an independent contractor.

9. ☑ **D**. Public and private employers who handle at least $500,000 in business annually must comply with the provisions of the FLSA.

   ☒ **A, B**, and **C** are incorrect. The FLSA applies to both public and private employers at the appropriate level of revenue and organizations that engage in interstate commerce.

10. ☑ **A**. A red circle rate is when an employee's pay is above the pay range for the position.

    ☒ **B, C**, and **D** are incorrect. **B** is incorrect because $9 an hour is a green circle rate (below the pay range for the position). **C** and **D** are incorrect because they are within the pay range.

11. ☑ **A**. This is an example of pay compression. Pay compression is present when the difference between a more senior employee's pay and a newer employee's pay is small because of rising starting salaries.

    ☒ **B, C**, and **D** are incorrect. **B** is incorrect because pay regression does not refer to an established concept in the human resource field. **C** is incorrect because a pay adjustment describes a process companies engage in that may increase an employee's pay if related to a performance rating or decrease an employee's pay as a result of an organization's pay calibration exercise. **D** is incorrect because a seniority increase refers to a company practice of increasing an employee's pay based on longevity. Seniority increases happen fairly often in a union shop or most public service positions.

12. ☑ **C.** A cost of living adjustment (COLA) is paid to employees to protect against inflation. A COLA is usually offered in cases where an employee is relocating from a market with a lower cost of living to an area where the cost of living is markedly higher.

   ☒ **A, B**, and **D** are incorrect. **A** is incorrect because differential pay is dependent on performance and is paid to employees who assume more risk. **B** is incorrect because a market-based increase is a pay strategy where a company increases employees' pay rates to remain competitive with the market. This strategy is often used by companies to attract top talent. **D** is incorrect because a lump-sum increase is the same as a performance bonus used to reward employees.

13. ☑ **C.** A stock option provides the executive with the right to purchase company stock at a predetermined price.

   ☒ **A, B**, and **D** are incorrect. **A** is incorrect because paying an executive with phantom stock entails paying the executive the equivalent value of shares of stock without granting the employee stock ownership. **B** is incorrect because a stock purchase plan is a broad-based plan that allows the employee to purchase company stock at a discounted rate. If the plan is not broad based, it does not receive a favorable tax treatment. **D** is incorrect because a restricted stock grant is the gifting or transfer of stock to an employee.

14. ☑ **B.** Commissions are the only way to motivate sales staff to increase sales rapidly.

   ☒ **A, C**, and **D** are incorrect. Any salary outlay still requires the company to pay the salesperson whether or not the primary objective of increasing sales is met.

15. ☑ **C.** A flat or single-rate system pays each employee the same regardless of seniority or performance.

   ☒ **A, B**, and **D** are incorrect. **A** and **D** are incorrect because a performance/merit-based system pays an employee based on individual performance. **B** is incorrect because a step-rate system is one in which an employee receives pay increases based on a predetermined pay schedule. This kind of base pay system is often observed in union shops.

16. ☑ **A.** Pay for performance (P4P), also known as merit pay systems, results in a permanent increase in payroll costs because employees' base salaries are increased.

   ☒ **B, C**, and **D** are incorrect. **B** is incorrect because in P4P systems performance improvement is incentivized. **C** is incorrect because all employees receiving the same pay regardless of seniority is a feature of a flat-rate system. **D** is incorrect because scheduled incremental pay increases is a characteristic of a step-rate system.

17. ☑ **B.** A differential piece-rate system is a productivity-based pay system where an employee is paid per piece up to a certain benchmark. If Lancelot exceeds the target, then he will earn a higher piece-rate.

   ☒ **A, C**, and **D** are incorrect. **A** is incorrect because a person-based system pays an employee based on their personal characteristics. For example, a person may be paid more as the subject-matter expert (SME) in a discipline. **C** is incorrect because a piece-rate system is a productivity-based system where an employee is paid a set rate per piece. **D** is incorrect because a competency-based system is a type of person pay-based system where an employee's pay is based on their ability to demonstrate the job competencies.

18. ☑ **A**. Time-based differential pay is when employees are paid different rates based on the time of day that they work.

    ☒ **B, C,** and **D** are incorrect. **B** is incorrect because incentive pay is used to encourage employees to improve performance. **C** is incorrect because COLA is paid to employees to protect against inflation. **D** is incorrect because a pay adjustment describes a process companies engage in that may increase an employee's pay if related to a performance rating or decrease an employee's pay as a result of an organization's pay calibration exercise.

19. ☑ **B**. A total rewards statement is a personalized document that provides the overall value of tangible rewards. An employer may want to send this statement to employees annually or more frequently such as quarterly. These statements may also be called compensation or benefits statements.

    ☒ **A, C,** and **D** are incorrect. **A** is incorrect because a balance sheet that reports on company assets, liability, and owners' equity is a financial statement used to communicate the financial health of an organization. **C** is incorrect because a formal summary of the objectives and values of an organization is a mission statement, and **D** is incorrect because a statement that identifies what an organization would like to be in the future is called a vision statement. It is not relevant to the total rewards statement.

20. ☑ **D**. A key purpose for why employers choose to provide employees with a periodic total rewards statement is to increase employee engagement and ultimately drive business results.

    ☒ **A, B,** and **C** are incorrect. **A** is incorrect because this statement is simply not true. The Equal Employment Opportunity Commission (EEOC) does not require a total rewards statement to be produced. **B** is incorrect because this is statement is only partially true. A total rewards statement communicates the value of wages as well as benefits, perks, and other cash items such as bonuses. **C** is incorrect because this statement is not true.

21. ☑ **C**. A total rewards statement typically includes elements such as the value of wages, benefits, allowances, holidays, and voluntary benefits.

    ☒ **A, B,** and **D** are incorrect. **A** is incorrect because years of experience, date of hire, and benefits enrollment date, while needed to track employment and benefits records, are irrelevant to the total rewards statement. **B** is incorrect because benefits enrollment date, benefits selected, and dependents information may be drivers behind some of the costs of benefits, but these data points are not generally included in the total rewards statement. **D** is incorrect because job title, job classification, status, wages, and employee name are the data required for the management of compensation programs; these are not generally considered key elements of a total rewards statement.

22. ☑ **A.** To maximize the value of a total rewards statement, it is best to personalize it as much as possible and ensure the contents are accurate. Great care should be applied to the accuracy of the statements; otherwise, employees will question the statement and the employer and HR will lose credibility. When the statement is personalized and accurate, the outcome is one of trust and engagement.

☒ **B, C,** and **D** are incorrect. **B** is incorrect because this statement is simply not true. As stated, great care is needed when compiling total rewards statements. It is a poor assumption that employees will be grateful when they receive another piece of paper in the mail, let alone if the content is incorrect. **C** is incorrect because there is no reason to require employees to sign a total rewards statement. A statement is intended for informational purposes only, and there is no need to require signing and returning the document. **D** is not the best answer because while giving raises will certainly boost the morale of the workforce, it is not necessary to maximize the value of a total rewards statement.

23. ☑ **A.** A thank-you letter is an example of an intangible reward. Other examples of intangible rewards are a private lunch out or a public acknowledgment of a job well done. Intangible rewards are difficult to quantify and include in a total rewards statement.

☒ **B, C,** and **D** are incorrect. **B** is incorrect because a bonus check is a tangible reward. It can be quantified and included in a total rewards statement. **C** is incorrect because a gift card is a tangible reward, and **D** is incorrect because a wage raise is also a tangible reward, which is something that can be converted to a cash value. An intangible reward is something that can't be quantified.

24. ☑ **C.** A fringe benefit is an example of a tangible reward. Health benefits, gift cards, and merchandise are additional examples of a tangible reward.

☒ **A, B,** and **D** are incorrect. **A** is incorrect because a pat on the back is not tangible. It is not something that can be converted to cash. **B** is incorrect because a public thank-you is also not a tangible reward, and **C** is incorrect because development coaching is also not an intangible reward. While it can be motivating to have the opportunity for career development, it is not considered a tangible reward.

25. ☑ **D.** A company car is considered a perk. Also called a perquisite, a perk is something employees receive in addition to wages and benefits. On-site daycare, dry cleaning, and country club memberships are examples of perks.

☒ **A, B,** and **C** are incorrect. **A** is incorrect because a perk is something offered to an employee in addition to wages and benefits. Health benefits are considered a standard option for employment. **B** is incorrect because participating in a pension plan is considered part of the benefit package offered to employees, and **C** is incorrect because a paycheck is considered wages. A perk is something offered in addition to wages or benefits.

26. ☑ **B.** To ensure employees can fully understand the total rewards statement, an employer may want to create an interactive platform such as a company forum. This gives employees a chance to ask questions and get a better understanding about the total rewards statement. Organizations are also using online web platforms to enable employees to ask questions virtually.

☒ **A, C,** and **D** are incorrect. **A** is incorrect because there are ways to ensure employees have the opportunity to ask questions and get a clear understanding of the statement. **C** is incorrect because simply sending a statement to the homes of employees may not get the value intended. The risk is that employees may overlook the statement or mistake it for junk mail and throw it out. **D** is incorrect because a generic total rewards statement will not be as meaningful for employees as a personalized statement would.

27. ☑ **A.** The Affordable Care Act (ACA) requires applicable large employers that offer health insurance to provide employees with a 1095-C form. This benefits form provides information of the coverage an employer offered the previous year whether or not an employee chooses to participate in benefits. Employees can use this form to file taxes. While the ACA may require this form today, this may change over future years given the hotly contested nature of the law. A savvy human resource professional will keep an eye on this law and watch for changes as it may impact the employer.

☒ **B, C,** and **D** are incorrect. **B** is incorrect because an EEO-1 report is a required form from the Equal Employment Opportunity Commission (EEOC). This report is used to track employee race and gender by job categories. **C** is incorrect because an I-9 is a required form used to verify eligibility to work in the United States. **D** is not correct because a 5500 form is a tax form used to file employee benefit plan information with the Department of Labor (DOL).

28. ☑ **C.** Establishing an employee stock option plan (ESOP) is a viable option for an organization's owner who wants to fund employees' retirement, including the owner's, without having to sell the company to outside investors. An ESOP is a defined contribution plan in which a firm sets up a trust and makes tax-deductible contributions to it. An ESOP enables employees to purchase shares in an organization from the selling owners.

☒ **A, B,** and **D** are incorrect. **A** is incorrect because a 401(k) does not offer stock ownership of an organization. **B** is incorrect because there is a noncash compensation option that is more effective than simply trying to convince relatives of the owner to take over a company. **D** is incorrect because an ESOP is a viable alternative to selling the company to outside investors.

29. ☑ **A.** If money is left over in an employee's account at the deadline for FSA, all remaining funds will be forfeited.

☒ **B, C,** and **D** are incorrect. These choices, while disadvantages, are mere inconveniences compared to losing money if not used during the plan year.

30. ☑ **B.** A fiduciary is one who exercises discretionary decision-making over a group health plan. The Department of Labor (DOL), specifically the Employee Retirement Income Security Act (ERISA), outlines who is a fiduciary and the responsibilities of fiduciaries.

☒ **A, C,** and **D** are incorrect. **A** is incorrect because profitability responsibility is not an ERISA compliance responsibility. **C** is incorrect because recruitment is not tied to health benefit fiduciary responsibilities. **D** is incorrect because talent satisfaction is not an ERISA compliance responsibility.

31. ☑ **A.** Wellness programs are established to promote health and wellness. Utilization of wellness programs correlate to a reduction in healthcare premium costs to the employer. Therefore, it is common to incentivize wellness programs.

☒ **B, C,** and **D** are incorrect. **B** is incorrect because an EAP is a service employers offer that helps employees work through certain personal matters or work-related matters that may affect performance. **C** is incorrect because disability benefits are paid to employees when they are physically unable to work. **D** is incorrect because workers' compensation pays employees in cases where injuries are sustained on the job.

32. ☑ **B.** Once short-term disability expires (if applicable in the state in which the employee resides), long-term disability will apply (if enrolled at the time of diagnosis). It is important to coordinate with Social Security disability benefits to avoid duplication of coverage.

☒ **A, C,** and **D** are incorrect. These choices may help the employee, but they are not the next step in the benefit coverage process.

33. ☑ **A.** A benefits needs assessment concludes with a gap analysis. A gap analysis involves comparing the organizational needs, employee needs, and existing benefits.

☒ **B, C,** and **D** are incorrect. A review of the organizational strategy, philosophy, and analysis of design and utilization data all happen earlier in the benefits needs analysis process.

34. ☑ **D.** The main purpose of an international Social Security agreement (totalization agreement) is to eliminate dual Social Security taxation, which occurs when a worker from one country works in another country where workers are required to pay Social Security taxes on the same wages.

☒ **A, B,** and **C** are incorrect. None of the choices represents the purpose of an international Social Security agreement.

35. ☑ **D.** A health savings account (HSA) is a mandatory feature of a high-deductible health insurance plan. An HSA is intended to cover medical expenses that occur when the employee is still meeting the deductible of the plan. An HSA is funded through pretax payroll deductions.

☒ **A, B,** and **C** are incorrect. **A** and **B** are incorrect because providing employees with the option to enroll in a vision or dental plan are not mandatory features of an HSA. **C** is incorrect because a health reimbursement arrangement (HRA) is intended to cover all medical costs up to a certain limit. It is not health insurance, and it is funded by employer contributions.

36. ☑ **B.** Care for a dependent such as an elder or a child that is provided so that the employee can work is a qualified expense reimbursable from the employee's dependent-care FSA.

☒ **A, C,** and **D** are incorrect. **A** is incorrect because babysitting is a qualified expense only if it is provided by a nondependent caregiver and the services performed are done so that the employee can work. An example of a dependent caregiver is a spouse or a 16-year-old son or daughter who the employee financially supports. **C** is incorrect because nursing home expenses are qualified only if the elder care in this case is provided to allow the employee to work or look for work. **D** is incorrect because even though the lessons take place after school, they are not part of an after-school care program where the after-school care is being provided to allow a parent to work.

37. ☑ **D**. Paid time off (PTO) is a bank of hours in which the employer provides time that employees use for illness, vacation, and holidays. It may also be called personal time off. Essentially employers may adopt one of two ways to provide employees paid time off. One way is they may have them in separate banks such as a sick bank and a separate vacation bank. Another way is when the employer combines sick, vacation, holidays, and personal time into one bank called PTO. Typically, the bank of hours is accrued (or earned) every full pay period an employee works for an organization.

    ☒ **A**, **B**, and **C** are incorrect. While all are time-off provisions, vacation, personal, and sick time stated and accrued separately is not PTO or an all-in-one bank of hours.

38. ☑ **B**. Jury duty is when an employer provides paid time off for employees who are summoned to participate in a judicial proceeding. Often employers will pay for the time off to serve on jury duty through a special jury duty leave or through an earned paid time off (PTO) bank.

    ☒ **A**, **C**, and **D** are incorrect. **A** is incorrect because sick time is a bank of hours dedicated to cover an employee who may fall ill and need the time off work to recover. **C** is incorrect because family medical leave (FMLA) is used to entitle an employee to time off to recover from a serious medical condition or tend to a family member's serious medical condition. **D** is incorrect because military leave is used to entitle an employee to serve active duty in the Armed Forces or National Guard.

39. ☑ **C**. Personal leave is when an employer wants to grant an employee optional time off for purposes that are unrelated to illness, vacation, or holidays. Many employers recognize that "life happens" and employees may need time off from work to deal with a situation or participate in educational pursuits that may go beyond mandated leaves such as family medical leave (FMLA). This is a way that employers may choose to earn an employee's long-term loyalty to the organization.

    ☒ **A**, **B**, and **D** are incorrect. **A** is incorrect because family medical leave (FMLA) is a mandated unpaid 12 weeks of leave for employers who have 50 or more employees and applies to employees who worked 1,250 hours and may have a serious medical condition or must tend to a family member who has a serious medical condition. **B** is incorrect because sick leave is a bank of hours accrued that employees may use for the purposes of illness. This is a specific paid time off reason versus a general need for time off that may not fall into a specific category. **D** is incorrect because military leave is mandated time off for those who serve in the Armed Forces or National Guard. In this question, we were looking for an answer that fell outside of mandated time off or the usual paid time-off categories such as sick, vacation, or holiday.

40. ☑ **D**. Minimum wage is the lowest amount an employer can pay an employee mandated under federal and state laws.

    ☒ **A**, **B**, and **C** are incorrect. **A** is incorrect because an annual salary is a pay rate set by an employer based on experience, skills, education, and job level. An employer can set the annual salary so long as it doesn't fall below the minimum wage hourly rate and is not discriminatory against any protected Equal Employment Opportunity (EEO) class such as gender, race, or age. **B** is incorrect because similar to the annual salary, the base rate is set by the employer based on experience, skills, education, and job level. **C** is not the best answer because overtime pay is a rate paid 1.5 times the base rate and is triggered for any time worked over 40 hours in a week.

41. ☑ **A**. A sign-on bonus is additional pay given to a prospective employment candidate to entice them to work for an employer. Typically, an employer will offer a sign-on bonus in exchange for the employee's commitment to work for the employer. Otherwise, if the employee quits, he or she would be required to pay back the sign-on bonus in full or a prorated amount calculated by how long he or she worked for the employer.

    ☒ **B**, **C**, and **D** are incorrect. **B** is incorrect because overtime pay is a mandated pay for eligible nonexempt employees paid at 1.5 times the employee's regular pay. **C** is incorrect because base rate pay is the initial rate of pay an employee is paid in exchange for services, and **D** is incorrect because an annual salary is a standard rate of pay that is calculated on an annual basis.

42. ☑ **C**. Employees who are eligible for overtime as mandated by the Fair Labor Standards Act (FLSA) are categorized as nonexempt. Nonexempt employees may also be called hourly. Regulations can change over time. HR professionals, business owners, and managers should regularly check government web sites. Savvy HR professionals stay up on shifting laws to ensure their employer is compliant and pay employees correctly no matter the legislative and judicial changes that may occur.

    ☒ **A**, **B**, and **D** are incorrect. **A** is incorrect because managerial is a classification that may be used to exempt employees from overtime eligibility. **B** is incorrect because technical is a classification that is used for Equal Employment Opportunity (EEO-1) reports, and **D** is incorrect because salaried is another term often used for exempt. Exempt employees are not eligible for overtime.

43. ☑ **B**. Base earnings are used to determine the employee's regular rate of pay. This is an important concept to know when determining benefit values, determining time-off accruals, and calculating overtime rate of pay.

    ☒ **A**, **C**, and **D** are incorrect. **A** in incorrect because overtime pay is in addition to the regular rate of pay after 40 hours of work in a week and calculated at 1.5 times the regular rate of pay. **C** is incorrect because bonuses are additional pay that are paid above and beyond the regular rate of pay, and **D** is incorrect because stock options are a benefit given to employees allowing them to buy stock in the company at a discount or a fixed price.

44. ☑ **B**. A pay range is a set of pay rates that is defined by minimum, midpoint, and maximum rates of pay and is assigned to any job. Employers use pay ranges to gauge their competitiveness in the market for any job. Employees are placed into the pay range based on years of experience and education.

    ☒ **A**, **C**, and **D** are incorrect. **A** is incorrect because bonuses are discretionary pay amounts that are used to incentivize employees to accomplish certain goals and objectives or agree to work for an employer for a certain time frame. **C** is incorrect because a base rate is a single dollar amount paid to an employee on an hourly basis. **D** is incorrect because overtime is a single pay rate paid to an employee who works 40 or more hours in a week.

45. ☑ **D**. Commission is incentive pay that is connected to a percentage of sales achieved by an employee. Employers will use this pay structure to incentivize employees to sell product or services.

    ☒ **A, B, and C** are incorrect. **A** is incorrect because regular pay is a rate of pay given to an employee in exchange for services. Regular rate pay is a set pay and not connected to sales accomplishments. **B** is incorrect because overtime is a mandated pay for eligible nonexempt employees who work 40 or more hours in a week. **C** is not correct because a differential pay is extra pay when an employee may work off-shifts such as graveyard or weekend shifts. For example, an employee may earn an extra $1 or $2 an hour for working the weekend shift.

46. ☑ **C**. The main purpose why employers conduct salary surveys is to set competitive wages. By watching closely what the market pays for jobs, employers can set wages that will enable them to attract and retain talented staff within their fiscal constraints.

    ☒ **A, B, and D** are incorrect. Keeping HR busy, ignoring market trends, and compressing wages are not correct and do not describe why employers would go through the expense and time to conduct or participate in market surveys.

47. ☑ **A**. The Sherman Antitrust Act of 1890 prohibits employers from price fixing. Employers are prohibited from working with other employers to keep wages at a certain level, also called colluding. Avoiding this legal pitfall is another reason why employers purchase or participate in third-party sponsored surveys.

    ☒ **B, C, and D** are incorrect. **B** is incorrect because the Americans with Disabilities Act 1990 is a law that prohibits discrimination in employment on the basis of disability. **C** is incorrect because the Affordable Care Act of 2010 is a law intended to increase healthcare coverage and reduce the costs of healthcare. **D** is incorrect because the Fair Labor Standards Act 1938 established the 40-hour workweek, minimum wage, and overtime.

48. ☑ **C**. Industries and geographical regions usually organize compensation and benefit survey data results. Some surveys may also drill down to specific location regions and specific jobs or job classes. Having the ability to attract and retain hard-to-fill or highly skilled talent is a key driver for what kind of survey data an employer may value.

    ☒ **A, B, and D** are incorrect. How many products or services, how many policies, and Equal Employment Opportunity (EEO) classifications are irrelevant to wage and benefit surveys. In fact, it is critically important to ensure the survey data being obtained is based on objective criteria to avoid discrimination or a useless survey.

49. ☑ **D**. Ensuring the employer job profile matches the market job profile is an important step to obtain an accurate comparison of the organization's jobs to the survey data. Comparing "apples to apples" and "oranges to oranges" helps an employer make competitive wage determinations that fit within financial constraints.

    ☒ **A, B, and C** are incorrect. We are looking to match as many jobs to market data as possible. Creating random or deleting jobs or making guesses do not improve the accuracy of the data and comparison. A good wage and benefit survey process takes careful planning, appropriate job profile information, and a solid compensation philosophy.

50. ☑ **A**. If an organization chooses to focus on the 75th percentile of the market, it has adopted a market leader compensation or pay philosophy. The 75th percentile indicates that the pay is better than 74 percent of the organizations participating in the survey.

   ☒ **B, C**, and **D** are incorrect. **B** is incorrect because a lag-lead pay philosophy is when an organization chooses to lag in the market the first part of the year and catch up and lead the market the second part of the year. **C** is incorrect because matching the market means the employer intends to align the midpoint of the pay ranges to the 50th percentile of the market, and **D** is incorrect because market lag means the employer intends to align the midpoint of its pay ranges to the 25th or lower percentile.

51. ☑ **D**. If an organization chooses to focus on the 25th percentile of the market, it has adopted the market lag pay philosophy. The 25th percentile means that 75 percent of the survey participants pay at higher rates.

   ☒ **A, B**, and **C** are incorrect. **A** is incorrect because a market leader is when an employer chooses to focus on paying employees at the 75th percentile or higher. **B** is incorrect because lag-lead is when an employer chooses to pay employees at the lower end of the market the first part of the year and then catch up to lead the market the second part of the year, and **C** is incorrect because a market lag pay philosophy is when an employer chooses to pay less than what the market pays.

52. ☑ **B**. When an organization chooses to focus on the 25th percentile of the market for the beginning of the year and then catch up to the 75th percentile in the second half of the year, it has adopted a lag-lead compensation philosophy.

   ☒ **A, C**, and **D** are incorrect. **A** is incorrect because a market leader is a philosophy that means the employer will consistently lead the market in pay throughout the year. **C** is incorrect because matching the market pay philosophy means the employer will focus on the 50th percentile consistently throughout the year. **D** is incorrect because market lag pay philosophy means the employer pays less than the market consistently throughout the year.

53. ☑ **C**. Cross-validation of data is the benefit of utilizing multiple data sources to obtain market information. Employers may use multiple surveys to ensure the data is valid and fill in the blanks that one survey may lack.

   ☒ **A, B**, and **D** are incorrect. These are all false statements. Managers rarely have access to the actual surveys as it is typically HR's or the compensation professional's responsibility to analyze the data and report it in a format that management understands and can take action on. While surveys can keep HR busy, that is hardly a reason or benefit for utilizing multiple surveys. As we've discussed, there is indeed a benefit of utilizing multiple surveys.

54. ☑ **A**. When an employer can't afford to purchase a wage survey every year, they may age the old data to obtain new market data. This method is also called trending. The market continuously moves ahead regardless if an employer participates in surveys.

Compensation professionals can age data by learning the average percent of the market's movement for that particular year and increasing the old data by that amount.

☒ **B, C,** and **D** are incorrect. **B** is incorrect because searching the Internet for wages may not yield precise or correct wage information. **C** is incorrect because simply assuming the old data as fact is incorrect because the market is always moving forward, rendering old market data as obsolete. Calling competitors for wage data can violate the Sherman Antitrust Act of 1890. Under this law the U.S. Department of Justice (DOJ) and the Federal Trade Commission (FTC) have determined that organizations conducting their own salary surveys could be seen as practicing illegal price-fixing.

55. ☑ **B.** The Americans with Disabilities Act broadly defines a disability.

☒ **A, C,** and **D** are incorrect. **A** is incorrect because Title VII of the Civil Rights Act prohibits employers from discriminating against employees on the basis of sex, race, color, national origin, and religion. **C** is incorrect because the Age Discrimination in Employment Act protects people who are 40 or older from discrimination because of age. **D** is incorrect because the Family Medical Leave Act requires covered employers to provide employees job-protected and unpaid leave for qualified medical and family reasons.

56. ☑ **A.** A physical or mental impairment that causes substantial limitation to a major life activity is the broad definition of a disability under the ADA.

☒ **B, C,** and **D** are incorrect. These may be factors, but they are not the definitions of a disability under the ADA.

57. ☑ **B.** Short- and long-term disability protects employees from loss of wages because of illness or injury.

☒ **A, C,** and **D** are incorrect. **A** is incorrect because this is not a true statement. Short-term disability would not protect an employer from loss of profits. **C** and **D** are incorrect because these would be tenants of accidental death and dismemberment insurance.

58. ☑ **D.** Long-term disability could last until age 65 because that is the age that Social Security disability benefits could begin.

☒ **A, B,** and **C** are incorrect because these are untrue statements.

59. ☑ **B.** When paying a workers' compensation claim, the seriousness is decided before paying a monetary value. A more serious injury could be assigned a higher dollar value.

☒ **A, C,** and **D** are incorrect. Although they will be looked at when investigating a workers' compensation claim, none is the best answer.

60. ☑ **C.** When a particular state pays the total cost of any injuries or illnesses when they occur instead of paying insurance premiums for workers' compensation, it is called self-funded.

☒ **A, B,** and **D** are incorrect. **A** and **B** are incorrect because they are not correct terms in HR. **D** is incorrect because risk management is the overall process of managing risk in an organization.

61. ☑ **C** is incorrect. Workers' compensation is regulated by each individual state.

☒ **A, B,** and **D** are incorrect. These are untrue of who workers' compensation is regulated by. The federal government has left it up to each individual state to regulate its own businesses in terms of workers' compensation. Also, the state government governs this, not the city or company.

62. ☑ **A**. The man's family would be entitled to workers' compensation benefits and payments.

   ☒ **B, C**, and **D** are incorrect. **B** and **C** are incorrect because these benefits would be paid if an employee was temporarily unable to work, not because of death. **D** is incorrect because family medical leave is not a paid benefit.

63. ☑ **B**. Under workers' compensation plans, the employer assumes all costs of injuries regardless of who is to blame. This helps to reduce the number of court cases and improve safety overall on the job.

   ☒ **A, C**, and **D** are incorrect. They would not be responsible for workers' compensation claims or costs because that is paid for by the employer, not the government.

64. ☑ **D**. Because of advances in technology, this allows employees to work from home and affords them many more flex work options.

   ☒ **A, B**, and **C** are incorrect. These answers are just part of doing business and not related directly to why telecommuting is more common.

65. ☑ **C**. Working four 10-hour days is an example of a compressed workweek.

   ☒ **A, B**, and **D** are incorrect. **A** is incorrect because working from home would be an example of telecommuting. **B** is incorrect because sharing job responsibilities with another colleague would be job sharing. **D** is incorrect because working 20 hours a week would be considered part-time.

66. ☑ **C**. An employee who comes into work at 10 a.m. to miss heavy traffic and take her children to school is utilizing a flex-time work-life balance program.

   ☒ **A, B**, and **D** are incorrect. **A** is incorrect because a compressed workweek would be working 40 hours in a compressed amount of time. **B** is incorrect because job sharing would be when two part-time employees share one job. **D** is incorrect because telecommuting would be when employees use technology to work remotely or from home.

67. ☑ **B**. Time off granted with pay is typical with a sabbatical.

   ☒ **A, C**, and **D** are incorrect. These are untrue tenets of a sabbatical.

68. ☑ **A**. Educational institutions are where sabbaticals began and are most often found.

   ☒ **B, C**, and **D** are incorrect. Sabbaticals are starting in other industries, but these are not where they are most commonly found.

69. ☑ **D**. Two part-time employees who are assigned to the same job, equivalent to one full-time employee, is an example of job sharing.

   ☒ **A, B**, and **C** are incorrect. These are all examples of what a flex work arrangement might look like.

70. ☑ **C**. Performance review scores would not increase because of implementing a flex work arrangement.

   ☒ **A, B**, and **D** are incorrect. **A** is incorrect because a flex work arrangement could enhance recruitment efforts by attracting more qualified candidates. **B** is incorrect because a flex time schedule could reduce costs by cutting down on the expenses of having an office (in cases of telecommuting, for example). **D** is incorrect because flex-time arrangements could improve attendance because workers would have more time to see the doctor or attend to family matters in their off time.

71. ☑ **B.** Loss of productivity is not a challenge. Studies show that in fact productivity can increase because of telecommuting.

☒ **A, C,** and **D** are incorrect. **A** is incorrect because a challenge is a heightened feeling of being "owned" by the organization, in that the company now has a virtual presence in the employee's home when telecommuting. **C** is incorrect because a challenge of telecommuting is that a negative impact on career advancement and perception is that employees away from the office are not as available as those working in a traditional office setting. **D** is incorrect because distraction by spouse, children, pets, and others in the workspace could be a challenge of telecommuting.

72. ☑ **A.** Hoteling is having telecommuters reserve an office or workstation for their in-office days in lieu of assigning them a permanent workspace.

☒ **B, C,** and **D** are incorrect. They are not part of hoteling or any other flex work relationship.

Human Resource Development and Retention

This functional area includes coverage of the following responsibilities and knowledge objectives:

- **01** Applicable laws and regulations related to training and development activities (for example, Title VII, ADA, Title 17 [copyright law])

- **02** Training delivery format (for example, virtual, classroom, on the job, microlearning)

- **03** Techniques to evaluate training programs (for example, participant surveys, pre- and post-testing, after-action review)

- **04** Career development practices (for example, succession planning, dual career ladders)

- **05** Performance appraisal methods (for example, ranking, rating scales)

- **06** Performance management practices (for example, setting goals, benchmarking feedback)

Human resource development (HRD) focuses on the development of the knowledge, skills, and abilities employees need to be successful in their current and potentially future roles. This can include various training opportunities, coaching, mentoring, identifying high-potential employees, and preparing them for future roles as in the case of succession planning. Additionally, HRD concerns itself with performance management measures. Retention refers to the organization's ability to reduce attrition. Retention is affected by a company's culture and approach to performance management. Setting goals, creating benchmarks, and having an effective feedback loop establish expectations for employees and identify the mechanism by which meeting those expectations will be measured. Additionally, employee engagement strategies focus on what impact various activities and programs have on improving engagement, thereby increasing retention. In this chapter, you will review the knowledge you have gained regarding the federal laws that affect training and development opportunities for a diverse workforce and learning and development best practices.

Objective 01   Applicable Laws and Regulations Related to Training and Development Activities

1. Rohit is a quality assurance engineer at TransPacific Coders (TPC). He developed a set of requirements for records management that has revolutionized TPC testing processes. Rohit considers resigning from TPC to begin his own QA testing company using the records management process he developed. He did not sign a nondisclosure agreement (NDA) during the time he worked for TPC. With respect to the Copyright Act of 1976, what should Rohit consider before moving forward with his decision?

    A. Public domain

    B. That the process was created as part of regular job duties

    C. That the work is trademarked by TPC

    D. That the process was developed during nonwork hours

2. Sundar Batta is the learning and development manager at Professional Advisors, LLC. He is developing consulting skills training for employees. The HR director informed Sundar that there have been complaints that training has not been offered to minority groups in the company for the past 2 years. What is the most likely reason that the HR manager shared this information with Sundar?

    A. Concern that minorities find the training too difficult

    B. Concern that minorities will resign

    C. Concern that minorities will become disengaged

    D. Concern that training selection practices might adversely impact minorities

3. Family Resources is a nonprofit that provides back-to-work training resources (specifically, CompTIA courses) to individuals below the poverty line taught by employees of Family Resources. The organization wants to ensure that they are complying with the fair use provision of the U.S. Copyright Act. What is the best course of action?

A. Develop a copyright compliance policy and educate employees on the organization's intent to comply with the law

B. Tell trainers they may use copyrighted material without asking for permission because they are a not-for-profit organization

C. Allow pages of magazines to be copied and used in training but not pages from a book

D. Allow trainers to use copyrighted material only for those courses they do not charge for

4. RSV Parachuting is hosting a training class for all employees at a historic hotel. The hotel is not ADA compliant. As the HR director, what advice would you give to the CEO?

A. Employees have the responsibility of providing their own accommodation when training is being held in a non-ADA-compliant facility.

B. The employer is not liable if employees are not required to attend training.

C. The employer is liable if training is provided in a non-ADA-compliant facility.

D. Employees have the responsibility of providing their own accommodation when training is not held at the employer's facility.

5. Sarah works for International Visions Publishing as a travel writer. She recently authored a book for ex-pats on relocating and opening a restaurant in Paraguay. Who is the owner of the copyright?

A. Sarah, because she is the original author of the work

B. International Visions Publishing, which paid Sarah for this work as part of her normal job duties

C. The Paraguay government, because of an agreement with International Visions Publishing

D. Sarah, because no one can replicate the original works of an author without their permission

6. Which type of patent protects new processes, machines, manufacture, or composition of matter?

A. Design

B. Plant

C. Utility

D. Re-issue

7. Which of the following is an example of work that can be replicated without the author's permission?

A. Works in the public domain

B. Works protected under the fair use provision

C. Work-for-hire domain

D. Works protected under the U.S. Patent and Trademark Office

8. Work-for-hire creations are protected under the guidelines of the Copyright Act of 1976 for _____ years.

   A. The author's life plus 70

   B. 120

   C. 90

   D. 100

9. The recently revised job description of an Administrative Assistant III at the Unified School District of Montage, which has 6,500 employees, lists as one of the essential functions that applicants must be able to lift up to 50 pounds. Jonathon is a 56-year-old Administrative Assistant II who was denied a promotion to Administrative Assistant III because of his medically supported inability to lift more than 10 pounds. His performance evaluations over the past 15 years have been average to above average, and there are other Administrative Assistant IIIs with various documented limitations that the school district has made accommodations for. Which of the following laws would be most applicable in this case?

   A. Title VII of the Civil Rights Act of 1964

   B. Americans with Disabilities Act

   C. Age Discrimination in Employment Act of 1967

   D. Fair Labor Standards Act of 1938

10. Which of the following describes a process in training, why it happened, and what can be done to make training better?

   A. Peer review

   B. Performance review

   C. After-action review

   D. Session review

Objective 02   Training Delivery Format

11. Learning conducted through electronic media often delivered through the Internet is called:

   A. Discussion

   B. Lecture

   C. Classroom

   D. E-learning

12. What is a key advantage of e-learning over classroom training?

   A. It allows trainees to learn at their own pace.

   B. It requires the trainee to learn spreadsheet skills.

C. There is no advantage to e-learning training.

D. It limits the number of participants.

13. Training that is designed to mimic certain processes, events, or scenarios of the participant's job is called:

   A. Lecture

   B. E-learning

   C. Simulation

   D. Classroom

14. Training that entails point scoring, competition with others, and rules of engagement is called:

   A. Lecture

   B. Classroom

   C. Gamification

   D. E-learning

15. When trainees act out a situation with a problem to solve, it is called:

   A. E-learning

   B. Role-playing

   C. Lecture

   D. Classroom

16. A common form of training that utilizes more experienced and skilled employees to train less skilled and experienced employees is called:

   A. E-learning

   B. Simulation

   C. On-the-job training

   D. Scenario

17. A method of teaching and delivering content to trainees in small and specific bursts is called:

   A. Microlearning

   B. Pop quiz

   C. Simulation

   D. Gamification

18. What is a key advantage of the microlearning training delivery method?

    A. It takes up a lot of space on network servers.

    B. It keeps people out of classrooms.

    C. It is required training to meet regulations.

    D. It delivers training just in time.

19. A training program that combines online digital media with traditional classroom methods is called:

    A. Simulation

    B. Blended learning

    C. E-learning

    D. Computer-based training

20. Which training delivery method is most useful when trainees lack any knowledge of the topic and may possess attitudes or habits contrary to desired objectives?

    A. Lecture

    B. E-learning

    C. Simulation

    D. Microlearning

Objective 03   Techniques to Evaluate Training Programs

21. The HR manager at a midsize software company is conducting a training evaluation after new product training recently took place. She is analyzing data from observations, interviews, tests, and surveys to see whether new skills were successfully transferred to the job. The analysis she is completing is an example of _____ evaluation.

    A. Behavior

    B. Results

    C. Learning

    D. Reaction

22. Your company has tasked the training department to determine whether and what learning has occurred after the in-depth 4-week series on achieving customer satisfaction. Which of the following would the best method to measure if and what learning has actually taken place?

    A. Pre/post-test

    B. Group discussion

    C. Lower turnover rates

    D. Increased employee morale

23. Which of the following would be most effective in evaluating training effectiveness?

   A. Small-group discussion

   B. Large-group discussion

   C. Measurement of enhanced job performance

   D. Grade-in-training program

24. Which of the following data-gathering methods would help the HR manager determine whether employee behavior has changed after training?

   A. Checklist

   B. 360-degree feedback

   C. Post-measure test

   D. ROI analysis

25. Prior to rolling out training on the use of the new point-of-sale (POS) system to all 50 stores, a beauty-supply store decides to train just those employees at its Pennsylvania location. Attendees are asked to evaluate the effectiveness of the training session, and HR uses the feedback to make modifications to future training sessions. Which of the following best describes this type of evaluation?

   A. Summative evaluation

   B. Trainer evaluation

   C. Formative evaluation

   D. Results evaluation

26. A trainer developed a new customer service development program to achieve organizational customer satisfaction goals. The trainer wants to measure the results of the training. Which of the following measures best describes the results evaluation method?

   A. A 360-degree feedback process is implemented after the training program.

   B. An online evaluation is distributed to participants to complete and return.

   C. The number of customer complaints is measured before and after the training.

   D. A test is distributed to participants before and after the training session.

27. An organization has implemented a mandatory service excellence training organization-wide. The desire of leadership is to see a change in customer service behavior after the training session. Essentially, they want to see employees smiling more in front of customers. Which question would best measure the success of training?

   A. Is there a change in performance observed in the participant after the training session?

   B. Is there a reduction in customer service complaints after the training session?

   C. Did the participants learn what the intended objectives were in the training session?

   D. Did the participants consider the training relevant and a good use of their time?

28. After the completion of a six-module computer-based test, participants are asked to complete a 30-minute online test. What aspect of summative evaluation is this?

   A. Learning

   B. Behavior

   C. Results

   D. Reaction

29. During the development phase of the purchase order module training of a financial software implementation, it was determined that participants would be secretly observed while doing their jobs at set intervals of 6 and 12 weeks. Trainers would use this information to determine whether training was effective and what supplemental training would need to be developed. What level of summative evaluation is described here?

   A. Learning

   B. Results

   C. Behavior

   D. Reaction

30. Determining the ROI of training is a task that requires a high degree of critical thinking skills. If an HR department can isolate the effect of training and assign a monetary value, the manager will be measuring training effectiveness at which Kilpatrick evaluation level?

   A. Reaction

   B. Learning

   C. Behavior

   D. Results

Objective 04   Career Development Practices

31. A process for identifying and developing new leaders who can replace leaders when they leave an organization is called:

   A. Strategic planning

   B. Contingency planning

   C. Goal setting

   D. Succession planning

32. A career development plan that allows upward advancement for employees without requiring they be placed into managerial roles is called:

   A. Transfer

   B. Promotion

C. Dual career ladder

D. Succession planning

33. An employee who works in the marketing department is assigned a few weeks of training in the finance department to gain knowledge of a different skill. This is known as what type of development practice?

A. Job rotation

B. E-learning

C. Transfer

D. Succession planning

34. When a more experienced person helps to guide a less experienced person, the relationship is known as:

A. Lecture

B. Transfer

C. Training

D. Mentorship

35. Encouraging development using formal education and providing financial assistance to accomplish educational goals are practices known as:

A. Employee development

B. Classroom training

C. Tuition reimbursement

D. Cross-training

36. A tool that helps employees think strategically about their career paths and how to meet career goals is called:

A. Self-assessment

B. Career mapping

C. Performance evaluation

D. Corrective counseling

37. A challenge in the traditional career ladder is when an employee reaches a point where there is no more upward mobility. This career challenge is called:

A. Career plateau

B. Career burnout

C. Career change

D. Career training

38. On-the-job projects or tasks that allow employees to develop new skills, knowledge, and competencies necessary for higher-level positions is called:

    A. Delegation

    B. Stretch assignments

    C. Career promotion

    D. Transfer

39. The development method of having an employee follow a colleague around all day is known as:

    A. Transfer

    B. Career ladder

    C. Job shadowing

    D. Job rotation

40. Which of the following is a key factor that can derail effective organizational career development plans?

    A. Lack of alignment between development programs and business strategy.

    B. Organizations are always too busy to implement career development plans.

    C. Career development programs are always not seen as value added.

    D. It's impossible to have a good program in a multigenerational workplace.

Objective 05   Performance Appraisal Methods

41. Which of the following is *not* true of a performance appraisal?

    A. Employees know exactly where they stand in relation to achieving goals and reaching performance milestones that contribute to career development and promotions.

    B. Managers gain insights into the motivations of the people working for them through the required conversations.

    C. Employees know how long they will be allowed to stay with the company.

    D. The organization retains motivated employees who understand their role and the roles of others in contributing to the overall success of the organization.

42. The _____ performance appraisal method lists all employees in a designated group from highest to lowest in order of performance.

    A. Competency-based

    B. 360-degree feedback

    C. Ranking

    D. Forced distribution

43. The _____ performance appraisal method is when ratings of employees in a particular group are disbursed along a bell curve, with the supervisor allocating a certain percentage of the ratings within the group to each performance level on the scale.

   A. Forced distribution

   B. Ranking

   C. 360-degree feedback

   D. Competency based

44. _____ is a process that collects information from the employee's supervisor, colleagues, and subordinates about an individual's work.

   A. 360-degree feedback

   B. Competency based

   C. Ranking

   D. Forced distribution

45. The _____ type of performance appraisal system focuses on performance as measured against specified qualities (as opposed to specific tasks or behaviors) that are identified for each position.

   A. 360-degree feedback

   B. Competency based

   C. Ranking

   D. Forced distribution

46. The _____ type of performance appraisal is a process through which goals are set collaboratively for the organization as a whole, various departments, and each individual member. Employees are evaluated annually based on how well they have achieved the results specified by the goals.

   A. 360-degree feedback

   B. Competency based

   C. Management by objectives

   D. Forced distribution

47. _____ appraisals list several factors, including general behaviors and characteristics (e.g., attendance, dependability, quality of work, quantity of work and relationships with people), on which a supervisor rates an employee.

   A. 360-degree feedback

   B. Competency based

   C. Graphic rating scale (GRS)

   D. Forced distribution

48. Which of the following is the most widely used form of a performance appraisal?

   A. 360-degree feedback

   B. Competency based

   C. Behaviorally anchored rating scales

   D. Graphic rating scale (GRS)

49. The _____ appraisal tool generally contains a set of specific behaviors that represent gradations of performance and are used as common reference points for rating employees on various job dimensions.

   A. 360-degree feedback

   B. Competency based

   C. Behaviorally anchored rating scales

   D. Graphic rating scale (GRS)

50. Which of the following is the main drawback of using the behaviorally anchored rating scales (BARS) system?

   A. It's expensive.

   B. Employees do not like the process.

   C. Managers do not like the process.

   D. The process is seen by executives as busywork.

Objective 06   Performance Management Practices

51. Which of the following is critical in achieving effective performance results?

   A. Setting clear and specific performance criteria

   B. Telling employees what to focus on

   C. Explaining to employees the vision of the company

   D. Teaching employees about the mission of their department

52. The process of establishing objectives to be achieved over a period of time is called:

   A. Discussions

   B. Goal setting

   C. Performance appraisals

   D. Microlearning

53. What is a SMART goal?

   A. Smart, measurable, attainable, realistic, target

   B. Smart, measurable, affirmation, realistic, time bound

   C. Smart, measurable, attainable, realistic, time bound

   D. Smart, meaningful, attainable, realistic, time bound

54. Who should be involved in the development of goals?

    A. Employee

    B. Employee's manager

    C. Employee and manager

    D. Manager's manager

55. When using a SMART goal, which of the following is a tenet of the *R* (realistic)?

    A. Concrete

    B. Resources

    C. Detailed

    D. Focused

56. When using a SMART goal, which of the following is a tenet of the *S* (specific)?

    A. Detailed

    B. Equipment

    C. Staff

    D. Skills

57. Achievable objectives should be:

    A. Outcomes based on goals

    B. Aspirations for the next 5 to 10 years

    C. Your vision for the future

    D. Something you can realistically do within the time frame set

58. What is the difference between a goal and an objective?

    A. Goals are narrow, and objectives are broad.

    B. Managers set goals, and companies set objectives.

    C. Goals are short term, and objectives are long term.

    D. Goals are long range, and objectives are short term.

59. When setting time-oriented objectives, all the following questions should be asked except which one?

    A. "What are the earliest—yet achievable and realistic—dates for this objective to be started and to be completed?"

    B. "Have I included these dates in the statement of the objective?"

    C. "Are there other projects/objectives that must be completed first? Are other individuals or objectives reliant on the completion of this objective?"

    D. "Do I have the resources to accomplish this objective?"

60. When setting realistic objectives, all the following questions should be asked except which one?

    A. "Have I included these dates in the statement of the objective?"

    B. "Do I have the resources to accomplish this objective?"

    C. "Do I need to rearrange my priorities to accomplish this objective?"

    D. "Is it possible to complete this objective?"

1. B	21. A	41. C
2. D	22. A	42. C
3. A	23. C	43. A
4. C	24. B	44. A
5. B	25. C	45. B
6. C	26. C	46. C
7. A	27. A	47. C
8. B	28. A	48. D
9. B	29. B	49. C
10. C	30. D	50. A
11. D	31. D	51. A
12. A	32. C	52. B
13. C	33. A	53. C
14. C	34. D	54. C
15. B	35. C	55. B
16. C	36. B	56. A
17. A	37. A	57. D
18. D	38. B	58. D
19. B	39. C	59. D
20. A	40. A	60. A

1. ☑ **B.** The Copyright Act of 1976 allows for an exception for employers who hire employees to create the original works as part of their normal job duties.

   ☒ **A, C,** and **D** are incorrect. These are not exceptions to the Copyright Act.

2. ☑ **D.** Title VII of the Civil Rights Act of 1964 requires that employers prohibit discrimination based on color, race, religion, national origin, and gender in all aspects of employment, including selection for training. This is likely the reason that the HR manager decided to discuss the training data with Sundar.

   ☒ **A, B,** and **C** are incorrect. **A** is incorrect because training difficulty experiences can't validly be correlated to racial or ethnic categories. **B** and **C** are incorrect because while retention and engagement should always be the concern of an HR manager, the specific statistic of number of minorities trained in the past 2 years was likely shared because of the legal impact that the perception of a lack of minority training opportunities can have on the company.

3. ☑ **A.** To stay compliant, an organization must develop a copyright policy and train employees on the intent and expectation that the organization will comply with the law.

   ☒ **B, C,** and **D** are incorrect. **B** is incorrect because nonprofit organizations are not exempt from copyright laws. **C** is incorrect because the fair use provision will only cover an excerpt that is extremely short, and a magazine article would not always qualify under that doctrine. Also, pages from a book cannot be copied and used without permission. **D** is incorrect because it is untrue that just because you are not charging for a training course that you can use copyrighted material at your discretion.

4. ☑ **C.** RSV Parachuting is required to provide a location that is readily accessible to employees with disabilities unless doing so would pose an undue hardship.

   ☒ **A, B,** and **D** are incorrect. ADA applies whether training is required or regardless of location where the training is held.

5. ☑ **B.** International Visions Publishing paid Sarah for this work as part of her normal job duties. An exception to the Copyright Act of 1976 is when an employee creates original work in the normal course of their duties, the employer is the owner of the copyright.

   ☒ **A, C,** and **D** are incorrect. These are all incorrect because of the reason stated earlier.

6. ☑ **C.** A utility patent protects new processes, machines, manufacture, and composition of matter.

   ☒ **A, B,** and **D** are incorrect. **A** is incorrect because a design patent is granted for the ornamental design of a functional item. **B** is incorrect because a plant patent protects an asexually reproduced variety of plants. **D** is incorrect because a re-issue patent is granted to correct an error in an already issued utility, design, or plant patent.

7. ☑ **A.** Works that are in the public domain do not require permission to be used.

   ☒ **B, C,** and **D** are incorrect. **B** is incorrect because the fair use provision refers to the copying of copyrighted material done for a limited purpose. **C** is incorrect because the work-for-hire domain refers to the U.S. legal principle that states that if an employee creates something in the normal course of doing work for their employer, the employer is considered the author of the work. **D** is incorrect because the U.S. Patent and Trademark Office is the agency that oversees all U.S. patents and trademarks.

8. ☑ **B.** Works for hire are protected for 120 years.

    ☒ **A, C,** and **D** are incorrect. **A** is incorrect because original works are protected for the life of the author plus 70 years. **C** and **D** are incorrect because they are not the numbers of years related to the Copyright Act of 1976.

9. ☑ **B.** Title I of the American with Disabilities Act requires employers with 15 or more employees to provide qualified individuals with disabilities an equal opportunity to benefit from the full range of employment-related opportunities available to others. It requires that employers make reasonable accommodation to the known physical or mental limitations of otherwise qualified individuals with disabilities, unless it results in undue hardship.

    ☒ **A, C,** and **D** are incorrect. **A** is incorrect because Title VII of the Civil Rights Act of 1964 does not mention disabled Americans. It prohibits unlawful employment practices with respect to race, color, religion, sex, or national origin. **C** is incorrect because if Jonathon were being denied this promotion because of age, then the Age Discrimination in Employment Act of 1967 may be applicable. The act prohibits denial of promotions and other unlawful employment practices on the basis of a person's age. **D** is incorrect because the Fair Labor Standards Act of 1938 establishes minimum wage, overtime pay, record-keeping, and youth employment standards affecting all full-time and part-time workers in the private sector and in federal, state, and local governments. The act makes no mention of employees with disabilities specifically.

10. ☑ **C.** An after-action review is a process for evaluating training effectiveness by analyzing what happened in training, why it happened, and what can be done to make training better.

    ☒ **A, B,** and **D** are incorrect. **A** is incorrect because a peer review is a review of your work by someone in the same industry (peer). **B** is incorrect because a performance review is a periodic evaluation of an employee's work performance. **D** is incorrect because a session review is not a commonly used term in the HR profession.

11. ☑ **D.** Learning conducted through electronic media often delivered through the Internet is called e-learning. Leveraging technology, e-learning is delivered in the form of distance learning, computer-based training (CBT), or web-based training (WBT).

    ☒ **A, B,** and **C** are incorrect. **A** is incorrect because discussion is a training delivery method that involves a two-way conversation between trainees and teacher. **B** is incorrect because lecture is a training delivery method that involves the teacher providing information verbally with minimal, if any, interaction with trainees. **C** is incorrect because classroom is training that occurs in a location where trainees and teacher are physically present.

12. ☑ **A.** One key advantage of e-learning over classroom training is that it allows trainees to learn at their own pace. In classroom training, the learning is directed at the teacher's pace.

    ☒ **B, C,** and **D** are incorrect. **B** is incorrect because trainees learning spreadsheets is very narrow. E-learning can teach unlimited topics and skills. **C** is incorrect because this statement is incorrect. There are many advantages to e-learning, including trainees learning at their own pace and being cost effective. **D** is incorrect because e-learning can reach a wide audience without space limitations.

13. ☑ **C.** Training that is designed to mimic certain processes, events, or scenarios that may occur on the participant's job is called simulation training. Simulation training is used by healthcare professionals, airline pilots, and military professionals to aid in the critical decision-making they need on the job.

    ☒ **A, B,** and **D** are incorrect. **A** is incorrect because lecture is a one-way information-sharing method typically occurring in a classroom. **B** is incorrect because e-learning is computer-based or online training that may not involve simulation training. **D** is incorrect because classroom training is in a physical room that may not include training that is based on scenarios that may occur on the job.

14. ☑ **C.** Training that entails point scoring, competition with others, and rules of engagement is called gamification. This method of training is designed to engage participants and motivate them to learn and achieve higher levels of learning.

    ☒ **A, B,** and **D** are incorrect. **A** is incorrect because lecture is a one-way information-sharing method typically occurring in a classroom. **B** is incorrect because classroom training is in a physical room that may not include training that is based on scenarios that may occur on the job. **D** is incorrect because e-learning is computer-based or online training that may not involve gamification.

15. ☑ **B.** Role-play (or role-playing) is when trainees act out a situation with a problem to solve. Typically, trainees are given a situation, character definitions, and a problem to solve.

    ☒ **A, C,** and **D** are incorrect. **A** is incorrect because e-learning is a course given online and rarely has the ability to allow role-playing. **C** is incorrect because a lecture does not allow for interactivity between teacher and trainees. **D** is incorrect because classroom training is in a physical room and does not necessarily involve role-playing as part of the training curriculum.

16. ☑ **C.** A common form of training that utilizes more experienced and skilled employees to train less skilled and experienced employees is called on-the-job training (OJT).

    ☒ **A, B,** and **D** are incorrect. E-learning, simulation, and scenario don't necessarily involve using more experienced and skilled workers to train those who are less skilled and experienced. While each of those can be used train people on the job, one of the most common forms of training seen today is on-the-job training that involves knowledge transfer from a more experienced employee to a less experienced employee.

17. ☑ **A.** A method of teaching and delivering content to trainees in small and specific bursts is called microlearning. Microlearning is becoming more popular because it delivers the right amount of information just as an employee needs it.

    ☒ **B, C,** and **D** are incorrect. **B** is incorrect because a pop quiz is unannounced and tests the trainee's knowledge of a particular topic. **C** is incorrect because simulation is a full training session that develops decision-making skills in a safe setting. **D** is incorrect because gamification is an online training delivery method that creates a sense of competition and accomplishment through learning.

18. ☑ **D.** A key advantage of the microlearning training delivery method is that it delivers information just in time, meaning it provides trainees with a small amount of information just as they need it.

 ☒ **A, B,** and **C** are incorrect. Too much server space, limited classroom space, and regulations do not apply to microlearning. Often microlearning can be delivered in small amounts of information online.

19. ☑ **B.** A training program that combines online digital media with traditional classroom methods is called blended learning. Blended learning is a way to keep the training interesting and maintain the trainees' attention throughout the session.

 ☒ **A, C,** and **D** are incorrect. Simulation, e-learning, and simulation training are all broad training terms. They may or may not include multiple forms of methods such as digital media and are also online or computer based.

20. ☑ **A.** Lecture is a training delivery method that is most useful when trainees lack any knowledge of the topic and may possess attitudes or habits contrary to desired objectives.

 ☒ **B, C,** and **D** are incorrect. E-learning, simulation, and microlearning often assume the trainee has a certain level of knowledge.

21. ☑ **A.** Conducting observations, interviews, tests, and surveys describes the behavior evaluation method.

 ☒ **B, C,** and **D** are incorrect. **B** is incorrect because an example of the results evaluation method is "a 20% decrease in customer complaints over a 12-month period," which answers the question of whether training had an impact on business results. **C** is incorrect because an example of learning evaluation is a pre/post-test that answers the question of whether learning took place. **D** is incorrect because an example of the reaction evaluation method is measuring the initial reaction of the training participants. It doesn't measure organization impact but provides feedback for the trainer as far as presentation of the material.

22. ☑ **A.** Pre/post-test is the most effective way to evaluate as it measures knowledge before the training takes place and then measures knowledge after the training has taken place.

 ☒ **B, C,** and **D** are incorrect. **B** is incorrect because a group discussion is not an effective way to evaluate effectiveness; it is subjective and not quantifiable. **C** is incorrect because lower turnover rates could mean that learning has taken place, but it is likely a small percentage of the reason why lower turnover is occurring. **D** is incorrect because employee morale could be because of a multitude of things, not an effect of learning conducted by the training program.

23. ☑ **C.** Measurement of enhanced job performance is the best way to measure training effectiveness as it can quantifiably measure the desired outcome of the training.

 ☒ **A, B,** and **D** are incorrect. **A** and **B** are incorrect because large- and small-group discussion cannot be quantifiably measured as a desired outcome of training. **D** is incorrect because an employee's grade in a training program is not necessarily a valid indicator of training success; it is merely an indicator of how well a participant can study rather than what they learned.

24. ☑ **B**. A 360-degree feedback process is a data-gathering method that supports Kilpatrick's behavior training effectiveness measure, which is level 3.

    ☒ **A**, **C**, and **D** are incorrect. **A** is incorrect because a checklist is a data-gathering method of level 1, reaction. **C** is incorrect because a post-measure test is a data-gathering method for level 2, learning. **D** is incorrect because an ROI analysis is a data gathering method for level 4, results.

25. ☑ **C**. Formative evaluation is done during the design phase of instructional design. It involves participants taking part in a training session and providing feedback. The evaluations are then reviewed, and the feedback is used to modify future training sessions.

    ☒ **A**, **B**, and **D** are incorrect. **A** is incorrect because summative evaluations happen at the conclusion of training. They may be at the reaction, learning, behavior, or results level. **B** is incorrect because trainer evaluation refers to the assessment of the trainer's delivery. **D** is incorrect because results evaluation is a method that compares an objective statement to an end result.

26. ☑ **C**. Capturing a before and after picture of the number of customer complaints is a results training evaluation type. Using key performance indicators such as customer complaints is a popular method of measuring training effectiveness.

    ☒ **A**, **B**, and **D** are incorrect. **A** is incorrect because the 360-degree feedback is typically used to measure behavior after the training session. **B** is incorrect because it measures a participant's impression of the training, which is associated with the reaction evaluation type. **D** is incorrect because pre- and post-tests are typically used for the learning evaluation method.

27. ☑ **A**. This method measures behavior changes after the training is complete, which is consistent with the behavior evaluation method.

    ☒ **B**, **C**, and **D** are incorrect. **B** is incorrect because this question is answered by using the results evaluation method. **C** is incorrect because this question is answered by using the learning evaluation method. **D** is incorrect because this question is answered by using the reaction evaluation method.

28. ☑ **A**. The learning evaluation method involves administering a test to participants to determine whether participants learned the material presented. It does not measure improvements in job performance due to training.

    ☒ **B**, **C**, and **D** are incorrect. **B** is incorrect because the behavior evaluation method measures training effectiveness at predetermined intervals. This does tell the trainer whether training transferred to effectiveness on the job. **C** is incorrect because the results evaluation method measures training effectiveness at predetermined intervals and what effect the training had on actual business performance. This also tells the trainer whether training transferred to effectiveness on the job. **D** is incorrect because the reaction evaluation method involves providing participants with a survey immediately after the completion of training. It does not measure improvements in job performance due to training.

29. ☑ **B**. The results evaluation method measures training effectiveness at predetermined intervals and what effect the training had on actual business performance. This also tells the trainer whether training transferred to effectiveness on the job.

☒ **A**, **C**, and **D** are incorrect. **A** is incorrect because the learning evaluation method involves administering a test to participants to determine whether participants learned the material presented. It does not measure improvements in job performance due to training. **C** is incorrect because the behavior evaluation method measures training effectiveness at predetermined intervals. This does not tell the trainer if training transferred to effectiveness on the job. **D** is incorrect because the reaction evaluation method involves providing participants with a survey immediately after the completion of training. It does not measure improvements in job performance due to training.

30. ☑ **D**. At the results level, HR uses quantifiable metrics to determine whether training has affected organizational goals. Some data-gathering methods at this stage include performance appraisals and ROI analysis.

☒ **A**, **B**, and **C** are incorrect. **A** is incorrect because reaction is the first level and is characterized by checklists and questionnaires. **B** is incorrect because learning is at level 2, and training effectiveness is measured with pre- and post-tests. **C** is incorrect because level 3 is behavior, and some data-gathering methods used include the number of critical incidents, simulators, 360-degree feedback, and so on.

31. ☑ **D**. A process for identifying and developing new leaders who can replace leaders when they leave an organization is called succession planning. Effective succession plans focus on a 1- to 3-year plan that prepares employees for future roles.

☒ **A**, **B**, and **C** are incorrect. **A** is incorrect because strategic planning refers to the overall plan for the organization. **B** is incorrect because a contingency plan refers to a pre-thought-out strategy for addressing scenarios that may disrupt normal business operations. **C** is incorrect because goal setting is individualized or organizational objectives to achieve. Goal setting may be an outcome of succession planning once skill gaps are identified as part of the succession plan process.

32. ☑ **C**. A career development plan that allows upward advancement for employees without requiring they be placed into managerial roles is called a dual career ladder. Typically ladders enable employees to choose advancement paths other than through the managerial path such as a technology knowledge achievement path. More recently, the concept of career lattices has been implemented in some organizations that allow employees to advance in numerous directions vertically or horizontally.

☒ **A**, **B**, and **D** are incorrect. **A** is incorrect because a transfer is simply moving from one job to another that may not be tied to a career development plan. **B** is incorrect because a promotion is certainly upward movement but may not be tied to a specific career development plan. **D** is incorrect because while a succession plan may involve career planning, it doesn't necessarily utilize dual career ladders to achieve objectives.

33. ☑ **A**. An employee who works in the marketing department and is assigned a few weeks of training in the finance department to gain knowledge of a different skill is an example of job rotation. This may also be called functional cross-training. Typically, a formalized

job rotation program enables employees to have a view of the entire business and may stretch out for a year or more.

☒ **B, C,** and **D** are incorrect. **B** is incorrect because e-learning refers to online training through the Internet. **C** is incorrect because a transfer is when an employee moves from one department or job to another and may not be tied to a formal job rotation or career development program. **D** is incorrect because succession planning is an overarching plan that strategizes the replacement of key leadership positions.

34. ☑ **D.** A relationship between a more experienced person that helps to guide a less experienced person is known as mentorship. An effective mentorship program enables key knowledge transfer to a less experienced person and helps mitigate what is sometimes called brain drain. Brain drain refers to what happens when someone with a great deal of experience and knowledge leaves an organization.

☒ **A, B,** and **C** are incorrect. Lecture, transfer, and training do not describe any relationship.

35. ☑ **C.** Encouraging development through the use of formal education and providing financial assistance to accomplish educational goals is a practice known as tuition reimbursement. This is also known as tuition assistance. Typically, these programs are offered with a promissory note requiring an employee commitment to the organization over a period such as 2 years. In addition, it typically requires an employee to provide receipts and transcripts to show proof of accomplishment to receive funds from the employer.

☒ **A, B,** and **D** are incorrect. **A** is incorrect because employee development is an overarching term that may or may not include tuition reimbursement. **B** is incorrect because classroom training may be part of the equation but is not the definition of tuition reimbursement; also, classroom training does not necessarily occur as part of a formal education program. **D** is incorrect because as with classroom training, cross-training does not occur as part of a formal education program. Cross-training is an internal method used to train employees on other functions and tasks that may fall outside of their normal role.

36. ☑ **B.** A tool that helps employees think strategically about their career paths and how to meet career goals is called career mapping. Career mapping provides a visual representation for both employer and employee and the various career development options available. It helps clear any ambiguity as to what career advancement opportunities exist within organizations.

☒ **A, C,** and **D** are incorrect. **A** is incorrect because self-assessment is a vague term that can be used for the purposes of coaching but also could be used in the performance evaluation process. **C** is incorrect because a performance evaluation refers to the feedback process of an employee's performance throughout a period of time. **D** is incorrect because corrective counseling is a tool or process used to correct a performance or behavioral issue.

37. ☑ **A.** A career plateau is when an employee reaches a point where there is no more upward mobility. A career may plateau when there are fewer upward positions available or there are more people competing for upward roles. Often this is where stretch assignments or dual career options come into play to keep plateau employees engaged.

☒ **B, C,** and **D** are incorrect. **B** is incorrect because career burnout is when someone grows weary of the role and career path that they are on. **C** is incorrect because a career change may be a result of a career plateau. **D** is incorrect because career training is an irrelevant term and does not apply to the definition of a career plateau.

38. ☑ **B.** On-the-job projects or tasks that allow employees to develop new skills, knowledge, and competencies necessary for higher-level positions are called stretch assignments. Stretch assignments can come in the form of leading a team to solve an organizational problem, or a specific task that may challenge an employee's existing knowledge of how things work. Providing stretch assignments is a great way to keep skilled employees engaged.

☒ **A, C,** and **D** are incorrect. Delegation, career promotion, and transfer are all generic terms that are not on-the-job training projects. As such, they are not relevant to a stretch assignment. Delegation refers to assigning a task to an employee and may not necessarily teach a new skill or knowledge. A promotion is the advancement to the next level in a career. Transferring refers to moving from one department or job to another.

39. ☑ **C.** Job shadowing is the development method of having an employee follow a colleague around all day. This is a career development method that enables an employee to see firsthand what it's like to work in a particular role.

☒ **A, B,** and **D** are incorrect. Transfers, career ladders, and job rotation are not relevant to the definition of job shadowing. **A** is incorrect because a transfer is moving from one job to another and perhaps without the benefit of job shadowing. **B** is incorrect because a career ladder refers to upward mobility. **D** is incorrect because job rotation refers to a systematic shift from one role to another for the purposes of expanding on organizational knowledge.

40. ☑ **A.** Lack of alignment between development programs and business strategy is a key factor that can derail effective organizational career development plans. To ensure long-term growth and development, it is critical to ensure career development plans are aligned with the direction the organization is going in.

☒ **B, C,** and **D** are incorrect. **B** is incorrect because while it's true that some organizations are too busy, this statement is not always true. **C** is incorrect because although it's true that sometimes programs not seen as value added can be hindrances, this statement is not always true. Well-crafted programs can engage employees and deliver future talent. **D** is incorrect because it is possible to have an effective career development program for a multigenerational workforce. If anything, there are more options today that appeal to different audiences. It takes a savvy professional to understand multigenerational needs and to develop a career plan that delivers long-term value.

41. ☑ **C.** Employees knowing how long they will be allowed to stay with the company is not true of a performance appraisal because most states are at-will employment; therefore, an employer would not promise or talk about how long an employee can stay at the company. At-will employment is a term used in U.S. labor law for contractual relationships in which an employee can be dismissed by an employer for any reason (that is, without having to establish "just cause" for termination) and without warning.

☒ **A, B,** and **D** are incorrect. **A** is incorrect because with performance appraisals employees know exactly where they stand in relation to achieving goals and reaching performance milestones that contribute to career development and promotions. The outcome of the performance appraisal is that employees will know what is needed to reach their milestones. **B** is incorrect because through performance appraisals managers gain insights into the motivations of the people working for them through the required conversations. **D** is incorrect because with performance appraisals the organization retains motivated employees who understand their role and the roles of others in contributing to the overall success of the organization.

42. ☑ **C.** Ranking is a performance appraisal method that lists all employees in a designated group from highest to lowest in order of performance.

    ☒ **A, B,** and **D** are incorrect. **A** is incorrect because a competency-based system focuses on performance as measured against specified competencies (as opposed to specific tasks or behaviors) that are identified for each position. A competency is the capability to apply or use a set of related knowledge, skills, and abilities required to successfully perform "critical work functions" or tasks in a defined work setting. Competencies often serve as the basis for skill standards that specify the level of knowledge, skills, and abilities required for success in the workplace as well as potential measurement criteria for assessing competency attainment. **B** is incorrect because 360-degree feedback is a process that collects information from the employee's supervisor, colleagues, and subordinates about an individual's work-related behavior and its impact. Other names for this approach include multirater feedback, multisource feedback, or group review. **D** is incorrect because forced distribution is when ratings of employees in a particular group are disbursed along a bell curve, with the supervisor allocating a certain percentage of the ratings within the group to each performance level on the scale.

43. ☑ **A.** The forced distribution performance appraisal method is when ratings of employees in a particular group are disbursed along a bell curve, with the supervisor allocating a certain percentage of the ratings within the group to each performance level on the scale.

    ☒ **B, C,** and **D** are incorrect. **B** is incorrect because ranking is a performance appraisal method that lists all employees in a designated group from highest to lowest in order of performance. **C** is incorrect because 360-degree feedback is a process that collects information from the employee's supervisor, colleagues, and subordinates about an individual's work-related behavior and its impact. Other names for this approach include multirater feedback, multisource feedback, or group review. **D** is incorrect because a competency-based system focuses on performance as measured against specified competencies (as opposed to specific tasks or behaviors) that are identified for each position.

44. ☑ **A.** The process that collects information from the employee's supervisor, colleagues, and subordinates about an individual's work is the 360-degree process.

    ☒ **B, C,** and **D** are incorrect. **B** is incorrect because a competency-based system focuses on performance as measured against specified competencies (as opposed to specific tasks or behaviors) that are identified for each position. **C** is incorrect because ranking is a performance appraisal method that lists all employees in a designated group from highest to lowest in order of performance. **D** is incorrect because forced distribution is a performance appraisal method when ratings of employees in a particular group are disbursed along a bell curve, with the supervisor allocating a certain percentage of the ratings within the group to each performance level on the scale.

45. ☑ **B.** The competency-based type of performance appraisal is a system that focuses on performance as measured against specified competencies/qualities (as opposed to specific tasks or behaviors) that are identified for each position.

☒ **A, C, and D are incorrect. A** is incorrect because 360-degree feedback is a process that collects information from the employee's supervisor, colleagues, and subordinates about an individual's work-related behavior. **C** is incorrect because the ranking performance appraisal method lists all employees in a designated group from highest to lowest in order of performance. **D** is incorrect because forced distribution is a performance appraisal method when ratings of employees in a particular group are disbursed along a bell curve, with the supervisor allocating a certain percentage of the ratings within the group to each performance level on the scale.

46. ☑ **C.** Management by objectives is a process through which goals are set collaboratively for the organization as a whole, various departments, and each individual member. Employees are evaluated annually based on how well they have achieved the results specified by the goals.

☒ **A, B, and D are incorrect. A** is incorrect because 360-degree feedback is a process that collects information from the employee's supervisor, colleagues, and subordinates about an individual's work-related behavior. **B** is incorrect because the competency-based type of performance appraisal is a system that focuses on performance as measured against specified competencies (as opposed to specific tasks or behaviors) that are identified for each position. **D** is incorrect because forced distribution is a performance appraisal method when ratings of employees in a particular group are disbursed along a bell curve, with the supervisor allocating a certain percentage of the ratings within the group to each performance level on the scale.

47. ☑ **C.** A graphic rating scale (GRS) appraisal is a number of factors, including general behaviors and characteristics (e.g., attendance, dependability, quality of work, quantity of work, and relationships with people), on which a supervisor rates an employee.

☒ **A, B, and D are incorrect. A** is incorrect because 360-degree feedback is a process that collects information from the employee's supervisor, colleagues, and subordinates about an individual's work-related behavior. **B** is incorrect because the competency-based type of performance appraisal is a system that focuses on performance as measured against specified competencies (as opposed to specific tasks or behaviors) that are identified for each position. **D** is incorrect because forced distribution is a performance appraisal method when ratings of employees in a particular group are disbursed along a bell curve, with the supervisor allocating a certain percentage of the ratings within the group to each performance level on the scale.

48. ☑ **D.** A graphic rating scale (GRS) is the most frequently used form of performance appraisal because the rating is usually based on a scale of three to five gradations (e.g., unsatisfactory, marginal, satisfactory, highly satisfactory, and outstanding). This type of system allows the rater to determine the performance of an employee along a continuum.

⊠ **A**, **B**, and **C** are incorrect. **A** is incorrect because 360-degree feedback is a process that collects information from the employee's supervisor, colleagues, and subordinates about an individual's work-related behavior and can be time consuming for all team members. **B** is incorrect because the competency-based type of performance appraisal is a system that focuses on performance as measured against specified competencies (as opposed to specific tasks or behaviors) that are identified for each position and can be labor intensive to create. **C** is incorrect because behaviorally anchored rating scales attempt to assess employee behavior rather than specific characteristics. The appraisal tool generally contains a set of specific behaviors that represent gradations of performance and that are used as common reference points, called anchors, for rating employees on various job dimensions. It can also be labor intensive and take a great deal of time to create and complete.

49. ☑ **C**. The behaviorally anchored rating scales appraisal tool generally contains a set of specific behaviors that represent gradations of performance and are used as common reference points, called anchors, for rating employees on various job dimensions.

    ⊠ **A**, **B**, and **D** are incorrect. **A** is incorrect because 360-degree feedback is a process that collects information from the employee's supervisor, colleagues, and subordinates about an individual's work-related behavior. **B** is incorrect because the competency-based type of performance appraisal is a system that focuses on performance as measured against specified competencies (as opposed to specific tasks or behaviors) that are identified for each position. **D** is incorrect because a graphic rating scale (GRS) is an appraisal that lists a number of factors, including general behaviors and characteristics (e.g., attendance, dependability, quality of work, quantity of work, and relationships with people), on which a supervisor rates an employee.

50. ☑ **A**. The main drawbacks of using a behaviorally anchored rating scale (BARS) system are that the process is expensive and it is time consuming because it is based on extensive job analysis and the collection of critical incidents for each specific job.

    ⊠ **B**, **C**, and **D** are incorrect. These are not tenets of the BARS system.

51. ☑ **A**. Setting clear and specific performance criteria is crucial to the success of the employee achieving effective performance results.

    ⊠ **B**, **C**, and **D** are incorrect. These items could be part of performance management, but they would not be critical to achieving effective performance results.

52. ☑ **B**. The process of establishing objectives to be achieved over a period of time is called goal setting.

    ⊠ **A**, **C**, and **D** are incorrect. **A** is incorrect because discussion is not a formal process of establishing objectives; it is too vague. **C** is incorrect because the process of establishing objectives to be achieved over a period of time is not a performance appraisal. A performance appraisal is usually an annual process where all performance is looked at and then noted, with a meeting to go over the results with a manager and an employee. **D** is incorrect because microlearning is an emergent learning strategy known for quickly closing skill and knowledge gaps.

53. ☑ **C.** SMART stands for smart, measurable, attainable, realistic, and time bound.

☒ **A, B,** and **D** are incorrect. **A** is incorrect because target is not correct, as the *T* should be time bound. **B** is incorrect because affirmation is not correct; the *A* should be attainable. **D** is incorrect because meaningful is not correct; the *M* should be measurable.

54. ☑ **C.** The employee and manager should be involved in the development of goals to ensure understanding and commitment.

☒ **A, B,** and **D** are incorrect. **A** and **B** are incorrect because just an employee or a manager alone would not be sufficient in creating goals. The process should include both. **D** is incorrect because a manager's manager would be out of touch for what the employee needs to do.

55. ☑ **B.** When speaking of the *R* (realistic) as it relates to a SMART goal, the employee would need to have the necessary resources available for the goal to be realistic.

☒ **A, C,** and **D** are incorrect. They are all incorrect because they are all tenets of *S*, which is specific.

56. ☑ **A.** When speaking of the *S* (specific) as it relates to a SMART goal, detailed would be a tenet of specific.

☒ **B, C,** and **D** are incorrect. They are tenets of the realistic component of a SMART goal.

57. ☑ **D.** An achievable goal should be something you can realistically do within the set time frame.

☒ **A, B,** and **C** are incorrect. These are the opposite of what an achievable goal should be.

58. ☑ **D.** Goals are long term, and objectives are short term.

☒ **A, B,** and **C** are incorrect. Goals are general, intangible, broad, and abstract, and long-term directions are generally set by senior leaders. Objectives are specific, measurable, narrow, and concrete. They are short-term plans generally set by managers to accomplish goals.

59. ☑ **D.** Having the resources to accomplish the objective would be a tenet of the *R* SMART goal, which is realistic.

☒ **A, B,** and **C** are incorrect. You would want to ask these questions for objectives that are time oriented.

60. ☑ **A.** This is a tenet of *T*, a time-oriented SMART goal.

☒ **B, C,** and **D** are incorrect. These are questions you would want to ask yourself for a realistic SMART goal.

6

Employee Relations

This functional area includes coverage of the following responsibilities and knowledge objectives:

- **01** Applicable laws affecting employment in union and nonunion environments, such as laws regarding antidiscrimination policies, sexual harassment, labor relations, and privacy (for example, WARN Act, Title VII, NLRA)

- **02** Employee and employer rights and responsibilities (for example, employment at will, privacy, defamation, substance abuse)

- **03** Methods and processes for collecting employee feedback (for example, employee attitude surveys, focus groups, exit interviews)

- **04** Workplace behavior issues (for example, absenteeism, aggressive behavior, employee conflict, workplace harassment, bullying)

- **05** Methods for investigating complaints or grievances

- **06** Progressive discipline (for example, warnings, escalating corrective actions, termination)

- **07** Off-boarding or termination activities

- **08** Employee relations programs (for example, recognition, special events, diversity programs)

- **09** Workforce reduction and restructuring terminology (for example, downsizing, mergers, outplacement practices)

This functional area weighs in as the second largest section on the Associate Professional in Human Resources (aPHR) exam at 16 percent of the test's questions. Employee relations focuses on understanding the methods organizations use to monitor and address morale, performance, and retention. It balances the operational needs of the organization with the well-being of the individual employee.

Employees are no doubt extremely important to any organization in any industry. Without them, companies cease to exist. Employees who are happier at work tend to be more productive, say good things about the company in the community, and refer family and friends to work there. The area of employee relations seeks to understand applicable laws affecting employment and employee and employer rights and responsibilities such as employment at will and privacy.

Employee relations affects the employees by imploring recognition, special events, and diversity programs, as well handling all off-boarding and termination events. HR is seen as the employee relation expert when it comes to matters of progressive discipline and workplace behavior standards.

Use this chapter to test your understanding of employee relation matters.

Objective 01   Applicable Laws Affecting Employment in Union and Nonunion Environments

1. John was offered a job at Rubber Makers International on the condition that he not join the union. His supervisor suggested that there might be a financial incentive after 90 days for adhering to this verbal contract. As the HR director, what concerns you most about this interaction?

    A. This is a potential violation of the Wagner Act.

    B. This is a potential violation of the Taft-Hartley Act.

    C. This is a potential violation of the Norris-LaGuardia Act.

    D. This is a potential violation of the WARN Act.

2. A company reaches an agreement with a labor union that states that only union members will be employed with the company. Which of the following laws makes it illegal to establish a closed shop except in the construction industry?

    A. National Labor Relations Act

    B. Wagner Act

    C. Taft-Hartley Act

    D. Labor-Management Reporting and Disclosure Act

3. Which of the following established that employers can be held vicariously liable for the actions of their employees in sexual harassment cases?

    A. *Burlington Industries v. Ellerth*

    B. *Meritor Savings Bank v. Vinson*

C. *Harris v. Forklift Systems*

D. *Oncale v. Sundowner Offshore Services, Inc.*

4. A mine workers' union provides free printing services to a candidate running for union president. Which entity would be most likely to investigate these activities?

   A. Office of Labor-Management Standards (OLMS)

   B. National Labor Relations Board (NLRB)

   C. Department of Labor (DOL)

   D. Department of Justice (DOJ)

5. A nonunion company implemented a freeze on raises for the next 3 years. The tool and dye makers at this plant are unhappy with this decision and begin meeting in small groups to discuss confronting management and possibly forming a union. Which of the following would most likely be used to lead a discussion with management?

   A. Labor Management Reporting and Disclosure Act

   B. Labor Management Relations Act and Wagner Act

   C. National Labor Relations Act

   D. Wagner Act and the Norris-LaGuardia Act

6. Farai, an African-American woman, resigns her position as account manager citing that she was harassed by the team leader who supervises her on a daily basis. The team leader has no authority to take tangible employment actions in regard to Farai. The sales director claims no knowledge of the events leading up to Farai's resignation. As the HR director, how would you advise senior management regarding the company's liability in this case?

   A. There is no liability because Farai did not report the incidents that led up to her decision to resign.

   B. The company is vicariously liable because the team leader meets the definition of a supervisor as established by the *Ellerth* and *Faragher* cases on sexual harassment.

   C. The company is not liable for the team leader's actions because the Supreme Court in *Vance v. Ball State University* narrowly defined *supervisor* as the person who may take tangible employment actions such as demotion or termination of employment.

   D. The company is liable because the team leader meets the definition of supervisor as established by the Equal Employment Opportunity Commission (EEOC).

7. Which of the following are covered under the Worker Adjustment and Retraining Act (WARN)?

   A. Employers with 50 or more employees

   B. Public and quasi-public entities only

   C. Employers with 100 or more employees

   D. Employers that employ only part-time employees

8. With respect to sexual harassment, what is quid pro quo?

   A. A favor for a superior in return for a special favor

   B. Hostile work environment

   C. Harassment directed at a female manager by a subordinate

   D. Exchange of sexual favors between peers

9. A healthcare consulting company is laying off 60 employees. They have a total of 180 full-time employees prior to the layoff. According to provisions of the WARN Act, what must they do?

   A. Nothing. The WARN Act does not apply to private companies.

   B. Notify the DOL State Dislocated Workers' Unit only.

   C. Nothing. The company is not closing.

   D. Notify employees 60 days prior because the company is laying off more than 33 percent of its workforce.

10. An African-American employee objects to his co-worker's display of the Confederate flag. He reports to HR that he feels like the display of this flag creates a hostile work environment. Which of the following legislation should HR consider while evaluating this complaint?

    A. National Labor Relations Act (NLRA)

    B. Fair Labor Standards Act (FLSA)

    C. Equal Employment Opportunity Commission (EEOC)

    D. Title VII

Objective 02 Employee and Employer Rights and Responsibilities

11. Which of the following describes an employment-at-will exception?

    A. Employee terminated after filing a workers' compensation claim.

    B. A candidate discusses salary range, job title, and level with HR.

    C. An employee on long-term disability leave is terminated from employment.

    D. An employee is fired for no stated reason.

12. All Meat Fast Food Company is in the process of setting in place guidelines for responding to reference checks of former employees. Which of the following strategies would you recommend?

    A. Provide dates of employment and title only

    B. Provide only job-related information that is truthful, clear, and supported by the former employees' evaluations

C. Provide dates of employment and the reason for discharge only

D. Provide job-related information that prevents the new employer from making a negligent hire

13. Gina's supervisor included the following on her last evaluation: "Keep up the good work and you'll have this job for life." How could this statement have affected the concept of employment at will?

A. Contract exception

B. Statutory exception

C. Public-policy exception

D. Fraudulent misrepresentation

14. Which data privacy principle refers to the employer demonstrating a need to collect data and obtaining the employee's consent prior to data collection?

A. Proportionality

B. Notice

C. Finality

D. Legitimacy

15. The good faith and fair dealing exception to employment at will establishes that:

A. The employment-at-will doctrine is null if an employee termination is without cause.

B. The employment-at-will doctrine is null when an employer makes a verbal promise to an employee.

C. The employment-at-will doctrine is null in cases where the employer performs unjust and malicious acts against the interest of the employee.

D. Employees can't be fired without cause when doing so violates a legal protection of employees.

16. When is the best time to adopt a union avoidance strategy?

A. When union wages outpace management wages

B. During union-organizing events

C. After a union is established at the employer site

D. Before a union is established at the employer site

17. An organization wants to remain union-free. The newly hired HR leader is expected to be proactive in union avoidance strategies. Which of the following actions would contribute significantly to the organization's objectives?

A. Implement a generous retirement plan

B. Give every employee a pay raise

C. Hire employees with a positive attitude

D. Conduct a vulnerability assessment

18. A company facilitates a program that assists ex-offenders with transitioning back into society. As the HR director, you want to ensure that the company does not hire anyone who may have had a violent past. What strategy would you put in place to prevent negligent hiring?

   A. Ensure that all employees submit to a review of motor vehicle records

   B. Ensure that all employee submit to a fingerprint-based criminal background check

   C. Ensure that all employees submit to a drug screen

   D. Ensure that employees are discharged immediately if violent behavior is exhibited

19. An employee notifies HR that he is a recovering alcoholic. One day he arrives at work impaired and his manager suspects that he is inebriated. The manager wants to fire him immediately citing the at-will-employment doctrine. What should be considered?

   A. Labor Relations Act and Drug Free Workplace Act

   B. American with Disabilities Act (ADA) and the Drug Free Workplace Act

   C. Drug Free Workplace Act and Civil Rights Act

   D. Civil Rights Act and American with Disabilities Act

20. A school district decides to purchase absence management software, which eliminates the need to have an administrative assistant contact and assign substitute teachers on a daily basis. The administrative assistant who currently performs this job was notified that her position will be eliminated at the close of the school year. She files a grievance with the secretarial union, which has an active contract with the district for the next 4 years. What is the likely outcome of an arbitration proceeding on this matter?

   A. The school district must retain the administrative assistant's current position until the end of the contract term.

   B. The school district would be engaging in an unfair labor practice by accepting this iron-clad contract.

   C. The union would be engaging in an unfair labor practice (ULP) if it does not guarantee the administrative assistant retain employment because she is a dues-paying member.

   D. The union would be engaging in an unfair labor practice if it tried to force the school district to keep this position.

Objective 03   Methods and Processes for Collecting Employee Feedback

21. Surveys that solicit employee ideas and feedback for improving the organization is called:

   A. Competitor surveys

   B. Manager surveys

   C. Opinion surveys

   D. Customer surveys

22. Small groups of employees who are asked questions by a facilitator regarding any element of the workplace are called:

   A. Focus groups

   B. Customer groups

   C. Peer groups

   D. Employer groups

23. A policy that removes all barriers that may discourage free communication between employees and managers is called:

   A. Solicitation policy

   B. Open door policy

   C. Social media policy

   D. Anti-harassment policy

24. A container with an opening that is used for collecting employee input, ideas, or suggestions for workplace improvements is called a(n):

   A. Offering box

   B. Voting box

   C. Mail box

   D. Suggestion box

25. Ensuring an effective use of the suggestion box that encourages employees' continuous participation involves which of the following key steps?

   A. Regularly checking the box for suggestions and communicate answers

   B. Making sure there are plenty of suggestion slips available

   C. Placing numerous suggestion boxes around the workplace

   D. Sending an e-mail and reminding everyone about the suggestion box

26. A style of management that involves managers randomly visiting employee workplaces and engaging in informal discussions about how things are going is called:

   A. Laissez-faire

   B. Manage by walking around

   C. Democratic

   D. Autocratic

27. Which of the following is a primary reason for conducting exit interviews?

   A. To follow company policy that requires conducting exit interviews

   B. To find out whether the exiting employee is planning to sue the company

   C. To learn reasons why the employee chose to leave the company

   D. To learn about the employee's career and development goals

28. An interview that helps managers understand why employees stay and why they may leave a company is called a(n):

   A. Group interview

   B. Job interview

   C. Exit interview

   D. Stay interview

29. Which of the following is a key advantage of adopting the stay interview process?

   A. It's proactive and may prevent employee turnover.

   B. It can develop a counteroffer when the employee leaves.

   C. It can learn why the employee is leaving the company.

   D. It can talk the employee into giving a longer resignation notice.

30. A short and frequent survey method that gives quick insight into any particular workplace topic is called a(n):

   A. Engagement survey

   B. Pulse survey

   C. Satisfaction survey

   D. Attitude survey

Objective 04 Workplace Behavior Issues

31. Unwelcome sexual advances, requests for sexual favors, and other verbal or physical conduct of a sexual nature is known as what type of misconduct?

   A. Drug use in the workplace

   B. Sexual harassment

   C. Retaliation

   D. Employee conflict

32. An employee's willful disregard of an order or direction given by a supervisor is known as:

   A. Forgetfulness

   B. Accidental injury

   C. Heavy workload

   D. Insubordination

33. Mean-spirited joking designed to highlight a co-worker's weaknesses or yelling at or sabotaging a co-worker is behavioral conduct known as:

   A. Bullying

   B. Nonsocial

C. Rudeness

D. Negative

34. What is a key step in preventing workplace bullying?

    A. Sending an e-mail to everyone requesting it to stop

    B. Ignoring the behavior so it will go away

    C. Training supervisors to discourage bullying

    D. Writing a human resource policy

35. Pervasive, long-lasting behavior or communication that makes it difficult to perform normal job duties or advance in a career progression is known as:

    A. Defensiveness

    B. Laziness

    C. Team playing

    D. Hostile work environment

36. Two employees breaking out in a yelling match in the workplace over local election results is an example of:

    A. Employee conflict

    B. Political campaigning

    C. Harassment

    D. Poor performance

37. Regularly staying away from work without good reason is known as:

    A. Absenteeism

    B. Presenteeism

    C. Tardiness

    D. Vacation

38. Moral principles that govern a person's behavior or way of conducting business is known as:

    A. Values

    B. Mission

    C. Ethics

    D. Policies

39. A list of rules that outline expectations of behavior in the workplace is called:

    A. Procedures

    B. Code of conduct

    C. Vision

    D. Policies

40. What federal regulation prohibits sexual harassment?

   A. National Labor Relations Act

   B. Occupational Safety and Health Act

   C. Fair Labor Standards Act

   D. Title VII of the Civil Rights Act of 1964

Objective 05   Methods for Investigating Complaints or Grievances

41. A top mistake in handling complaints or grievances is which of the following?

   A. Conducting a timely investigation

   B. Ensuring objectivity

   C. Ignoring the complaints

   D. Outsourcing the investigation

42. To help overcome "he said, she said" complaints, it is best to include which of the following key steps?

   A. Utilize aggressive tactics to intimidate one side to tell the truth

   B. Talk to friends of the complainant to see whether he or she lies

   C. Ask about the workplace gossip channels for information

   D. Gather physical evidence that might validate the complaint

43. What should HR do with the employee who complains regularly?

   A. Ignore the employee. Enough is enough.

   B. Investigate as if it were the first complaint.

   C. Delay the investigation because of other priorities.

   D. Conduct a shortened version of the investigation.

44. According to the Equal Employment Opportunity Commission (EEOC), which of the following factors will help determine witness credibility?

   A. Plausibility, demeanor, motive, corroboration, past record

   B. Likeability, how many friends the witness has, social networks

   C. Attendance history, relationship with supervisor and co-workers

   D. Employment tenure, personnel record history, number of EEOC cases

45. When choosing an investigator, it is important to be mindful of which of the following potential issues?

   A. Any conflicts of interest

   B. Attitude of the investigator

C. Where the investigator went to school

D. How the investigator asks questions

46. An employee's written rebuttal about a perceived violation of collective bargaining agreement or workplace dissatisfaction is known as a:

A. Memo

B. Suggestion

C. Presentation

D. Grievance

47. Most grievance procedures have what kind of common component?

A. Employees may initiate grievance procedures for safety concerns only.

B. The grievance procedure is used only in unionized companies.

C. Employees can discuss concerns with multiple levels of management.

D. The grievance procedure involves only the employee and supervisor.

48. In a nonunion employer, grievances may be subject to federal regulations under the National Labor Relations Act (NLRA) under what circumstances?

A. When the grievance is filed in HR within 14 days

B. When the grievance is deemed to be a protected concerted activity

C. When the grievance is sent to the chief executive officer

D. When the grievance is in written form

49. In a unionized workplace, if a grievance is filed during open labor negotiations, what key best step should HR take?

A. Acknowledge the grievance and begin to collect facts regarding the matter

B. Ignore the grievance because the negotiation process will resolve all issues

C. Submit the grievance to the National Labor Relations Board (NLRB)

D. Gather the unionized employees together and ask them for more information

50. What is an important feature of a good grievance-handling procedure?

A. Requiring employees to meet with the CEO

B. Requiring employees to write a report of issues

C. Being slow because it involves complicated steps

D. Being simple and easily understood by all

Objective 06   Progressive Discipline

51. An employer has discovered alleged misconduct from an employee that may lead to termination. What is the first step HR should take once discovering the alleged misconduct?

   A. Investigate promptly and thoroughly

   B. Move to termination

   C. Suspend the employee with pay pending investigation

   D. Suspend the employee without pay pending investigation

52. What is the main advantage to an organization using the alternative dispute resolution process?

   A. Decreases HR/management time spent on disputes

   B. Decreases costs related to conducting investigations

   C. Decreases conflict within the organization

   D. Decreases the number of disputes that might end up in court

53. What is the *best* way a manager can take preventative measures to avoid disciplinary action?

   A. Talk to each employee on a monthly basis

   B. Provide positive results on yearly performance reviews

   C. Lead the market with salary rates

   D. Set clear expectations

54. A restaurant employee in a nonunion environment has had repeated tardiness and customer complaints. What should the manager's *first* step be in the disciplinary process?

   A. Oral warning

   B. Termination

   C. Open dialogue and problem-solving

   D. Written warning

55. An employee has been caught using the company credit card for fraudulent purchases and profiting from the purchases in excess of $10,000. What step should HR recommend in this case?

   A. Oral warning

   B. Termination

   C. Problem-solving

   D. Written warning

56. An organization is being threatened with a lawsuit from an employee who was recently terminated. The claim is that the employer terminated him because of his race. However, the employer states that the termination was "for cause." Which of the following would be the best proactive approach to preventing a possible lawsuit?

   A. Have a written disciplinary policy and follow it uniformly

   B. Survey terminated employees to see whether they feel discriminated against

   C. Train all employees on cultural awareness and diversity

   D. Create a leadership development program on diversity awareness

57. An organization wants to establish a formal progressive disciplinary policy. Which of the following will most likely be included as disciplinary steps in the policy?

   A. Management discretion in issuing verbal, written, and final warnings

   B. A meeting with the employee, supervisor, and senior leader

   C. First, second, and third offense before taking action

   D. Minor, intermediate, and severe policy violations

58. An organization's leaders have decided that it must conduct a reduction in force (RIF) to remain financially viable. As the HR leader, you must decide how to select employees to lay off that would minimize any adverse impact. Which of the following are the best criteria to use for an RIF selection?

   A. Complaint or grievance history, troublemaker reputation, team-player status

   B. Popularity, co-worker friendliness, and team-playing activity

   C. Attendance, meeting participation, and project completion timeliness

   D. Job categories, prior disciplinary actions, seniority, and skill set

59. A supervisor has approached the HR leader expressing interest in terminating an employee because of ongoing performance issues. Which of the following is the best first step to take?

   A. Include the employee in a future reduction in force to minimize risk.

   B. In the termination meeting, tell the employee she is being laid off.

   C. Check the personnel record for documentation of previous and current performance issues.

   D. There are no actions to take because the performance issue will correct itself.

60. A nursing home employee who has been with the company for 5 years has been out of work for 4 consecutive days without notice of her status. The manager is writing up a disciplinary action for the time missed from work. The manager brings it to HR for review. What step should HR take at this point?

   A. Call the employee and let her know she has been terminated for no call/no show.

   B. Find out whether the employee has been out of work for FMLA, USERRA, or another state law–protected leave of absence.

   C. Have the manager deliver the disciplinary action with HR present.

   D. Find out whether the employee is missing work because of dissatisfaction with her position.

Objective 07 Off-boarding or Termination Activities

61. Which of the following is a *not* an HR best practice when terminating an employee or potentially terminating an employee?

   A. Look at all investigation materials and then make a decision

   B. Make a decision on the spot after the accusation has been made

   C. Document witness testimony

   D. Give outplacement information to employee

62. When is the best time to involve legal counsel during termination proceedings?

   A. When an employee voluntarily resigns

   B. After a performance improvement plan

   C. After a performance improvement plan and the employee asks to see copies of the HR files

   D. At the termination meeting

63. An employee brings a licensed firearm to work in a concealed carry state. The same employee had a verbal altercation with a vendor 2 weeks before and made statements regarding the company not doing business with this particular vendor because he might just have to hurt him. What is the best course of action for this company?

   A. Write the employee up because an immediate termination may result in an accusation of wrongful termination

   B. Terminate his employment immediately because he poses a threat to the workplace

   C. Suspend the employee pending investigation

   D. Write the employee up because these incidents have to be documented before termination can be considered

64. An employee filed a workers' compensation claim that cost the company almost $2 million. He is subsequently terminated. The employee believes the termination is related to the filing of the workers' compensation claim. What is this an example of?

   A. Wrongful termination

   B. Constructive discharge

   C. Hostile work environment

   D. Constructive dismissal

65. What is HR's strategic role in involuntary employee terminations?

   A. Conduct the termination meeting

   B. Counsel and coach before the meeting to ensure proper documentation and proper ways to conduct the actual meeting

   C. Ensure company property is returned

   D. Ensure that the employee's access to company technology is terminated

66. How should an involuntary employee termination be handled?

   A. Cite the work policy or rule violated.

   B. No explanation should be given. That will only lead to more problems.

   C. Give a written letter of all the rules broken.

   D. Read through the job description to discuss job functions.

67. Who should be present during an involuntary termination?

   A. The employee and a member of the HR team

   B. The employee and the manager

   C. The employee and the CEO

   D. The employee, the manager, and a member of the HR team

68. When an employee resigns from a company, which of the following essential part of the exit process will help the organization reduce future turnover?

   A. Distribution of HIPAA and COBRA notices

   B. Final payment of wages

   C. Exit interview

   D. Promotion of qualified employees to the vacated position

69. When should an investigation of employee misconduct take place?

   A. 1 to 2 months after accusation.

   B. No later than 72 hours after accusation.

   C. 1 to 2 weeks after accusation.

   D. An investigation is usually not needed.

70. When an employee provides a resignation stating her intention to leave the organization within a specified period of time, what is it called?

    A. Involuntary

    B. Lay-off

    C. Downsizing

    D. Voluntary

Objective 08   Employee Relations Programs

71. A CEO receives conflicting reports from HR regarding the reason for high turnover in the finance department. He wants to take a more hands-on approach to gathering feedback. Which employee engagement measurement tool would you recommend?

    A. Skip-level interviews

    B. Employee focus groups

    C. Employee surveys

    D. Exit interviews

72. Which of the following is the best description of the overall purpose of an effective employee relation program?

    A. Establish employee dispute resolution techniques

    B. Maximize employee performance

    C. Increase employee feedback to management

    D. Improve employee communication to management

73. HR wants to encourage the number of innovative ideas submitted by employees throughout the year. Which of the following employee relation strategies work best to achieve increased employee participation?

    A. List the names of people with the most innovative ideas on the company intranet

    B. Recognize employees who submitted innovative ideas and then recognize them in a public forum, preferably with an incentive that they find valuable

    C. List the names of employees with the most innovative ideas in the company newsletter

    D. Recognize employees with the most innovative ideas at their department's staff meeting

74. Which of the following helps to promote inclusion and diversity in the workplace?

    A. Recognition events

    B. Work/life balance programs

    C. Employee committees

    D. Job share

75. At the cornerstone of a positive employee relations strategy is _____.

    A. Mutual trust between employees and management

    B. Adherence to all common law statutes

    C. Exclusively communicating positive outcomes to employees

    D. Consistent vocalization of the company's nonunion message

76. Which of the following has the most impact on increasing employee productivity?

    A. Increase pay raises

    B. Review the total rewards package, including health benefits

    C. Increase the number of ways that an employee can be recognized

    D. Treat employees with dignity and respect

77. A procedure that provides clear guidance for supervisors and employees to systematically and fairly resolve complaints is known as which of the following?

    A. An open-door policy

    B. An HR resolution policy

    C. A grievance process

    D. A team-building process

78. What is the main benefit to a company using employee involvement (participative management) for companies and employees to receive mutual benefit?

    A. Employees' morale improves

    B. Provides positive results on yearly performance reviews

    C. Active participation fosters employee commitment

    D. Sets clear expectations for company

79. The following are all needed for a successful employee recognition program except which one?

    A. Funded sufficiently

    B. Timely

    C. Tax implications considered

    D. Taxes given to employees to offset costs

80. _____ is given immediately upon witnessing outstanding employee performance.

    A. A spot award

    B. An employee-of-the-month award

    C. A retirement award

    D. A length-of-service award

Objective 09   Workforce Reduction and Restructuring Terminology

81. Half of a manager's department is slated to be laid off. As the HR manager, how would you advise the manager to handle the layoff meeting?

    A. Because so many people are affected, a group meeting with time for questions would be most efficient.

    B. Hold a group meeting with the affected employees. Be sure to be completely clear regarding the conditions of the layoff. Show compassion.

    C. Hold individual meetings. Provide the employee with a clear message regarding the conditions of the layoff. Show compassion. Meet with the remaining employees to offer support.

    D. Hold individual meetings with affected employees. Give them a few weeks to properly say good-bye to their co-workers.

82. A contracted service supplied by companies that specialize in helping employees prepare for job searching after a layoff or job loss is defined as which of the following?

    A. Search firm

    B. Outplacement firm

    C. Brokerage firm

    D. Outsourcing firm

83. Which of the following describes what happens when a firm purchases the assets of another outright, resulting in expanding the acquiring company's employee base and facilities?

    A. Strategic alliance

    B. Equity partnership

    C. Joint venture

    D. Acquisition

84. Which restructuring driver is in place when a company is experiencing a reduction in revenue?

    A. Strategy

    B. Downsizing

    C. Structure

    D. Expansion

85. A company decides to close four of its North American locations in 3 months. The layoff affects 2,500 full-time employees, 200 of which are on leaves of absence. Is the organization subject to the provisions of the Worker Adjustment and Retraining Notification Act?

   A. Yes, because the WARN Act requires that organizations provide 60 days' notice to employees or their union representatives if the organization has 100 or more employees

   B. Yes, because the WARN Act requires that organizations provide 30 days' notice to employees or their union representatives if the organization has 100 or more full-time employees

   C. No, because the WARN Act is applicable only to companies that operate large manufacturing plants

   D. No, because the WARN Act applies in this case only if the employer counts the 200 employees who are on leave in its total employee count

86. A corporation determines that 10 percent of its workforce in specific business units has to be laid off in order for the company to remain profitable. As the HR director, you are asked to craft the criteria by which employees will be selected for layoff. What criterion would most likely be included?

   A. Performance as determined by performance appraisals of employees in the targeted business units

   B. The cost of a reasonable severance package

   C. The cost of outplacement services and unemployment compensation

   D. The company cost of COBRA to continue to provide health benefits for affected employees

87. The act of reorganizing legal, ownership, operational, or other organizational structures is called _____.

   A. Restructuring

   B. Reorganizing

   C. Divesting

   D. Strategy

88. Which of the following poses a risk to a company because of downsizing?

   A. Leadership realignment

   B. Increased resignations by valued employees

   C. Refocused training and development

   D. Job security

89. Which of the following describes a post-termination financial consideration or benefit that aids impacted employees in the areas of résumé writing and accepting job loss?

   A. Severance

   B. Divestiture

   C. Retraining

   D. Outplacement

90. When must an employer pay severance?

   A. Never

   B. In right-to-work states

   C. To union members

   D. When there's an executed contract between the employee and the employer where severance terms were detailed

1. C	31. B	61. B
2. C	32. D	62. C
3. A	33. A	63. C
4. A	34. C	64. A
5. B	35. D	65. B
6. C	36. A	66. A
7. C	37. A	67. D
8. A	38. C	68. C
9. D	39. B	69. B
10. D	40. D	70. D
11. A	41. C	71. A
12. B	42. D	72. B
13. A	43. B	73. B
14. D	44. A	74. C
15. C	45. A	75. A
16. D	46. D	76. D
17. D	47. C	77. C
18. B	48. B	78. C
19. B	49. A	79. D
20. D	50. D	80. A
21. C	51. A	81. C
22. A	52. D	82. B
23. B	53. D	83. D
24. D	54. C	84. B
25. A	55. B	85. A
26. B	56. A	86. A
27. C	57. A	87. A
28. D	58. D	88. B
29. A	59. C	89. D
30. B	60. B	90. D

1. ☑ **C.** Even though verbal, this is potentially an example of a yellow-dog contract, which was deemed unenforceable by the Norris-LaGuardia Act. A yellow-dog contract is one in which an employer makes an offer of employment contingent upon the employee agreeing not to join a union.

   ☒ **A, B,** and **D** are incorrect. **A** is incorrect because the Wagner Act, also known as the National Labor Relations Act (NLRA), protects the rights of employees to form unions and collectively bargain for wages, benefits, hours, and other working conditions. **B** is incorrect because the Labor Management Relations Act (LMRA), also known as the Taft-Hartley Act, provides the employer with the right to promote an anti-union message in the workplace as long as the employer is not threatening employees or bribing employees to discourage them from forming a union. **D** is incorrect because the Worker Adjustment and Retraining Notification Act (WARN) requires that employers provide notice 60 days in advance of covered plant closings during covered mass layoffs.

2. ☑ **C.** The Taft-Hartley Act amended the National Labor Relations Act and outlawed closed shops. A closed shop is a company where employees are required to join a union as a condition of employment.

   ☒ **A, B,** and **D** are incorrect. **A** and **B** are incorrect because the National Labor Relations Act, also known as the Wagner Act, established the basic rights of employees to form unions. **D** is incorrect because the Labor-Management Reporting and Disclosure Act established reporting requirements for unions, union officers, employees, and employers; set standards for electing union officers; and established safeguards for protecting the assets of labor organizations.

3. ☑ **A.** *Burlington Industries v. Ellerth* established that an employer can be held responsible for the unlawful acts of its employees. This is a legal concept known as vicarious liability.

   ☒ **B, C,** and **D** are incorrect. **B** and **C** are incorrect because the issue in both *Meritor Savings Bank v. Vinson* and *Harris v. Forklift Systems* is the existence of a hostile work environment with sexual harassment. **D** is incorrect because *Oncale v. Sundownder Offshore Services, Inc.* established the standard for same-sex sexual harassment.

4. ☑ **A.** The Office of Labor-Management Standards (OLMS) provides oversight for the Labor-Management Relations Act (LMRA). Title IV of the LMRA establishes that union funds may not be used to support the candidacy of any candidate.

   ☒ **B, C,** and **D** are incorrect. **B** is incorrect because the National Labor Relations Board (NLRB) provides oversight for the National Labor Relations Act (NLRA). **C** is incorrect because the Department of Labor (DOL) provides oversight in multiple areas; the most common area of oversight is the proper execution of the Fair Labor Standards Act (FLSA). Additionally, since the OLMS is part of the DOL, the DOL has much broader authority. **D** is incorrect because the Department of Justice (DOJ) would not be the entity most likely to be a first responder to a situation like this. At some point, the DOJ may be involved depending on the complexity of the violation.

5. ☑ **B.** The Labor Management Relations Act (LMRA), also known as the Taft-Hartley Act, provides the employer with the right of employers to promote an anti-union message in the workplace so long as the employer is not threatening employees or bribing employees to discourage them from forming a union. The Wagner Act, also known as National Labor Relations Act (NLRA), protects the rights of employees to form a union and collectively bargain for wages, benefits, hours, and other working conditions. As the HR leader, it would be your responsibility in this case to arm management with this knowledge and recommend a dual approach to resolution. Management should carefully craft with their legal representatives a message that expresses the company's position on unions but be mindful that they should not infiltrate any attempt for the tool and dye makers to organize and bargain collectively.

   ☒ **A, C,** and **D** are incorrect. **A** is incorrect because the Labor-Management Reporting and Disclosure Act established reporting requirements for unions, union officers, employees, and employers; set standards for electing union officers; and established safeguards for protecting the assets of labor organizations. **C** is incorrect because the NLRA or Wagner Act takes into account only one side of this situation. The employer should also be proactive and exercise its right to clarify its position on the existence of unions in the workplace. **D** is incorrect because the Norris-LaGuardia Act, also known as the Anti-Injunction Bill, outlawed a specific kind of employment contract called yellow-dog contracts. Yellow-dog contracts are where employers make it a condition of employment that workers not join a union. Yellow-dog contracts have been determined as unenforceable in a court of law.

6. ☑ **C.** The Supreme Court decision in *Vance v. Ball State University* established that a person is a supervisor for the purposes of vicarious liability in cases of unlawful harassment under Title VII only if that person can take tangible employment actions against the accuser. The Supreme Court rejected the Equal Employment Opportunity Commission (EEOC) guidance that a supervisor may be an individual who has authority to direct an employee's daily work activities. However, the employee still maintains the right to sue the company for being negligent in preventing the harassment.

   ☒ **A, B,** and **D** are incorrect. **A** is incorrect because the assumption that Farai did not report the incidents is irrelevant. Also, the scenario does not indicate that she did not report the incidents, only that the sales director claims no knowledge of a report. Farai could have reported directly to HR or some other supervisory authority. **B** is incorrect because the *Ellerth* and *Faragher* cases, taken together, established that whether an employer is vicariously liable depends on what happened to the plaintiff and if the harassment resulted in tangible employment actions being taken. **D** is incorrect because the EEOC guidance is only guidance, but Title VII did not define *supervisor* for the purposes of unlawful harassment.

7. ☑ **C.** Generally, employers must have at least 100 employees to be covered by the WARN Act.

   ☒ **A, B,** and **D** are incorrect. **A** is incorrect because employers with 50 employees are not covered by the WARN Act. **B** is incorrect because WARN covers private, for-profit employers; private, nonprofit employers; and public and quasipublic entities that operate in a commercial context and are separately organized from the regular government. **D** is incorrect because part-time employees are not counted in the total number of employees with respect to WARN coverage.

8. ☑ **A.** *Quid pro quo* translates to "this for that" and describes anytime a superior demands a sexual favor of a subordinate in return for special favors such as raises or promotions.

   ☒ **B, C,** and **D** are incorrect. **B** is incorrect because hostile work environment is another type of sexual harassment. **C** is incorrect because it describes a form of bullying or illegal harassment but not sexual harassment. **D** is incorrect because an exchange of sexual favors between peers does not describe quid pro quo; however, if one of the parties is nonconsensual, it could be sexual harassment or sexual assault, which isn't necessarily rape but would include rape.

9. ☑ **D.** This layoff will affect more than 33 percent of the current workforce. In this case, employees must receive 60 days' notice prior to the layoff occurring. If the employer fails to do so, the employer may be fined.

   ☒ **A, B,** and **C** are incorrect. **A** is incorrect because WARN applies to private, for-profit employers; private, nonprofit employers; and public and quasipublic entities that operate in a commercial context and are separately organized from the regular government. **B** is incorrect because employees must also receive notification. **C** is incorrect because employees must be notified at least 60 days in advance of layoffs for both plant closings and layoffs that affect 33 percent or more of the workforce.

10. ☑ **D.** Title VII prohibits severe, pervasive, unwelcomed offensive conduct, such as racial or ethnic slurs, racial "jokes," derogatory comments, or other verbal or physical conduct based on an individual's race/color. Of the choices listed, Title VII addresses the creation of a hostile work environment for protected classes.

    ☒ **A, B,** and **C** are incorrect. **A** is incorrect because the NLRA protects the rights of employees to form unions and collectively bargain for wages, benefits, hours, and other working conditions. **B** is incorrect because the FLSA establishes minimum wage, overtime pay, record-keeping, and youth employment standards affecting employees in the private sector and in federal, state, and local governments. **C** is incorrect because the EEOC is the agency responsible for enforcing federal laws that make it illegal to discriminate against a job applicant or an employee because of the person's race, color, religion, sex (including pregnancy, gender identity, and sexual orientation), national origin, age (40 or older), disability, or genetic information.

11. ☑ **A.** Terminating an employee after filing a workers' compensation claim is a public policy exception to the at-will-employment doctrine.

    ☒ **B, C,** and **D** are incorrect. **B** is incorrect because discussing salary range, job title, and level is not an oral contract that would be considered an implied-contract exception to the at-will-employment doctrine. **C** is incorrect because an employee can be terminated while on any leave. This is not an exception to the at-will doctrine. **D** is incorrect because firing an employee for no reason is central to the employment-at-will doctrine.

12. ☑ **B.** Employers can share any information that is truthful, clear, and supported. An employer is covered by the concept of qualified privilege. Qualified privilege is a provision available under the law of libel and slander that allows a company to be immune from prosecution if the libelist of the slanderous act is committed in the performance of a legal or moral duty and is free of malice and words uttered or statements written are done in good faith.

☒ **A, C,** and **D** are incorrect. These are all good strategies. However, they are limited and do not allow the employer to give a meaningful reference. **D** also is so generic that the supervisor responding to the reference check may overstate information that could potentially cause the company to be guilty of defamation, which is any communication that willfully damages an employee's reputation and prevents the employee from obtaining employment or other benefits.

13. ☑ **A.** Gina's supervisor may have created an implied contract with this statement. Employment at will, in the purest sense, means that the employer may terminate employment with or without notice and for good reason or no reason at all. The employee, in turn, may resign with or without reason and for good reason or no reason at all. By making the statement "Keep up the good work and you'll have this job for life," Gina's supervisor may have invalidated the at-will doctrine.

☒ **B, C,** and **D** are incorrect. **B** is incorrect because a statutory exception exists if legislation changes the terms of the employment relationship. **C** is incorrect because a public-policy exception exists when the application of the at-will doctrine conflicts with public policy. For example, an employee should not be discharged under the at-will doctrine if she refuses to commit perjury by lying to protect an employer under investigation for racketeering. **D** is incorrect because fraudulent misrepresentation exists when an employer entices an employee to work for the organization by presenting the company in a more stable condition than currently exists. For example, if someone accepts a position based on the employer telling him that he would be promoted to general manager in 1 year while knowing that the company plans to close in 3 months, this is fraudulent misrepresentation.

14. ☑ **D.** Legitimacy is a data privacy principle that refers to the employer demonstrating a need to collect data and obtaining the employee's consent prior to data collection.

☒ **A, B,** and **C** are incorrect. **A** is incorrect because proportionality is a data privacy principle that refers to the collection of relevant and sufficient data only. **B** is incorrect because notice is a data privacy principle that refers to providing employees with proper notice that the employer is requesting employee data. **C** is incorrect because finality is a data privacy principle that refers to the employer ensuring the employee that the data will be used for a specific and limited purpose.

15. ☑ **C.** The good faith and fair dealing exception to the employment at will restricts against any employer action that is deemed malicious.

☒ **A, B,** and **D** are incorrect. **A** is incorrect because the employment-at-will doctrine allows for the termination of employment without cause. **B** is incorrect because the employment-at-will doctrine is null when an employer makes a verbal promise to an employee under the implied contract exception. **D** is incorrect because the public policy exception states that employees can't be fired when doing so violates a legal protection of the employee's such as being terminated after filing a workers' compensation claim.

16. ☑ **D**. The best time to adopt and promote a union avoidance strategy is before a union forms at a company.

☒ **A, B**, and **C** are incorrect. When union wages outpace management wages, during union-organizing events, and after a union is already established at the employer site are controversial times to adopt a union avoidance strategy. It may be perceived as adopting the strategy to directly defy the presence of a union or union-organizing activities, which is against the law. Additionally, **B** may also be an unfair labor practice (ULP).

17. ☑ **D**. Conducting a vulnerability assessment is a proactive strategy that provides an organization's leaders with insights into areas in which they are weak and susceptible to union organization attempts. A vulnerability assessment includes both internal and external insights that give an organization the ability to craft smart strategies to avoid union organizing.

☒ **A, B**, and **C** are incorrect. **A** is incorrect because implementing a retirement plan is not the best proactive action to take. In addition, giving benefits if you feel organizing is going on opens the organization to the charge of an unfair labor practice (ULP). **B** is incorrect because while giving everyone a pay raise may make everyone happy in the short term, it is not practical. In addition, union-organizing activity uses multiple platforms to convince employees to sign authorization cards, such as job security. There is a better proactive approach to take. **C** is incorrect because while trying to hire all employees with a positive attitude is noble, it is not an effective approach to union avoidance. This is particularly true when the work environment changes frequently, as do employee attitudes.

18. ☑ **B**. A fingerprint-based criminal background check will likely reveal any convictions for violent crimes such as battery. The HR director can then use this information to assist in determining whether to move forward with onboarding this candidate. The candidate must agree in writing prior to the background check being run, and the request can be made only after an offer of employment is extended.

☒ **A, C**, and **D** are incorrect. **A** and **C** are incorrect because a drug screen or motor vehicle records may or may not be relevant to performing this job effectively. However, in a business built on re-acclimating violent offenders into society, it is important to consider each potential new hire's criminal background as it relates to convictions for violent crimes. **D** is incorrect because this would occur after a person is already employed, so it has no bearing on the initial employment decision and therefore does not prevent negligent hiring.

19. ☑ **B**. Alcoholism is considered a disability under the provisions of the Americans with Disabilities Act (ADA). Additionally, an employer needs to balance its compliance with ADA with the need to maintain a drug-free workplace for the safety of all employees. While the employee appears under the influence of alcohol, a drug and alcohol test may also reveal the presence of illegal drugs. The employer, in this case, has the right to require a drug and alcohol test before that employee can be determined fit to return to work. In addition, the HR representative should not move forward with a termination if the test results reveal that the employee was under the influence of alcohol since the employee

reported he suffers from alcoholism. Rather, the employer needs to consider engaging in the interactive process to determine a reasonable accommodation once the employee is declared fit to return to work.

☒ **A**, **C**, and **D** are incorrect. **A** is incorrect because the National Labor Relations Act (NLRA) establishes the parameters for the creation and support of a union environment. **C** and **D** are incorrect because the Civil Rights Act does not speak to alcoholism.

20. ☑ **D**. If the union tried to force this issue, it would be guilty of an unfair labor practice (ULP) known as featherbedding. Featherbedding is a labor union practice where the union requires the employer to pay for the performance of unnecessary work to protect the job of its member.

☒ **A**, **B**, and **C** are incorrect. **A** and **C** are incorrect because the school district has no obligation to retain a specific employee simply because the person is a dues-paying member. **B** is incorrect because an iron-clad contract or yellow-dog contract is one that requires an employee to join a union as a condition of employment.

21. ☑ **C**. A survey that solicits employee ideas and feedback for improving the organization is called an opinion survey. It can also be called an employee engagement or employee satisfaction survey. Often these surveys are conducted periodically, and the results are compared to industry benchmark data to assess the level of employee engagement and determine improvement opportunities.

☒ **A**, **B**, and **D** are incorrect. Competitor, manager, and customer surveys do not solicit feedback directly from employees.

22. ☑ **A**. Small groups of employees who are asked questions by a facilitator are called focus groups. These are typically structured discussions that are facilitated and are designed to get feedback about specific elements of the workplace.

☒ **B**, **C**, and **D** are incorrect. Customer groups and employer groups are not employees. Peer groups are a group of people usually with similarities such as age, background, or social status.

23. ☑ **B**. A policy that removes all barriers that may discourage free communication between employees and managers is called an open-door policy. An open-door policy is usually adopted within companies to encourage open dialogue between managers and employees. When practiced consistently throughout the organization, this ultimately makes it safe to provide feedback to one another without fear of reprisal.

☒ **A**, **C**, and **D** are incorrect. Often these policies restrict what an employee can do or say in the workplace. A solicitation policy provides expectations on solicitation and distribution activities on company premises. A social media policy provides guidance and expectations around an employee's use of social network platforms such as Facebook, LinkedIn, or Twitter. An anti-harassment policy provides expectations around harassment in the workplace.

24. ☑ **D**. A container with an opening that is used for collecting employee input, ideas, or suggestions for workplace improvements is called a suggestion box. This can be a physical box, or today employers may be utilizing an e-suggestion box whereby employees can provide suggestions or feedback through electronic means.

☒ **A**, **B**, and **C** are incorrect. An offering, voting, or mailbox is not specific to the employee feedback process.

25. ☑ **A**. Regularly checking the box for suggestions and communicating answers to employees are key steps to ensuring employees' continuous participation in providing feedback. There are stories among HR circles of suggestion boxes that are forgotten and not checked eventually being filled with garbage, chewed gum, and candy wrappers to be discovered years later. Like any effective feedback process, it requires employer commitment of fresh two-way communication to keep the program alive and meaningful.

☒ **B**, **C**, and **D** are incorrect. Making paper slips and multiple boxes available and sending e-mails is a small component to an effective employee feedback program. However, these alone do not rise to an effective feedback program like fresh and meaningful interactive activities do.

26. ☑ **B**. A style of management that involves managers randomly visiting employee workplaces and engaging in informal discussions about how things are going is called manage by walking around (MBWA). This style is also called *manage by wondering around* or sometimes *rounding*. Having informal conversations with employees in their workspace often can yield important information about employee, equipment, or resource needs to ensure effective operations.

☒ **A**, **C**, and **D** are incorrect. **A** is incorrect because laissez faire refers to a management style that is opposed to government regulation and prefers little to no interference to operating. **C** is incorrect because a democratic style allows the employees to participate in the organizational decision-making process, and **D** is incorrect because an autocratic management style is one where the manager makes unilateral decisions without much regard to feedback from others.

27. ☑ **C**. A primary reason for conducting exit interviews is to learn why the employee chose to leave the company. Ideally, exit interviews are often conducted after the employee has given notice and before they actually leave the company. The exit interview seeks to understand what caused the employee to leave such as pay, benefits, supervisory, or co-worker relationship issues.

☒ **A**, **B**, and **D** are incorrect. **A** is incorrect because simply following a policy is not generally considered a key reason for why exit interviews are conducted. **B** is incorrect because finding out whether an employee is going to sue a company is not why exit interviews are utilized. **D** is incorrect because when an employee gives their notice to resign, learning about an employee's career and development goals is too late.

28. ☑ **D**. An interview that helps managers understand why employees stay and/or leave a company is called a stay interview. A stay interview asks employees before they give resignation notices key questions that are designed to help managers determine why they may want to leave. This enables managers to proactively put into place improvements that would encourage key employees to stay.

☒ **A**, **B**, and **C** are incorrect. Group interviews are too broad and may not apply to employees. Job interviews are conducted for applicants who are interested in working for the company. Exit interviews are just the opposite of stay interviews. Exit interviews are conducted after an employee has given a resignation notice.

29. ☑ **A.** A key advantage of adopting the stay interview process is that it's proactive and may prevent employee turnover. The stay interview finds out from key employees why they would be tempted to leave a company before they have given a resignation notice. This enables the employer to put into place improvements ultimately encouraging employees to stay.

☒ **B, C,** and **D** are incorrect. Each of these steps may be implemented upon the resignation notice of an employee. A counteroffer, finding out why they are leaving, and talking them into extending their notice of resignation may occur after the employee has decided to leave.

30. ☑ **B.** A short and frequent survey method that gives quick insight into any particular workplace topic is called a pulse survey. Pulse surveys minimize the complexity and number of questions asked of employees. The pulse survey is short, comprising 5 to 10 questions focused on a specific area of the workplace.

☒ **A, C,** and **D** are incorrect. Engagement, attitude, and satisfaction surveys are typically longer, more complex surveys that are conducted annually or over longer periods of time.

31. ☑ **B.** Unwelcome sexual advances, requests for sexual favors, and other verbal or physical conduct of a sexual nature are known as sexual harassment. The harasser can be any gender and be an organization's supervisor, co-worker, or those who are not an employee of the company such as a vendor or customer.

☒ **A, C,** and **D** are incorrect. While drug use in the workplace, retaliation, and employee conflict are certainly workplace issues, they may not be sexual infractions as sexual harassment implies. However, retaliation could be a subset of harassment and is considered equally egregious under the law.

32. ☑ **D.** An employee's willful disregard of an order or direction given by a supervisor is known as insubordination. At times managers may get confused as to what rises to the level of insubordination, especially when frustrated. A good way to remember this is that there is a difference between "can't do" and "won't do." When an employee can't do something, it may mean they lack the skills, knowledge, or abilities to do something and may need additional training. But when an employee "won't do" something, so long as it is not safety related, it might rise to the level of insubordination. Most HR professionals may want to involve legal counsel before terminating an employee to assess risk.

☒ **A, B,** and **C** are incorrect. Forgetfulness, accidental injury, and a heavy workload may not be intentional or showing willful disregard of an order.

33. ☑ **A.** Mean-spirited joking designed to highlight a co-worker's weaknesses or yelling at or sabotaging a co-worker is behavioral conduct known as bullying. This can also be called aggressive behavior. Bullying behavior can show its face in a variety of ways such as threatening, humiliating, intimidating, or sabotaging co-workers. If unchecked, pervasive bullying in the workplace can reduce productivity, create low morale, and produce high turnover.

☒ **B**, **C**, and **D** are incorrect. Nonsocial, rudeness, and negative are not necessarily mean-spirited actions or behaviors. Being nonsocial may mean an employee is simply introverted and prefers to work alone than with a team of people. Being rude is a subjective adjective that does not necessarily involve mean-spirited joking. For example, people can be considered "rude" when they don't respond to e-mails. Being negative also may not necessarily involve mean-spirited behavior.

34. ☑ **C**. A key step in preventing workplace bullying is to train supervisors to discourage bullying. Typically it's the first-line supervisors who know when bullying is occurring and can respond quicker at minimizing the problem. But to be effective, the best supervisors are trained on how to identify bullying and what to do about it when they see it.

☒ **A**, **B**, and **D** are incorrect. None of these is an effective step in combating workplace bullying.

35. ☑ **D**. Pervasive, long-lasting behavior or communication that makes it difficult to perform normal job duties or advance in a career progression is known as a hostile work environment. Bullying, if unchecked and if it becomes pervasive and long-lasting, can contribute to a hostile work environment.

☒ **A**, **B**, and **C** are incorrect. Behaviors such as defensiveness, laziness, or even positive team-playing would not necessarily make it difficult for others to perform normal job duties or advance in a career progression.

36. ☑ **A**. When two employees break out into a yelling match in the workplace over local election results, it is an example of employee conflict. Conflict is a natural occurrence in any workplace. Unaddressed conflict can also lower morale and productivity. HR professionals tend to step in when conflict turns into personal attacks, an employee threatens to quit over it, or morale is negatively impacted.

☒ **B**, **C**, and **D** are incorrect. Political campaigning is advocating for a politician or ballot initiative inside or outside of the workplace. Two employees erupting into a sudden yelling match does not fit the definition of harassment. Poor performance is relevant to an ongoing lack of performance that is evaluated by supervision.

37. ☑ **A**. Regularly staying away from work without good reason is known as absenteeism. Typically employers will outline attendance expectations in a policy giving details of progressive discipline if there are excessive absences. Excessive absences can negatively impact an employer's finances, morale, and staffing coverage needs. However, before leaping in to a corrective counseling session with an employee who is missing a lot of work, savvy HR professionals tend to first find out why the employee is missing work. For example, an employee who misses a lot of work may be doing so because they are experiencing bullying or harassment at work. It's best to find out why absences are occurring and then solve the actual problem.

☒ **B**, **C**, and **D** are incorrect. **B** is incorrect because presenteeism is when employees come to work even if they are sick or injured. **C** is incorrect because tardiness is the act of being late for a scheduled shift. **D** is incorrect because a vacation is scheduled time off.

38. ☑ **C.** Moral principles that govern a person's behavior or way of conducting business are known as ethics. Workplace ethics are based on having a sense of integrity and having the courage to do the right thing despite pressures to look the other way. Those who have disregard for ethics will display behaviors such as stealing, cheating, or ignoring regulatory rules.

☒ **A**, **B**, and **D** are incorrect. Values, mission, and policies are external written guidelines or stated principles. Ethics are an internal compass that guides a person's behavior.

39. ☑ **B.** A list of rules that outline expectations of behavior in the workplace is called a code of conduct. Typically this list is included in employee handbooks and used to communicate to new and existing employees expected behaviors in the workplace.

☒ **A**, **C**, and **D** are incorrect. Procedures, vision, and policies are not typically a list of rules that outline expectations of behavior.

40. ☑ **D.** Title VII of the Civil Rights Act of 1964 is a federal regulation that prohibits sexual harassment. The Equal Employment Opportunity Commission (EEOC) enforces the act.

☒ **A**, **B**, and **C** are incorrect. The National Labor Relations Act, Occupational Safety and Health Act, and Fair Labor Standards Act have primary purposes other than sexual harassment. The National Labor Relations Act (NLRA) guarantees basic private-sector employees' rights to organize a union. The Occupational Safety and Health Act (OSHA) was created to assure safe and healthful working conditions. The Fair Labor Standards Act (FLSA) establishes minimum wage and overtime provisions.

41. ☑ **C.** A top mistake in handling employee complaints or grievances is to ignore them. Ignoring employee complaints, no matter the reason, can make a bad situation worse and costly for the employer. This is particularly true if the complaints indicate serious work conditions such as harassment, hostile work environment, or discrimination. As with the case *Walsh v. National Computer Systems, Inc.*, the courts found that HR was neglectful in investigating disparate treatment and hostile work environment complaints from the employee, Shireen Walsh. HR cited the reason for not investigating the complaint was because they "didn't want to take sides" and feared an investigation would lead to more complaints. The cost was a $438,145 judgment against the employer and ultimately a damaged reputation.

☒ **A**, **B**, and **D** are incorrect. Conducting a swift and objective investigation is smart and a "must-do" strategy. In addition, some chief human resources officers may choose to outsource highly sensitive investigations, such as a matter relating to a high-ranking executive, to an outside third-party investigator to remove all appearances of bias.

42. ☑ **D.** To help overcome "he said, she said" complaints, it is best to gather physical evidence that might validate the complaint. It's not unusual for HR professionals to check time sheets, camera footage, or computer records to validate what did or did not happen relating to workplace complaints.

☒ **A**, **B**, and **C** are incorrect. The other methods such as aggressive tactics, talking to potentially biased friends with leading questions, and gossip are not reliable methods to determining the truth. Gathering physical evidence wherever possible is the best bet to getting to the bottom of things.

43. ☑ **B.** For an employee who complains regularly, HR should always investigate as if it were the first complaint. Granted, it can be annoying at times dealing with chronic complainers. However, the organization is best served by taking all complaints seriously and proceeding with any disruptive behavior concerns with great caution. There are growing laws that protect an employee's right to complain. From whistleblower laws to the National Labor Relations Board (NLRB) governing an employee's rights, employers need to exhibit great care in handling the chronic complainer.

☒ **A, C,** and **D** are incorrect. Each of these options indicates not taking the complaint seriously and can cause risk for the employer. It is best to always be swift and thorough in conducting investigations, regardless of how many times the employee has complained.

44. ☑ **A.** According to the Equal Employment Opportunity Commission (EEOC), plausibility, demeanor, motive, corroboration, and an employee's past record are key determining factors for witness credibility. HR often comes across witnesses who have their own biases or agendas when being questioned in any particular workplace circumstance. The factors that the EEOC offers in assessing witness credibility are good to keep in mind when conducting workplace investigations.

☒ **B, C,** and **D** are incorrect. These answers are not what the EEOC advises in assessing witness credibility.

45. ☑ **A.** When choosing an investigator, it is important to be mindful of any potential conflicts of interest. It is critically important that complaint investigations are completely objective. So, a compliant investigator who may be friends or related to those involved in the incident may be seen as biased. Further, this can throw the entire investigation into jeopardy and create additional risk for the employer. A great practice is to identify more than one potential compliant investigator and train them to freely self-disclose potential conflicts of interest should they come up.

☒ **B, C,** and **D** are incorrect. The attitude and how questions are asked may have some minor implication but can be corrected. A conflict of interest issue is not easily corrected, other than removing oneself from the investigation entirely. In addition, where the investigator went to school has no bearing on their ability to conduct a fair investigation.

46. ☑ **D.** An employee's written rebuttal about a perceived violation of collective bargaining agreement or workplace dissatisfaction is known as a grievance. Often grievance procedures are written into collective bargaining agreements (CBAs). In nonunionized environments, they may also call this a dispute resolution procedure.

☒ **A, B,** and **C** are incorrect. A memo, presentation, or suggestion may or may not have anything to do with a complaint or grievance.

47. ☑ **C.** Most grievance procedures allow employees to discuss concerns with multiple levels of management. Typically grievance procedures describe different levels along with timelines for filing a complaint and for management to respond.

☒ **A, B,** and **D** are incorrect. **A** is incorrect because initiating a grievance procedure for safety concerns only is not true. Grievance procedures are typically utilized for various workplace issues such as policy or collective bargaining agreement interpretation.

B is incorrect because a grievance procedure can be found in both union and nonunion environments, and **D** is incorrect because a grievance procedure typically allows employees to discuss concerns with multiple levels of management.

48. ☑ **B.** In a nonunion employer, grievances may be subject to federal regulations under the National Labor Relations Act (NLRA) when the grievance is deemed to be a protected concerted activity. The National Labor Relations Board (NLRB) concerns itself with employee rights regardless if in a union or nonunion environment. Employees have the protected right to express concerns about their work environment and working conditions without fear of retaliation from the employer, thus "protected concerted activity." A court case to note regarding "protected concerted activity" is *Saigon Gourmet Restaurant, Inc.*

    ☒ **A, C,** and **D** are incorrect. Whether the grievance is filed in HR under any timeline, whether it's sent to the CEO, or whether it's in written form is not what the NLRB would necessarily concern itself with so long as organizations are consistently following their own policy. The chief concern is whether employees are engaged in a protected concerted activity.

49. ☑ **A.** In a unionized workplace, if a grievance is filed during open labor negotiations, HR should acknowledge the grievance and begin to collect facts regarding the matter. Open negotiations or not, the employer is obligated to conduct an investigation and follow its policy or collective bargaining clause. The union representative or employer may discuss the matter at the bargaining table, but there should be no delay in following the established process.

    ☒ **B, C,** and **D** are incorrect. None of these options supports the established process and collective bargaining clause.

50. ☑ **D.** An important feature of a good grievance handling procedure is that it is simple and easily understood by all. Complexity of process does not make an effective practice. In fact, the more complex policies and procedures are, the less likely they will be followed consistently. Further, they may frustrate employees and managers alike.

    ☒ **A, B,** and **C** are incorrect. None of these options is considered a good feature of a grievance policy. If anything, they may frustrate the employees and managers.

51. ☑ **A.** Any misconduct that may result in termination should be investigated promptly and thoroughly.

    ☒ **B, C,** and **D** are incorrect. These choices are generally not the first step that HR should take without investigating first to see whether the alleged misconduct actually occurred.

52. ☑ **D.** ADR will reduce the number of disputes that end up in court.

    ☒ **A, B,** and **C** are incorrect. These choices are not the main advantage of using ADR. Each option is a factor and important but would not be a main advantage.

53. ☑ **D.** Setting clear expectations will help prevent disciplinary actions by managers and employees both having the same expectations; this can be done with the use of job descriptions.

☒ **A**, **B**, and **C** are incorrect. **A** and **B** are incorrect because although they may possibly help prevent disciplinary problems, these choices are not the best options. **C** is incorrect as leading the market with higher salary rates would have little to no bearing on preventing disciplinary action.

54. ☑ **C**. Having open dialogue and problem-solving will allow for two-way communication between manager and employee while figuring out what the performance issue is and to resolve it before it progresses any further.

☒ **A**, **B**, and **D** are incorrect. These choices are later steps in the progressive disciplinary process.

55. ☑ **B**. Since the severity of the offense is a severe violation, HR should recommend termination.

☒ **A**, **C**, and **D** are incorrect. These choices are advisable in this particular case.

56. ☑ **A**. The best proactive defense to any discrimination lawsuit is the implementation of a written disciplinary policy. It is critical to be able to demonstrate that the policy is being followed uniformly across the organization.

☒ **B**, **C**, and **D** are incorrect. **B** is incorrect because surveying exiting employees to see whether they feel discriminated against is not proactive or recommended. It would not be recommended at that time because discrimination should be discussed prior to termination and as soon after it occurs as possible. **C** is incorrect because while training employees on cultural awareness and diversity is a good idea, it is not the best proactive strategy to preventing a lawsuit. **D** is incorrect because training leaders on diversity is not the best proactive strategy for minimizing the success of a lawsuit.

57. ☑ **A**. Most progressive disciplinary policies include provisions for verbal, written, and final warnings in the event of a policy violation. The best policies have guidance on typical steps but also allow flexibility based on circumstance.

☒ **B**, **C**, and **D** are incorrect. **B** is incorrect because meeting with people is part of the procedures around handling a policy violation complaint, but it is not necessarily spelled out in a policy. **C** is incorrect because each violation typically requires some action even if it is just giving a verbal warning. **D** is incorrect because while there may be some language that speaks about the severity of a policy violation, it is not what is meant by a progressive disciplinary policy. Progressive discipline generally includes a series of increasingly severe penalties for repeated offenses, typically beginning with counseling or a verbal warning.

58. ☑ **D**. While going through a reduction in force is never pleasant, careful consideration of selection criteria is critical to minimize any disparate impact issues. The best selection criteria are those that can be clearly documented and are as objective as possible. Examples include job categories, prior disciplinary actions, seniority, and skill set.

☒ **A**, **B**, and **C** are incorrect. **A** is incorrect because simply selecting people for a reduction in force who have a record of complaining can set an organization up for whistleblower protection risks. **B** is incorrect because popularity is subjective at best. There are better selection criteria to use that would minimize risk. **C** is incorrect because you have to use caution around attendance as a selection criteria. Some attendance issues may be attributed to protected reasons such as Family Medical Leave (FMLA) purposes. Using attendance as blanket criteria for a reduction in force could lead to legal risk.

59. ☑ **C.** Among the first steps to take when a supervisor requests to terminate an employee is to review the personnel file for previous performance documentation. Additional steps include comparing this employee situation to written policies in place as well as checking for any protected status issues. Checking in with legal counsel before terminating an employee is also a good idea.

☒ **A, B,** and **D** are incorrect. **A** is incorrect because simply including an employee in a reduction in force does not resolve the performance issue but also causes risk or could result in increased risk. **B** is incorrect because giving the employee wrong information during the termination meeting not only causes legal risk but also damages the employer's reputation and credibility. **D** is incorrect because ignored performance issues tend to create more complex issues in the future. In addition, not taking corrective action impedes an organization's ability to compete in the marketplace for customers and skilled talent.

60. ☑ **B.** HR should contact the employee to find out whether the absences are because of a protected leave such as FMLA, USERRA, or other state or federal leave requirement.

☒ **A, C,** and **D** are incorrect. These choices are not advisable in this situation.

61. ☑ **B.** Making a decision on the spot after an accusation has been made would not be an HR best practice because it is always prudent to complete a thorough, dispassionate, and objective investigation first before deciding.

☒ **A, C,** and **D** are incorrect. **A** is incorrect because looking through all relevant documents and investigation findings before making a decision is the HR best practice. **C** is incorrect because getting all the facts and documenting witness information is prudent before making a decision. **D** is incorrect because giving outplacement information to an employee helps the employee who is being terminated to find another position.

62. ☑ **C.** When, after a performance improvement plan, an employee asks to see copies of their HR files, this could be a sign that the employee is planning on seeking legal counsel by gathering all the documents.

☒ **A, B,** and **D** are incorrect. Those would not be signs that legal counsel is needed for the employer.

63. ☑ **C.** The employee should be suspended pending investigation. The company can choose to suspend with or without pay. The reason for the suspension is to allow the company to perform a thorough and fair investigation. Even if the employee is subsequently terminated, the time away from the job may protect others from an incident of potential workplace violence as well as protect the employer if the employee follows up with legal action. The investigation gives a chance to make sure you have all of the facts before making a final decision.

☒ **A, B,** and **D** are incorrect. **A** and **D** are incorrect because a write-up is not serious enough of a response given the facts presented in the question, which are that the employee is carrying a firearm, has recently had an altercation with a vendor, and is reported to have made threatening statements. **B** is incorrect because the company should move to the termination phase in this case but not an immediate termination. Tempers can flare, and because the employee is armed, enraging him in this way may lead to unfortunate and unintended consequences.

64. ☑ **A.** This is an example of possible wrongful termination, also known as retaliatory discharge. When an employer terminates an employee in response to the employee doing something that is lawful or because they are part of a protected class, the employee may have a wrongful termination case.

☒ **B, C,** and **D** are incorrect. **B** and **D** are incorrect because constructive discharge or constructive dismissal occurs when an employer makes a work environment so intolerable to an employee that the employee is essentially forced to quit. **C** is incorrect because a hostile work environment is one where the employee is repeatedly harassed thereby making the work environment intolerable.

65. ☑ **B.** HR's primary role is to ensure adequate documentation to support the termination and to coach the supervisor on how to conduct the termination meeting.

☒ **A, C,** and **D** are incorrect. **A** is incorrect because as much as possible the supervisor should conduct the termination meeting. The supervisor is most familiar with the employee's work and the issue (or issues) for which he is being terminated, and the supervisor has had the most interaction with the employee regarding improving performance. **C** and **D** are incorrect because returning company property and disabling access to company records are both shepherded by HR but are not HR's primary function in the termination phase.

66. ☑ **A.** Cite the work policy or rule violated, verbally if possible, during the termination.

☒ **B, C,** and **D** are incorrect. **B** is incorrect because a short explanation will help answer any questions. **C** is incorrect because giving anything in writing besides a severance letter would not be advisable. **D** is incorrect because discussing job functions should have happened at prior meetings regarding performance.

67. ☑ **D.** The employee, the manager, and a member of the HR team would be advisable as there should always be more than one member from the employer side in the room when conducting a termination.

☒ **A, B,** and **C** are incorrect. These choices are not advisable as there should always be more than one person in the room, besides the person being terminated, to reduce risk. If there is more than one person in the room, then accurate notes can be taken of what was said from two different perspectives.

68. ☑ **C.** The exit interview is an extremely useful tool for a company. The information gathered should include the reason for leaving, suggestions for process and culture improvements, and issues that need to be addressed immediately. This information will help a company make decisions that will impact future turnover.

☒ **A, B,** and **D** are incorrect. **A** and **B** are incorrect because while these are significant parts of a smooth exit process, they have little impact on turnover. **D** is incorrect because the promotion of an employee into the vacated position may have the positive effect of retaining that employee, but that has little to no impact on the company's overall turnover ratio.

69. ☑ **B**. No later than 72 hours after the accusation would be ideal to collect the facts and let them know of the outcome.

   ☒ **A**, **C**, and **D** are incorrect. No later than 72 hours after the accusation would be ideal.

70. ☑ **D**. When an employee provides a resignation stating an intention to leave the organization within a specified period of time, it is a voluntary termination.

   ☒ **A**, **B**, and **C** are incorrect. **A** is incorrect because involuntary termination is at the direction of the employer. **B** is incorrect because a layoff is a suspension or termination of employment (with or without notice) by the employer or management. *Layoffs* are not caused by any fault of the employees but by reasons such as lack of work, cash, or material. **C** is incorrect because downsizing is reducing the number of employees on the operating payroll.

71. ☑ **A**. In a skip-level interview, an employee is interviewed by his or her manager's manager.

   ☒ **B**, **C**, and **D** are incorrect. **B** is incorrect because employee focus groups are a sampling of employees from various functional areas in a company that come together to provide input on employment matters. **C** is incorrect because employee surveys are used to gather information from large groups of people on a wide variety of topics. **D** is incorrect because exit interviews are surveys given when an employee is leaving the organization. It is likely that this is the data that HR has already provided to the CEO in this case. Because this information hasn't provided the answer the CEO seeks regarding the reason for turnover, it would be most beneficial for the CEO to perform skip-level interviews.

72. ☑ **B**. The overall goal of an employee relation program is to maximize employee performance. The employment relationship affects all parts of an employee's life because employees spend a significant amount of time at work.

   ☒ **A**, **C**, and **D** are incorrect. Establishing employee dispute resolution techniques, increasing employee feedback, and communicating to management are all excellent results that could result from having an effective employee relation program in place.

73. ☑ **B**. The most effective way to generate more participation in this program would be to recognize the employees in a public forum, preferably with an incentive that they find valuable (for example, money or paid time off).

   ☒ **A**, **C**, and **D** are incorrect. **A** and **C** are incorrect because listing the employee names on the intranet or in a newsletter is a form of recognition but not likely to be as effective as public recognition with a meaningful incentive associated with the recognition. **D** is incorrect because a department-level staff meeting does not have the global impact the HR department hopes to generate.

74. ☑ **C**. Employee committees are formed to address various organizational concerns and include members from cross-functional departments. This promotes inclusion and diversity because it gives employees a platform for sharing differing opinions, expertise, and knowledge to meet an organizational initiative.

☒ **A**, **B**, and **D** are incorrect. **A** is incorrect because recognition events provide a platform for the company to acknowledge the accomplishments of employees in a number of different areas. This does not directly promote workplace inclusion. **B** and **D** are incorrect because work/life balance programs such as job-share impact employee engagement and retention by enabling employees to benefit from creative work schedules to assist them in managing their overall life outside of work.

75. ☑ **A**. Mutual trust between employees and management is the premise upon which a positive employee relations strategy is built. This trust is built over time and exists when employees believe that management is completely honest with them regarding the positives and negatives of the company's initiatives.

☒ **B**, **C**, and **D** are incorrect. **B** is incorrect because adhering to all laws and statutes related to employee relations is the barest minimum that a company can do. To build a positive and effective employee relation strategy, there has to be a commitment by the company to be deliberate and honest in its desire to create a fair and equitable company culture and climate. **C** is incorrect because mutual trust is built when employees believe that management is being completely honest with them. Only sharing the positive aspects of any initiative is disingenuous. **D** is incorrect because stating the company's nonunion message does little to create positive employee relations without being coupled with an open-door policy message, recognition opportunities, and other positive aspects of working for the company.

76. ☑ **D**. Even in times of economic downturn, employers that have positive employee relation programs in place where employees feel like they are treated with dignity and respect have more productive employees.

☒ **A**, **B**, and **C** are incorrect. Making changes to compensation or rewards, including recognition, doesn't ensure employee productivity. Employees still leave organizations for a number of intrinsic reasons, such as a poor relationship with a boss or because they feel underutilized.

77. ☑ **C**. A grievance process is a systematic and fair procedure for supervisors and employees to resolve complaints that arise. It typically includes timelines, what is eligible, and the decision-making process involved.

☒ **A**, **B**, and **D** are incorrect. **A** is incorrect because an open-door policy refers to a communication philosophy indicating employees are free to voice their concerns to any level of management at any time. **B** is incorrect because while often supervisors mistake the grievance process as an HR-only procedure, it is a process that should be adopted wholeheartedly by the supervisors for it to be effective. **D** is incorrect because a team-building process is an overbroad concept, and it does not effectively reflect the grievance process.

78. ☑ **C**. If employees participate in the decision-making process for the company, they are more likely to stay committed to the decision.

☒ **A**, **B**, and **D** are incorrect. Although these choices may reflect an advantage, these would not be the main advantage.

79. ☑ **D.** Taxes given to an employee to offset other tax implications are not necessary for the success of an employee recognition program.

☒ **A**, **B**, and **C** are incorrect. These are all factors needed for success in an employee recognition program.

80. ☑ **A.** A spot award is given immediately upon witnessing outstanding employee performance; it's given "on the spot."

☒ **B**, **C**, and **D** are incorrect. **B** is incorrect because an employee-of-the-month award would be awarded after the month has ended. **C** is incorrect because a retirement award would be given after the employee has decided to retire. **D** is incorrect because a length-of-service award would be given after a specified period of time, for example, 1 year, 5 years, and 10 years.

81. ☑ **C.** To allow for the smoothest possible exit, managers should address affected employees individually with compassion. There should be complete clarity regarding the conditions of the layoff (indefinite, may be recalled, unemployment compensation eligibility). Following the completion of the individual meetings, managers should meet with the employees who survived the layoff collectively and answer questions candidly and clearly. This is an important emotional transition for those employees as well.

☒ **A**, **B**, and **D** are incorrect. **A** and **B** are incorrect because layoffs should rarely be done in a group setting. The effect on the employee is complicated and potentially devastating. It should not be about maintaining efficiency. The layoff meeting should be focused on ensuring a proper exit for affected employees. Some considerations for management are the occurrence of workplace violence and the retention of the employees left behind. **D** is incorrect because those who have been laid off should not be allowed to linger. Their understandable angst toward the company will have a negative impact on the remaining employees.

82. ☑ **B.** An outplacement firm is a contracted service supplied by companies that specialize in helping employees prepare for job searching after a layoff or job loss.

☒ **A**, **C**, and **D** are incorrect. **A** is incorrect because a search firm focuses on filling open positions for clients. **C** is incorrect because a brokerage firm is a liaison between a company and service providers. **D** is incorrect because an outsourcing firm is an outside organization that manages functional services for companies.

83. ☑ **D.** An acquisition happens when a firm purchases the assets of another outright, resulting in expanding the acquiring company's employee base and facilities.

☒ **A**, **B**, and **C** are incorrect. **A** is incorrect because a strategic alliance is an arrangement in which companies share assets, such as technology and sales, to accomplish a goal. **B** is incorrect because an equity partnership is an arrangement where one firm acquires partial ownership of the other through a purchase of shares. **C** is incorrect because a joint venture involves two or more companies that invest together in forming a new company that is jointly owned.

84. ☑ **B**. Downsizing is a restructuring driver that is employed when a company is experiencing a decline in revenue.

☒ **A**, **C**, and **D** are incorrect. **A** is incorrect because a change in strategy is a restructuring driver that organizations employ when they are interested in pursuing new markets. **C** is incorrect because structure refers to when an organization changes its business model to improve efficiencies. **D** is incorrect because expansion refers to when a company expands to accommodate new staff and departments.

85. ☑ **A**. The WARN Act provisions apply if an organization has 100 or more full-time employees or 100 or more full- and part-time employees who work an average of 4,000 or more hours per week. This would be considered a mass layoff by the definition provided in the WARN Act because the act defines a mass layoff as 500 or more affected employees.

☒ **B**, **C**, and **D** are incorrect. **B** is incorrect because the WARN Act requires that organizations provide 60 days' notice to employees or their union representatives if the organization has 50 or more full-time employees. **C** and **D** are incorrect because the WARN Act provisions are not exclusive to plants, and employees on leave are always considered part of the total employee count.

86. ☑ **A**. The use of performance appraisals to determine who remains employed and who is released is the most equitable way to document a layoff decision. If an affected employee were to subsequently raise an EEO concern, the use of performance appraisals to determine which employees are laid off would be legally defensible.

☒ **B**, **C**, and **D** are incorrect. **B** and **C** are incorrect because the cost of a severance package or outplacement services are of lesser concern at this point. Once you determine who will be laid off using a relatively objective tool such as a performance review, then you can review what it might cost if the company chooses to offer a severance package or outplacement services. **D** is incorrect because the cost of COBRA coverage for continued health benefits is almost exclusively that of the employee's.

87. ☑ **A**. Restructuring is the act of reorganizing legal, ownership, operational, or other organizational structures.

☒ **B**, **C**, and **D** are incorrect. **B** is incorrect because reorganizing is simply the act of placing something in a new order. **C** is incorrect because divesting is getting rid of a business interest. **D** is incorrect because strategy is simply a plan of action.

88. ☑ **B**. Following a layoff, employers risk losing valued employees to new jobs because they fear that their employment future is uncertain.

☒ **A**, **C**, and **D** are incorrect. These are not risks to an employer. **A** and **C** are incorrect because leader realignment and refocused training and development activities could exist pre- or post-layoff because of a reorganization or change in company strategic focus. **D** is incorrect because people experience job insecurity following a layoff as opposed to job security.

89. ☑ **D**. Outplacement services are sometimes offered to employees who experience a layoff. Services include workshops about accepting job loss and moving forward as well as résumé writing and job search support.

☒ **A**, **B**, and **C** are incorrect. **A** is incorrect because severance is a financial compensation package that some employers offer to employees to assist with their transition after a layoff. **B** is incorrect because a divestiture is when a company gets rid of a subsidiary or business unit. **C** is incorrect because retraining refers to a person engaging in training to learn new skills.

90. ☑ **D**. An employer must pay severance if it that has been agreed upon in writing by both the employee and employer.

☒ **A**, **B**, and **C** are incorrect. Severance pay is not required by law but may be agreed to by the employer and employee either before accepting a position or at the point of termination. Severance pay shows goodwill on behalf of the employer.

Health, Safety, and Security

This functional area includes coverage of the following responsibilities and knowledge objectives:

- **01** Applicable laws and regulations related to workplace health, safety, security, and privacy (for example, OSHA, Drug-Free Workplace Act, ADA, HIPAA, Sarbanes-Oxley Act)

- **02** Risk mitigation in the workplace (for example, emergency evacuation procedures, health and safety, risk management, violence, emergencies)

- **03** Security risks in the workplace (for example, data, materials, or equipment theft; equipment damage or destruction; cybercrimes; password usage)

Balance is essential for a tightrope walker to successfully cross the wire. The same is true for the human resource (HR) professional in the area of health, safety, and security. The HR professional must balance the call to influence a productive environment with minimizing risk and promoting a healthy and secure work environment.

It is not an easy balancing act. However, with knowledge and experience, an HR professional can be a successful performer. In fact, HR professionals can help organizations to navigate this specialized area.

This chapter will test your knowledge in all the health, safety, and security responsibilities and knowledge areas of the exam, covering items such as applicable federal laws and regulations, investigation procedures, workplace safety and security risks, and much more.

Go ahead and test your knowledge in health, safety, and security. You've got this!

Objective 01   Applicable Laws and Regulations Related to Workplace Health, Safety, Security, and Privacy

1. A retail business that operates 24 hours a day and 7 days a week has adopted a workplace violence prevention program. The company created a policy of zero tolerance for workplace violence. A reprisal-free reporting system has been set up to assure employees that no retaliation would take place if reporting a concern. The company also outlined a comprehensive security plan for its locations as well as established a relationship with local law enforcement representatives. In addition, the company's representatives conduct regular training sessions for all employees. This is an example of compliance under which of the following OSHA obligations?

   A. The General Duty Clause

   B. Code of Federal Regulations

   C. The Health and Safety Act

   D. Emergency Action Plans

2. An employee of a doctor's office often took a work laptop home. Information about patients is stored on the laptop for the employee's easy reference. While the employee was in a local grocery store, someone broke into his car and stole the laptop. Which federal law should the employer be concerned about?

   A. Federal Data Protection Act

   B. Sarbanes-Oxley Act of 2002

   C. Health Insurance Portability and Accountability Act

   D. Title 21 Code of Federal Regulations (21 CFR Part 11)

3. A job candidate completes an application for a position available at a company. At the end of the application, the candidate is informed that the company may want to run a background check. The applicant is informed of his rights and is provided with an opportunity to request a copy of any background check results. The company is complying with which of the following federal laws?

A. Merger/Acquisition Privacy Act of 1974

B. Freedom of Information Act of 1966

C. Right to Financial Privacy Act of 1978

D. Fair Credit Reporting Act of 1970

4. Drake, the lead groundskeeper, is off the company's premises, cleaning the back access road leading to the company's building. Drake slips, falls, and injures his back. Per the Occupational Safety and Health Act (OSHA), this situation requires:

A. All employees to be trained on safety protocols

B. Recording on the OSHA 300 log

C. The employee to seek medical attention

D. The employee to be sent home

5. A manufacturing plant has decided to utilize a temporary agency to help staff forklift drivers for a short-term staffing need. The forklift drivers will be moving glass, boxes, and chemicals periodically. Which of the following steps will best meet OSHA's Hazardous Communication (HAZCOM) standards?

A. The host company will provide generic hazard training, information concerning the categories of chemicals encountered, and site-specific information.

B. The temporary agency will provide generic hazard training, information concerning the categories of chemicals encountered, and site-specific information.

C. The temporary agency will provide generic hazard training, covering categories of chemicals encountered, and the host company will provide site-specific training.

D. The host company will provide generic hazard training, covering categories of chemicals encountered, and the temporary agency will provide site-specific training.

6. Which of the following requires that a publicly traded company's employment offers consistently meet internal approval requirements, that they are consistent with established salary ranges, and that salary increases are documented and approved in accordance with internal policies?

A. Occupational Safety and Health Act

B. Equal Employment Opportunity Commission

C. Sarbanes-Oxley Act

D. Fair Labor Standards Act

7. Which of the following statements regarding an employee's rights related to substance abuse is correct?

   A. Individuals who currently use illegal drugs are protected by the Americans with Disabilities Act (ADA).

   B. If the results of a pre-employment drug screen reveal use of prescription drugs, the employer must treat this as confidential information.

   C. An alcoholic is a person not protected by the Americans with Disabilities Act (ADA).

   D. Employers are prohibited from using the results of a pre-employment drug screen to determine final hiring decisions.

8. Which of the following is covered under the Drug-Free Workplace Act?

   A. Marijuana

   B. Controlled substances

   C. Abuse of prescription drugs

   D. Alcoholism

9. During new-hire orientation, employees at a food and beverage distribution company sign an e-mail policy stating that all electronic activity done during the normal course of business may be monitored. From her company-assigned laptop, Michelle used her personal Gmail account to e-mail a friend details of her plan to start a similar company and forwarded a confidential client list to herself from her work e-mail to her Gmail account. The transmission of client lists to noncompany e-mail addresses and the use of the company's electronic devices for personal business are strictly prohibited per company policy, which was detailed in the e-mail policy Michelle signed at orientation. You are made aware of the series of electronic communications via a routine monthly communications report from the IT department. As the HR director, what is your best next step?

   A. Nothing. Michelle has a reasonable expectation of privacy because she used her personal Gmail account.

   B. Have a conference with Michelle regarding the e-mail policy signed at orientation and take the appropriate disciplinary action.

   C. Nothing. Michelle has a reasonable expectation of privacy under the Electronic Communications and Privacy Act.

   D. Terminate Michelle's employment immediately because this is a direct violation of company policy.

Objective 02   Risk Mitigation in the Workplace

10. A startup company that manufactures organic sunscreen products is looking to see what safety measures need to put be in place to ensure safety for all employees while on the job. The CEO has asked the HR manager to conduct a needs analysis. What should the HR manager do first in the needs assessment?

   A. Propose solutions

   B. Calculate costs

   C. Gather data to identify needs

   D. Choose and implement findings

11. The HR department has concluded a needs assessment for safety risks for its medical billing company where most employees are working on their computers for 7 to 8 hours per day. Now that HR knows that musculoskeletal disorders are a potential hazard, what is the best solution for preventing this potential hazard?

   A. Offer employees time midshift to rest

   B. Have a compliant process in which employees feel comfortable letting management know whether potential injuries arise

   C. Involve senior management in the process

   D. Provide training to employees on the awareness of potential hazards

12. A midsize manufacturing company has uncovered a potential occupational injury hazard. The level of smoke from the exhaust machinery may be causing unsafe levels within the building. What should the safety manager's first priority be to rectify this issue?

   A. Provide employees with masks

   B. Install warning signs for people with respiratory problems

   C. Train employees about the problem and ways to reduce smoke

   D. Design a new ventilation system to reduce smoke to an acceptable level

13. A fire alarm sounded in a building of approximately 500 employees. During the exit process managers gave conflicting directions. Employees seemed confused as to what to do and where to go. Twenty minutes later, the entire building was vacated. What should immediately occur to minimize future liability?

   A. Create a process that accounts for all equipment, data, and other critical company property, and conduct training.

   B. Revise the evacuation plan, create a process that accounts for all employees and nonemployees, and conduct training.

   C. Create a map of where everyone is located in the building so that a report can be handed to emergency personnel.

   D. Be prepared to provide medical assistance when necessary, learn CPR, and train key personnel in CPR.

14. Rumors have been circulating that one of the employees has been receiving threatening calls at work from her former abusive spouse. Which of the following is the best immediate action the employer should take to minimize liability?

   A. Because rumors are circulating at this point, calm employees down and educate them about expectations against spreading gossip in the workplace.

   B. Meet with leadership, develop a "violence in the workplace" policy, and get supervisors involved in training employees on the new policy.

   C. Interview the employee allegedly receiving calls, assess whether there is a danger to her and others in the workplace, and take preventative steps.

   D. Establish an evacuation plan, train all employees on the new plan, conduct regular evacuation drills, and notify local authorities of the drills.

15. A large retail establishment has a workplace violence policy protecting employees from harm. The policy clearly states employees should not under any circumstance engage in violent acts, including fighting. One night while on a break, an employee spotted a woman being attacked by a man in the parking lot. He asked the woman if she needed help, and the attacker began hitting the employee. The employee fought back. What is the best course of action?

   A. Commend the employee for saving a customer's life, and review the policy to add exceptions

   B. Terminate the employee for violating company policy, and post the policy for all employees

   C. Provide the employee with a corrective action form, and conduct training for all employees

   D. Train all employees on expectations and safety procedures, and provide self-defense techniques

16. Your HR department has been tasked with formulating a disaster recovery plan. What is your first step?

   A. Inventory office equipment

   B. Make an inventory of all jobs that would need to be relocated to keep the business running

   C. Send files off-site for backup

   D. Contact an insurance agent to inquire about necessary coverage

17. _____ provides coverage to employers against claims made by employees alleging discrimination (based on sex, race, age, or disability, for example), wrongful termination, harassment, and other employment-related issues, such as failure to promote.

   A. General liability insurance

   B. Employment practices liability insurance

C. Workers' comp insurance

D. Professional liability

18. Which of the following is *not* an HR best practice when communicating with employees in an emergency?

   A. Have a boilerplate standby statement ready while you gather details.

   B. As soon as you hear something, let the employees know.

   C. Look at the positive side.

   D. Don't stop talking once the crisis ends.

Objective 03   Security Risks in the Workplace

19. To protect sensitive information and prevent identity theft, sabotage, or intellectual property loss, an employer may want to implement what type of policy?

   A. Hiring screening policy

   B. Records retention policy

   C. Social media policy

   D. Workplace monitoring policy

20. An organizational policy that describes expectations and protocols for using personal devices in the workplace is known as:

   A. Bring your own device

   B. Materials management

   C. Facility security

   D. Code of conduct

21. A fake e-mail sent to HR, seemingly from an organization's executive, requesting sensitive information such as Social Security numbers, salary, and dates of birth is known as what type of scam?

   A. Telemarketing scam

   B. Phishing scam

   C. Pyramid scam

   D. Chain letter scam

22. A form of malicious software that is designed to block access to a computer or network system until a specified amount of money is paid is called:

   A. Virus

   B. Ransomware

   C. Malware

   D. Trojans

23. Which of the following is a key step in preventing cyber-hacking attacks in the workplace?

   A. Prohibit mobile device use

   B. Remove all computers

   C. Test and train employees

   D. Write a policy

24. A key step to securing employees' computer passwords includes which of the following?

   A. Periodically reset passwords and require random alphanumeric and special characters

   B. Require employees to use the same password for all databases and platforms

   C. Allow predictable passwords such as words like *password* or personal dates

   D. Encourage employees to note all passwords and store them under the keyboard

25. Intellectual property refers to which of the following?

   A. Laptops, computers, tablets, and smart phones

   B. Reports, spreadsheets, presentations, and memos

   C. Internet, intranet, company software, and databases

   D. Patents, trademarks, copyrights, and trade secrets

26. Which of the following is a key step in protecting the company from potential liability in the event its laptops are stolen?

   A. Encrypt all laptops and provide training

   B. Buy leather cases for the laptops

   C. Allow employees to share passwords

   D. Don't allow the use of thumb drives

27. A feature that would enable an employer to track the precise location of equipment such as laptops in the event they are stolen is called:

   A. Social network link

   B. Specialized password

   C. Global Positioning System

   D. Remote shut-off

1. A	**10.** C	**19.** D
2. C	**11.** D	**20.** A
3. D	**12.** D	**21.** B
4. B	**13.** B	**22.** B
5. C	**14.** C	**23.** C
6. C	**15.** A	**24.** A
7. B	**16.** B	**25.** D
8. B	**17.** B	**26.** A
9. B	**18.** B	**27.** C

1. ☑ **A.** The General Duty Clause of OSHA requires an employer to do everything reasonably necessary to protect the life, safety, and health of employees. This includes the adoption of practices and processes reasonably adequate to create a safe and healthy workplace.

    ☒ **B, C,** and **D** are incorrect. **B** is incorrect because the Code of Federal Regulations (CFR) is produced annually and contains the general and permanent rules published in the Federal Register by the executive departments and agencies of the federal government. **C** is incorrect because the Health and Safety Act is not the name of a law or regulation in the United States. **D** is incorrect because an emergency action plan is limited in scope and not an obligation necessarily under the General Duty Clause.

2. ☑ **C.** The Health Insurance Portability and Accountability Act is a privacy rule that regulates the security and confidentiality of patient information. The issue in this case is whether the employer did all it could to protect patient medical information.

    ☒ **A, B,** and **D** are incorrect. **A** is incorrect because the Federal Data Protection Act does protect consumer information but does not apply specifically to private medical information. **B** is incorrect because the Sarbanes-Oxley (SOX) Act of 2002 does not apply to private medical information. SOX protects investors from the possibility of fraudulent accounting activities by corporations by requiring certain financial disclosures from them. **D** is incorrect because the Title 21 Code of Federal Regulations (21 CFR Part 11) governs food and drugs within the United States for the Food and Drug Administration (FDA), the Drug Enforcement Administration (DEA), and the Office of National Drug Control Policy (ONDCP).

3. ☑ **D.** The company is complying with the Fair Credit Reporting Act (FCRA) of 1970. The act was initially created to protect consumers from the disclosure of inaccurate information held by consumer reporting agencies. The act was later modified in 2003 to help address identity theft problems and make it easier for individuals to correct their credit information.

    ☒ **A, B,** and **C** are incorrect. **A** is incorrect because this law does not apply to job applicants. **B** is incorrect because the Freedom of Information Act is not applicable. **C** is incorrect because this does not apply to job applicants.

4. ☑ **B.** Providing medical assistance and giving time off are good practices; however, they are not considered required practices under the Occupational Safety and Health Act (OSHA). In addition, this scenario describes the employee being off-premises but conducting company business. Because the employee was conducting company business, the location is irrelevant. The employer is required to record this incident on the OSHA 300 log.

    ☒ **A, C,** and **D** are incorrect. **A** is incorrect because while training employees is a good practice, it is not a requirement upon an injury. **C** is incorrect because seeking medical attention is not a requirement. **D** is incorrect because sending the employee home is not a requirement.

5. ☑ **C.** The temporary agency is expected to provide generic hazard training and information concerning categories of chemicals employees may potentially encounter. Host companies would then be responsible for providing site-specific hazard training. OSHA sections 1910.1200(h)(1) and 1926.59 outline the employer's hazard communication standards.

☒ **A, B**, and **D** are incorrect. **A** is incorrect because both the host and temporary agency share hazard communication responsibilities. **B** is incorrect because, as in **A**, both the host and temporary agency share hazard communication responsibilities. **D** is incorrect because the host company is responsible for site-specific information, while the temporary agency is responsible for general information.

6. ☑ **C.** Section 404 of the Sarbanes-Oxley Act requires that public companies routinely review and test internal financial transaction controls (approval process). Thus, all salary offers, raises, or any other compensation must be documented and follow an established internal signature approval process.

☒ **A, B**, and **D** are incorrect. **A** is incorrect because the focus of the OSH Act is to protect employees from injury or illness. **B** is incorrect because the EEOC is the agency created by Title VII to promote equal opportunities in employment for protected classes. **D** is incorrect because the FLSA is a law that regulates employee status, overtime pay, child labor, minimum wage, record-keeping, and other wage-related administrative issues.

7. ☑ **B.** Per the ADA, if the results of a pre-employment drug screen reveal use of prescription drugs or other medical information, the employer must treat that information as confidential.

☒ **A, C**, and **D** are incorrect. **A** is incorrect because people who currently engage in the illegal use of drugs are specifically excluded from the definition of a "qualified individual with a disability" protected by the ADA when the employer acts based on the employee's drug use. **C** is incorrect because alcoholism is considered a medical condition and protected under the ADA. **D** is incorrect because pre-employment job testing can be done only after an offer of employment is made, but the offer can be contingent upon a satisfactory drug screen, which means the employer can act based on the results of the drug screen results.

8. ☑ **B.** The Drug Free Workplace Act (DFWA) covers defined controlled substances only.

☒ **A, C**, and **D** are incorrect. Marijuana is not covered in jurisdictions where it is legal, abuse of prescription drugs is not covered, and alcoholism is considered a disability under the American with Disabilities Act (ADA). Alcohol is not a controlled substance. Controlled substances are covered under the DFWA.

9. ☑ **B.** It would be appropriate to discuss these findings with the employee and engage in the disciplinary steps that are deemed appropriate per policy.

☒ **A, C**, and **D** are incorrect. **A** is incorrect because the e-mail use policy clarifies that any electronic communication made using the company's equipment can be reviewed. It is irrelevant that Michelle used her Gmail account. She transmitted this e-mail via the company laptop, so a record of the content of the e-mail exists and was discovered during a routine review of all the company's electronic communications. **C** is incorrect because there is no reasonable expectation of privacy under the ECPA. The bottom line is that Michelle used the company equipment to access her Gmail account and transmit this communication. Per the company's e-mail use policy, they are permitted to monitor. **D** is incorrect because it is advisable that the company closely review and evaluate Michelle's actions as they relate to the e-mail use policy before making any decision regarding continued employment. Immediate termination may or may not be appropriate and cannot be determined until after an in-depth conference with Michelle and a review of all the facts pertinent to the investigation.

10. ☑ **C.** Gathering data is the first step in a needs assessment. Data can be collected through the use of surveys, observations, advisory groups, and interviews.

    ☒ **A, B,** and **D** are incorrect. **A** is incorrect because proposing solutions is the third step in a needs assessment process. **B** is incorrect because calculating costs is the fourth step in a needs assessment. **D** is incorrect because it is the fifth and final step of a needs assessment.

11. ☑ **D.** Providing awareness training to employees on potential hazards will help employees notice signs and symptoms earlier on.

    ☒ **A, B,** and **C** are incorrect. These solutions are possible but not the best solution.

12. ☑ **D.** The first priority is to eliminate the hazard completely. This could be done by installing a new ventilation system.

    ☒ **A, B,** and **C** are incorrect. All of these choices are possible actions to mitigate the safety issue, but they are of lesser priority when compared to eliminating the hazard completely.

13. ☑ **B.** The ideal step to minimize liability is to revise the evacuation plan. Create a process that accounts for all employees and nonemployees, and conduct training on the plan. In addition, being able to account for all employees, nonemployees, customers, and suppliers is a critical component as part of an evacuation plan. This will enable emergency personnel to assess whether they need to rescue individuals from a building. Ideal evacuation plans include an orderly process to exit the building and a designation area where a head count can be taken.

    ☒ **A, C,** and **D** are incorrect. **A** is incorrect because the issue is with people exiting a building quickly and safely, not with the equipment. **C** is incorrect because having a map of where everyone sits is not an adequate approach to exiting the building safely. That said, having a head count ready and knowing who may still be in the building is good information to hand to emergency personnel after exiting the building. **D** is incorrect because providing medical assistance is unrelated to the fact that people need to exit a building quickly, safely, and orderly in an emergency.

14. ☑ **C.** Under the General Duty Clause of OSHA, the employer is required to provide "place[s] of employment which are free from recognized hazards that are causing or are likely to cause death or serious physical harm to his employees" (General Duty Clause, Section 5(a)(1)). In this case, the employer is hearing rumors of a possible threat that may or may not come into the workplace. The best step is to investigate and determine whether there is a viable threat and take appropriate preventative steps.

☒ **A**, **B**, and **D** are incorrect. **A** is incorrect because just calming employees down does not effectively address a possible threat to safety in the workplace. **B** is incorrect because while the employer may want to develop a "violence in the workplace" policy and train employees on the new policy as a good long-term practice, it doesn't address a possible eminent threat. **D** is incorrect because developing an evacuation plan is good for the long term but in the short term a threat needs to be assessed and dealt with immediately.

15. ☑ **A**. This real-life scenario provides a perfect example of how liability extends beyond just the employee but also to nonemployees, such as customers. Initially this employer terminated the employee who got involved in the altercation in the parking lot. The result was public outcry for punishing an employee for saving a customer's life and negative publicity for the company. The best course of action in this case is to commend the employee for saving someone's life but review the policy and consider exceptions that may apply that are aligned with the organization's overall objectives. Addressing what should happen if there is imminent danger to employees or nonemployees is a good practice.

☒ **B**, **C**, and **D** are incorrect. **B** is incorrect because taking negative steps toward the employee who saved a customer's life can result in negative publicity and deter employees from watching out for the customer's best interest. **C** is incorrect because providing a corrective action plan and training does not secure the customer's safety in this case. **D** is incorrect because just providing self-defense techniques is short-sighted in terms of protecting the organization's liability.

16. ☑ **B**. Taking inventory of all jobs needed for the business to operate is the most important and first thing HR should think about because without the proper staff, the business cannot operate. They should do this by coordinating with all departments.

☒ **A**, **C**, and **D** are incorrect. While these choices are applicable and needed during the process of disaster recovery planning, they are not the first step.

17. ☑ **B**. Employment practices liability insurance provides coverage to employers against claims made by employees alleging discrimination (based on sex, race, age, or disability, for example), wrongful termination, harassment, and other employment-related issues, such as failure to promote.

☒ **A**, **C**, and **D** are incorrect. **A** is incorrect because general liability insurance is coverage that can protect you from a variety of claims, including bodily injury, property damage, personal injury, and others, that can arise from your business operations. **C** is incorrect because workers' compensation insurance is a form of insurance providing wage replacement and medical benefits to employees injured in the course of employment in exchange for mandatory relinquishment of the employee's right to sue his or her employer for the tort of negligence. **D** is not correct because professional liability (more commonly known as errors and omissions [E&O] in the United States) is a form of liability insurance that helps protect professional advice- and service-providing individuals and companies from bearing the full cost of defending against a negligence claim made by a client and damages awarded in such a civil lawsuit.

18. ☑ **B**. HR's role in an emergency is to make sure everything you are hearing is true before spreading what could be just gossip or hearsay. So it is advisable to not tell employees unless you have fact-checked that it is true.

☒ **A**, **C**, and **D** are incorrect. **A** is not correct because having a boilerplate standby statement ready while you gather details is helpful. An example is "We're looking at the situation, and we'll be back in touch shortly." **C** is not correct because looking into the positive side can be helpful. An example is "Five of the employees who have been sent to the hospital have been treated and released, and the other two are expected to make a full recovery." **D** is not correct because you should keep talking after the crisis to see how you could have improved and continually revise your policies.

19. ☑ **D**. To protect sensitive information and prevent identity theft, sabotage, or intellectual property loss, an employer typically implements a workplace-monitoring policy. It may also be called a "computer use" policy. Employers may also use confidentiality or code of conduct policies to supplement behavior expectations around theft or damage of equipment or intellectual property.

☒ **A**, **B**, and **C** are incorrect. Hiring, records retention, and social media policies are not necessarily created to protect sensitive information. Rather, they are process- or conduct-related policies.

20. ☑ **A.** An organizational policy that describes expectations and protocols for using personal devices in the workplace is known as a bring-your-own-device (BYOD) to work policy. This policy is more about rules that govern access to the company network using personal devices such as smart phones and tablets. Many companies are utilizing apps to download on personal devices that control the employee's access to the company's network and track the device. The implementation and use of such apps without properly communicating the purpose of them to employees has been known to cause distrust and concern of "big brother is watching" among employees.

☒ **B**, **C**, and **D** are incorrect. A materials management, facility security, or a code of conduct policy may not explicitly discuss expectations around personal devices.

21. ☑ **B**. A fake e-mail sent to HR or anyone, seemingly from an organization's executive, requesting sensitive information is a phishing scam. Alarmingly, phishing scams are on the rise and unfortunately have been successful in fooling people, including those in HR, to share sensitive employee information. When organizations realize they have an information breach, they are obligated to notify those employees who are affected and to offer identity theft protection monitoring services.

☒ **A**, **C**, and **D** are incorrect. Telemarketing, pyramid, and chain letter scams are not necessarily in e-mail form.

22. ☑ **B**. A form of malicious software that is designed to block access to a computer or network system until a specified amount of money is paid is ransomware. Unfortunately, like phishing scams, this malicious activity is also on the rise and has successfully bilked hundreds of thousands of dollars from organizations and individuals.

☒ **A**, **C**, and **D** are incorrect. While viruses, malware, and Trojans can be equally damaging to organizations, they do not necessarily demand money to release access to systems.

23. ☑ **C.** Testing and training employees is a key step in preventing cyber-hacking attacks in the workplace. Keeping this issue top of mind for employees is critical. Otherwise, during a busy or hectic workday, it is easy for employees to forget and click hyperlinks that come from outside and unknown sources. Proactive information technology departments engage in test e-mails with links designed to pop up and warn employees that clicking unknown links is dangerous and reminding them of policies and protocols.

☒ **A**, **B**, and **D** are incorrect. These steps are may limit employee effectiveness in the workplace altogether such as removing computers and so on. These tools are great for efficient and effective productivity. However, they come with risks if employees are not trained to watch for and avoid malicious activity. Simply writing a policy alone will not prevent cyber-hacking in the workplace because often employees will either not know about them or read them without accompanying further action like training.

24. ☑ **A.** A key step to securing employees' computer passwords includes periodically resetting passwords and requiring random alphanumeric and special characters. Employees may groan about having to change and remember new passwords when they are reset, but it is well worth it to prevent cyber-hacking.

☒ **B**, **C**, and **D** are incorrect. All of these answers actually add risk by making it possible to hack an organization's systems.

25. ☑ **D.** Intellectual property refers to patents, trademarks, copyrights, and trade secrets. Intellectual property can be just as valuable to an organization as money in the bank. Organizations that are reliant on intellectual property are best served by having strong policies and limited-access protocols in place.

☒ **A**, **B**, and **C** are incorrect. All other answers may represent property but in a physical sense of the word and are not necessarily considered intellectual property.

26. ☑ **A.** Encrypting all laptops and providing training are key steps in protecting the company from potential liability in the event its laptops are stolen. Encrypting is the process of converting data into code that is designed to prevent unauthorized access. Also, providing training for employees that includes reminding them not to leave laptops visible in car seats and ensuring they shut down the laptop and requiring a password when they power up is a good practice.

☒ **B**, **C**, and **D** are incorrect. Buying laptop cases or preventing the use of thumb drives does not prevent laptop thefts. In addition, allowing employees to share passwords is a risk to an organization's security.

27. ☑ **C.** A Global Positioning System (GPS) is a feature that would enable an employer to track the precise location of equipment such as laptops in the event they are stolen. This feature enables employers to track the location of stolen equipment and alert law enforcement.

☒ **A**, **B**, and **D** are incorrect. Social network links and specialized passwords do not enable location tracking of items. Remote shut-off is a feature that enables information technology officials to control and shut down devices remotely, making it difficult to carry out unauthorized access.

About the CD-ROM

The CD-ROM included with this book comes complete with all of the practice questions loaded into Total Tester customizable practice exam software and a secured PDF copy of the book.

System Requirements

The software requires Windows Vista or higher and 30MB of hard disk space for full installation, in addition to a current or prior major release of Chrome, Firefox, Internet Explorer, or Safari. To run, the screen resolution must be set to 1024 × 768 or higher. The secured book PDF requires Adobe Acrobat, Adobe Reader, or Adobe Digital Editions to view.

Installing and Running Total Tester Premium Practice Exam Software

From the main screen you may install the Total Tester software by clicking the Total Tester Practice Exams button. This will begin the installation process and place an icon on your desktop and in your Start menu. To run Total Tester, navigate to Start | (All) Programs | Total Seminars, or double-click the icon on your desktop.

To uninstall the Total Tester software, go to Start | Control Panel | Programs And Features, and then select the Total Tester program. Select Remove, and Windows will completely uninstall the software.

Total Tester Premium Practice Exam Software

Total Tester provides you with a simulation of the aPHR exam. The test engine includes all of the 500+ practice questions from the book, and exams can be taken in Practice Mode, Exam Mode, or Custom Mode. Practice Mode provides an assistance window with hints, references to the book, explanations of the correct and incorrect answers, and the option to check your answers as you take the test. Exam Mode provides a simulation of the actual exam. The number of questions, the types of questions, and the time allowed are intended to be an accurate representation of the exam environment. Custom Mode allows you to create custom exams from selected functional areas, and you can further customize the number of questions and time allowed.

To take a test, launch the program and select aPHR PE from the Installed Question Packs list. You can then select Practice Mode, Exam Mode, or Custom Mode. All exams provide an overall grade and a grade broken down by domain.

Secured Book PDF

The entire contents of the book are provided in secured PDF format on the CD-ROM. This file is viewable on your computer and many portable devices.

- **To view the PDF on a computer**, Adobe Acrobat, Adobe Reader, or Adobe Digital Editions is required. A link to Adobe's web site, where you can download and install Adobe Reader, has been included on the CD-ROM.

 NOTE For more information on Adobe Reader and to check for the most recent version of the software, visit Adobe's web site at www.adobe.com and search for the free Adobe Reader or look for Adobe Reader on the product page. Adobe Digital Editions can also be downloaded from the Adobe web site.

- **To view the book PDF on a portable device**, copy the PDF file to your computer from the CD-ROM and then copy the file to your portable device using a USB or other connection. Adobe offers a mobile version of Adobe Reader, the Adobe Reader mobile app, which currently supports iOS and Android. For customers using Adobe Digital Editions and an iPad, you may have to download and install a separate reader program on your device. The Adobe web site has a list of recommended applications, and McGraw-Hill Education recommends the Bluefire Reader.

Technical Support

For questions regarding the Total Tester software or operation of the CD-ROM, visit **www.totalsem.com** or e-mail **support@totalsem.com**.

For questions regarding the secured book PDF, visit **http://mhp.softwareassist.com** or e-mail **techsolutions@mhedu.com**.

For questions regarding book content, e-mail **hep_customer-service@mheducation.com**. For customers outside the United States, e-mail **international_cs@mheducation.com**.

LICENSE AGREEMENT

THIS PRODUCT (THE "PRODUCT") CONTAINS PROPRIETARY SOFTWARE, DATA AND INFORMATION (INCLUDING DOCUMENTATION) OWNED BY McGRAW-HILL EDUCATION AND ITS LICENSORS. YOUR RIGHT TO USE THE PRODUCT IS GOVERNED BY THE TERMS AND CONDITIONS OF THIS AGREEMENT.

LICENSE: Throughout this License Agreement, "you" shall mean either the individual or the entity whose agent opens this package. You are granted a non-exclusive and non-transferable license to use the Product subject to the following terms:

(i) If you have licensed a single user version of the Product, the Product may only be used on a single computer (i.e., a single CPU). If you licensed and paid the fee applicable to a local area network or wide area network version of the Product, you are subject to the terms of the following subparagraph (ii).

(ii) If you have licensed a local area network version, you may use the Product on unlimited workstations located in one single building selected by you that is served by such local area network. If you have licensed a wide area network version, you may use the Product on unlimited workstations located in multiple buildings on the same site selected by you that is served by such wide area network; provided, however, that any building will not be considered located in the same site if it is more than five (5) miles away from any building included in such site. In addition, you may only use a local area or wide area network version of the Product on one single server. If you wish to use the Product on more than one server, you must obtain written authorization from McGraw-Hill Education and pay additional fees.

(iii) You may make one copy of the Product for back-up purposes only and you must maintain an accurate record as to the location of the back-up at all times.

COPYRIGHT; RESTRICTIONS ON USE AND TRANSFER: All rights (including copyright) in and to the Product are owned by McGraw-Hill Education and its licensors. You are the owner of the enclosed disc on which the Product is recorded. You may not use, copy, decompile, disassemble, reverse engineer, modify, reproduce, create derivative works, transmit, distribute, sublicense, store in a database or retrieval system of any kind, rent or transfer the Product, or any portion thereof, in any form or by any means (including electronically or otherwise) except as expressly provided for in this License Agreement. You must reproduce the copyright notices, trademark notices, legends and logos of McGraw-Hill Education and its licensors that appear on the Product on the back-up copy of the Product which you are permitted to make hereunder. All rights in the Product not expressly granted herein are reserved by McGraw-Hill Education and its licensors.

TERM: This License Agreement is effective until terminated. It will terminate if you fail to comply with any term or condition of this License Agreement. Upon termination, you are obligated to return to McGraw-Hill Education the Product together with all copies thereof and to purge all copies of the Product included in any and all servers and computer facilities.

DISCLAIMER OF WARRANTY: THE PRODUCT AND THE BACK-UP COPY ARE LICENSED "AS IS." McGRAW-HILL EDUCATION, ITS LICENSORS AND THE AUTHORS MAKE NO WARRANTIES, EXPRESS OR IMPLIED, AS TO THE RESULTS TO BE OBTAINED BY ANY PERSON OR ENTITY FROM USE OF THE PRODUCT, ANY INFORMATION OR DATA INCLUDED THEREIN AND/OR ANY TECHNICAL SUPPORT SERVICES PROVIDED HEREUNDER, IF ANY ("TECHNICAL SUPPORT SERVICES"). McGRAW-HILL EDUCATION, ITS LICENSORS AND THE AUTHORS MAKE NO EXPRESS OR IMPLIED WARRANTIES OF MERCHANTABILITY OR FITNESS FOR A PARTICULAR PURPOSE OR USE WITH RESPECT TO THE PRODUCT. McGRAW-HILL EDUCATION, ITS LICENSORS, AND THE AUTHORS MAKE NO GUARANTEE THAT YOU WILL PASS ANY CERTIFICATION EXAM WHATSOEVER BY USING THIS PRODUCT. NEITHER McGRAW-HILL EDUCATION, ANY OF ITS LICENSORS NOR THE AUTHORS WARRANT THAT THE FUNCTIONS CONTAINED IN THE PRODUCT WILL MEET YOUR REQUIREMENTS OR THAT THE OPERATION OF THE PRODUCT WILL BE UNINTERRUPTED OR ERROR FREE. YOU ASSUME THE ENTIRE RISK WITH RESPECT TO THE QUALITY AND PERFORMANCE OF THE PRODUCT.

LIMITED WARRANTY FOR DISC: To the original licensee only, McGraw-Hill Education warrants that the enclosed disc on which the Product is recorded is free from defects in materials and workmanship under normal use and service for a period of ninety (90) days from the date of purchase. In the event of a defect in the disc covered by the foregoing warranty, McGraw-Hill Education will replace the disc.

LIMITATION OF LIABILITY: NEITHER McGRAW-HILL EDUCATION, ITS LICENSORS NOR THE AUTHORS SHALL BE LIABLE FOR ANY INDIRECT, SPECIAL OR CONSEQUENTIAL DAMAGES, SUCH AS BUT NOT LIMITED TO, LOSS OF ANTICIPATED PROFITS OR BENEFITS, RESULTING FROM THE USE OR INABILITY TO USE THE PRODUCT EVEN IF ANY OF THEM HAS BEEN ADVISED OF THE POSSIBILITY OF SUCH DAMAGES. THIS LIMITATION OF LIABILITY SHALL APPLY TO ANY CLAIM OR CAUSE WHATSOEVER WHETHER SUCH CLAIM OR CAUSE ARISES IN CONTRACT, TORT, OR OTHERWISE. Some states do not allow the exclusion or limitation of indirect, special or consequential damages, so the above limitation may not apply to you.

U.S. GOVERNMENT RESTRICTED RIGHTS: Any software included in the Product is provided with restricted rights subject to subparagraphs (c), (1) and (2) of the Commercial Computer Software-Restricted Rights clause at 48 C.F.R. 52.227-19. The terms of this Agreement applicable to the use of the data in the Product are those under which the data are generally made available to the general public by McGraw-Hill Education. Except as provided herein, no reproduction, use, or disclosure rights are granted with respect to the data included in the Product and no right to modify or create derivative works from any such data is hereby granted.

GENERAL: This License Agreement constitutes the entire agreement between the parties relating to the Product. The terms of any Purchase Order shall have no effect on the terms of this License Agreement. Failure of McGraw-Hill Education to insist at any time on strict compliance with this License Agreement shall not constitute a waiver of any rights under this License Agreement. This License Agreement shall be construed and governed in accordance with the laws of the State of New York. If any provision of this License Agreement is held to be contrary to law, that provision will be enforced to the maximum extent permissible and the remaining provisions will remain in full force and effect.